IMAGES
of America

SONOMA COMMUNITY CENTER

ON THE COVER: Sonoma Grammar School was dedicated in May 1916. It was built at a cost of $30,000 during 1915, but weather and other delays pushed the opening back from January 1916 to May. The contractor, R.H. Ingraham, also had labor problems, which resulted in subcontractors filing numerous claims against him at the end of the project. It was put into use the following school year. (Courtesy Sonoma Valley Historical Society.)

IMAGES
of America

SONOMA COMMUNITY CENTER

Pamela Hallan-Gibson and Kathy Swett

ARCADIA
PUBLISHING

ISBN 978-1-4671-3259-6

Published by Arcadia Publishing
Charleston, South Carolina

Printed in the United States of America

Library of Congress Control Number: 2014941575

For all general information, please contact Arcadia Publishing:
Telephone 843-853-2070
Fax 843-853-0044
E-mail sales@arcadiapublishing.com
For customer service and orders:
Toll-Free 1-888-313-2665

Visit us on the Internet at www.arcadiapublishing.com

To Sandi Hansen, executive director of the Sonoma Valley Historical Society. Thank you. We could not have done this book without you.

Contents

Acknowledgments

As we researched this book, we marveled at the number of Sonoma residents who have served on the center's board of directors over the years. Even those who did not found a way to aid the center: helping out at the Fourth of July parade, volunteering as a server at a Thanksgiving or Christmas dinner, or assisting in an arts class or theater production. We are most grateful to this community, which shows such active interest in serving its fellow members.

As we noted in our dedication, we owe a tremendous debt to the hard work and resources made available to us by the Sonoma Valley Historical Society (SVHS) and Sandi Hansen of its Depot Museum. The group truly exemplifies the spirit of Sonoma—a place where volunteers keep civic, social, and cultural programs alive and where history and vintage buildings like the Sonoma Community Center are cherished.

Additionally, we thank the following people for the photographs, artifacts, stories, yarns, or technical assistance so freely given: Jason Bell of the Sonoma League for Historic Preservation; the Sonoma Community Center Archives (SCC); Jurine Biers; Karin Neihoff of the Crescent Montessori School; Ken Brown; David Goodison; Alex Cole; Lia Transue; Robert Parmelee; the *Sonoma Index-Tribune* (SIT); Mark Andrews; Bill Lynch; Melinda Kelley; Margaret Hatcher; Diane Mayo; Owen Orser; and Jared Nelson, our patient Arcadia editor, whose invaluable help got us through this process.

INTRODUCTION

Sonoma is known throughout the world for its world-class wines, its fine resorts and restaurants, and as the home of the Bear Flag Revolt. Visitors come yearly to visit Mission San Francisco Solano de Sonoma, the last mission in the California chain; to the plaza, where a flag was raised briefly and California declared an independent country; and to relax in the peace of the vineyard-covered countryside.

By 1915, when the first bricks were laid for the Sonoma Grammar School, the town had already gained a reputation as an education center. There were seven public school districts within Sonoma Valley, and before that, private schools with fine reputations flourished. When the grammar school was completed, it became an instant landmark that would educate decades of Sonoma's children and provide the basis for a lasting cultural tradition.

The Earthquake of 1936 drove the California legislature to pass strict laws on school construction, which required the closure of many of the grandest schools in the state. By 1949, Sonoma Grammar School was among them, but the community's love for the building protected it from demolition.

Dr. Carroll Andrews and his wife, Katherine, purchased the building in 1952, with the help of many friends, and then turned it over to the people of Sonoma. The building became the home of a community nonprofit called the Sonoma Community Center.

Through the years, the center has been the place where nonprofits get their start; where events celebrating births, marriages, and deaths occur; where visual and musical arts flourish; and where the valley comes together to put on events that define and sustain us. It has survived financial turmoil and building code updates, and today, the Sonoma Community Center is a place where the performing arts are alive; where creativity flourishes through ceramics, painting, and other media; and where people come to learn, to play, and to become revitalized. What was once only a school has become the realization of Dr. Andrews's dream: a true cultural center for the entire valley.

Happy birthday Sonoma Community Center. May you last another 100 years.

One

Sonoma's Educational Heritage

Fr. Jose Altimira founded Mission San Francisco Solano de Sonoma, the last of California's 21 missions, in a peaceful valley in 1823. Fears of Russian domination in the northern areas of California and a need to move missions into a warmer climate fueled the move, and the mission engaged in the chief activities of all missions—converting the native population to Catholicism, creating a Western European presence in a particular area, and beginning the task of teaching locals how to survive in a place that was now part of Mexico.

By 1833, the mission was secularized and momentarily abandoned, and Gen. Mariano Vallejo was put in charge of the tiny community called Sonoma. He established the town, supervised the construction of many buildings, and took up residence in a place that was part home and part garrison headquarters just north of the plaza. A believer in education, Vallejo is credited with bringing in the first tutor to the area, for his own children, and encouraging the establishment of private schools.

In 1846, the Bear Flag was raised over the plaza for a brief 26 days before the Stars and Stripes went up in its place. General Vallejo adapted, and so did the town. By the time that California became a state in 1850 and passed legislation allowing the formation of public school districts in 1851 and 1852, several private schools were already educating local children at all levels. In 1857, Sonoma Township—which was greater than its city limits today—petitioned for the establishment of public school districts. Initially there were four in the area: Ash Springs, Dunbar, Watmaugh, and Sonoma. Other schools in the valley, established later, were San Luis, Harvey, Enterprise, Flowery, Huichica, Verano, Tule Vista, and Summit Joint School. Some of these are still active today.

Sonoma was a town where schools were the cultural centers of their times. This legacy would carry forward and set the stage for the public school system in Sonoma Valley and the magnificent Sonoma Grammar School building that would eventually become the Sonoma Community Center—the heart and soul of the valley.

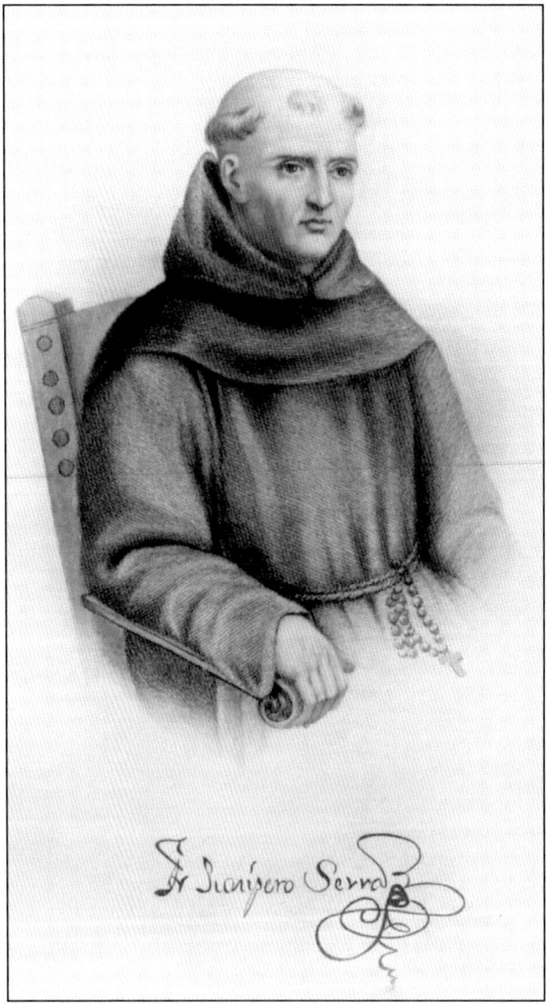

Fr. Junipero Serra was put in charge of the founding of the California Missions but only lived to establish the first seven. Fr. Jose Altimira founded Mission San Francisco Solano de Sonoma when it was thought that the Russians might seize Northern California. He chose the Sonoma Plain as a primary site, as it was near reliable water sources and numerous Miwok villages. These mission settlements often became the sites of future towns. (Author's Collection.)

Mission San Francisco Solano de Sonoma was established in 1823 as the last of the Franciscan Missions. It was the only one to be founded under Mexican rule. Like its sister missions, it was an early home for education and the first place in Sonoma Valley to provide instruction. The curriculum was based on religious principles, animal husbandry, agriculture, and other useful skills. Henry Chapman Ford supposedly made this etching in 1833. (Courtesy SVHS.)

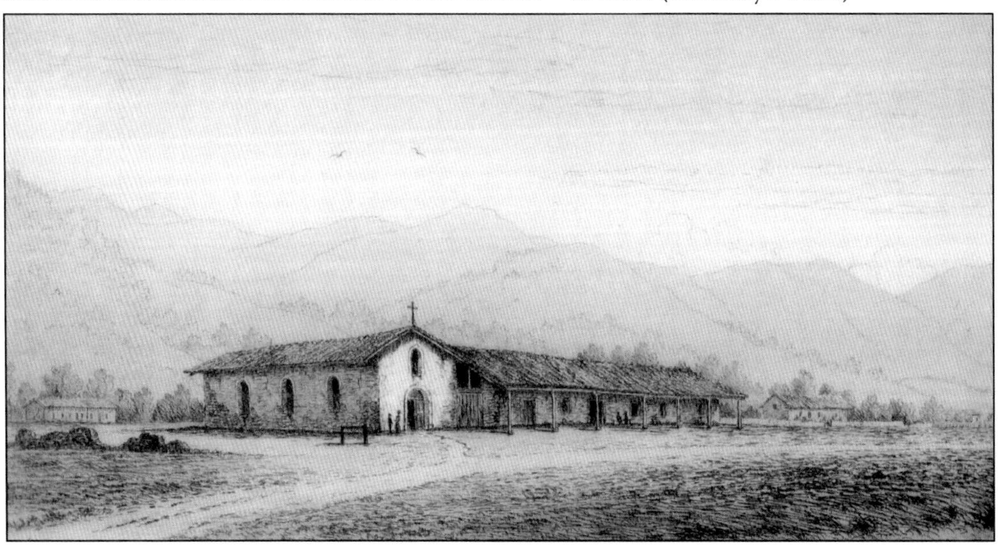

Mexican general Mariano Vallejo was put in charge of Sonoma's mission as early as 1833 and is credited with laying out the town of Sonoma. He believed strongly in education, and his children were tutored at home as early as 1849 by Frederik Reger and music master Andrew Hoeppner. He brought tutors and schools to Sonoma at a time when public education was not yet in place. (Courtesy SVHS.)

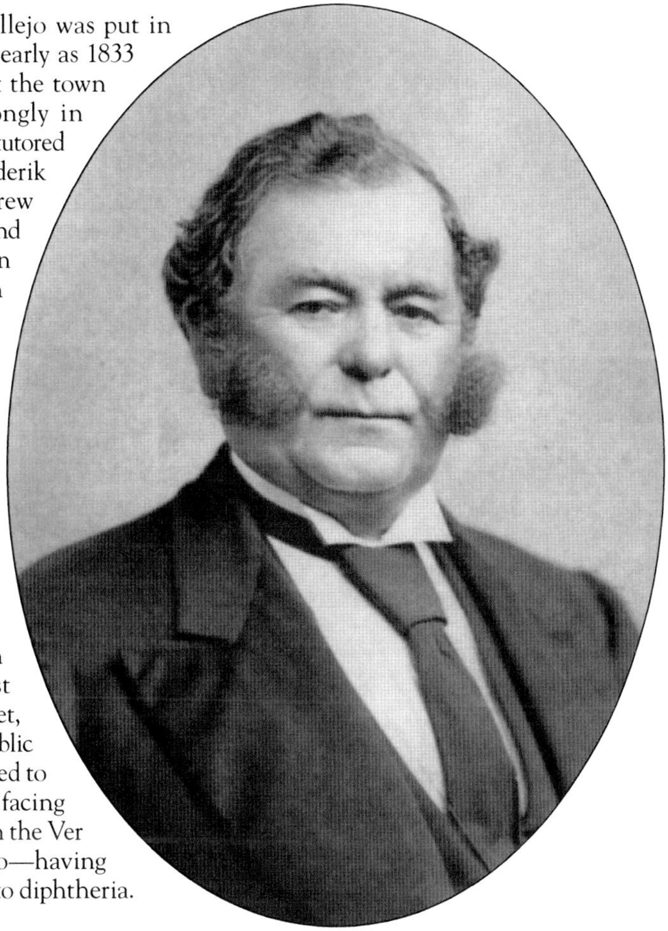

In the early 1850s, Dr. J.L. Ver Mehr opened St. Mary's Hall for Young Ladies in the Leese-Fitch Adobe, on the corner of First Street West and West Napa Street, prior to the establishment of a public school system. It eventually moved to General Vallejo's palatial home facing the plaza but closed in 1856 when the Ver Mehrs returned to San Francisco—having lost four of their nine children to diphtheria. (Courtesy SVHS.)

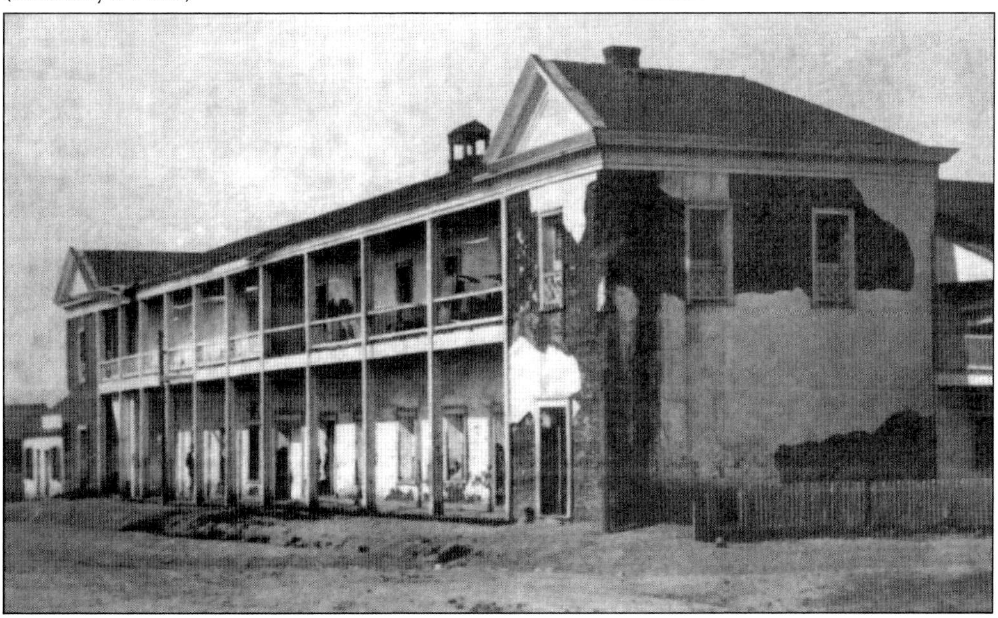

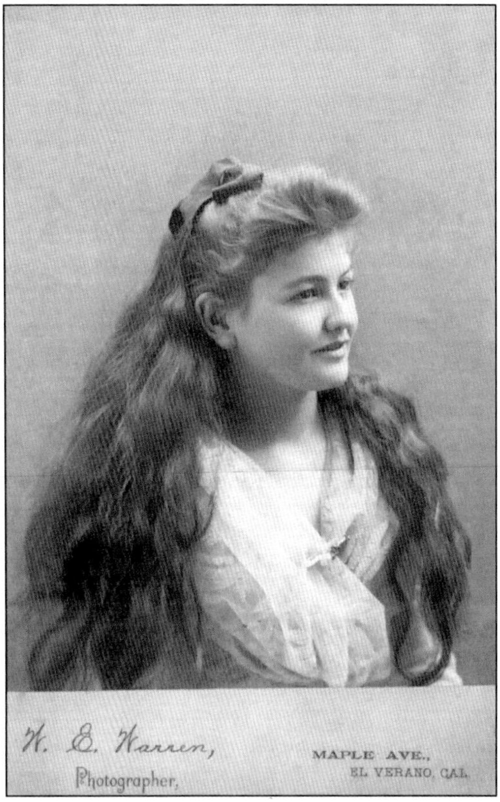

Natalia Vallejo—one of Mariano and Francesca's children—and her older sisters were students at the Ver Mehrs' school. Natalia remained in Sonoma after her marriage to Attila Haraszthy, whose father, Count Agoston Haraszthy, is credited with founding California's commercial wine industry at his Buena Vista Winery in Sonoma. (Courtesy SVHS.)

Natalia and Attila Haraszthy were married on June 1, 1863, in a double ceremony with her sister Jovita and Attila's brother Arpad at the Vallejo home. This stately building on Spain Street, now an event center, was once called Willows Wild and was Natalia's home for years. (Author's Collection.)

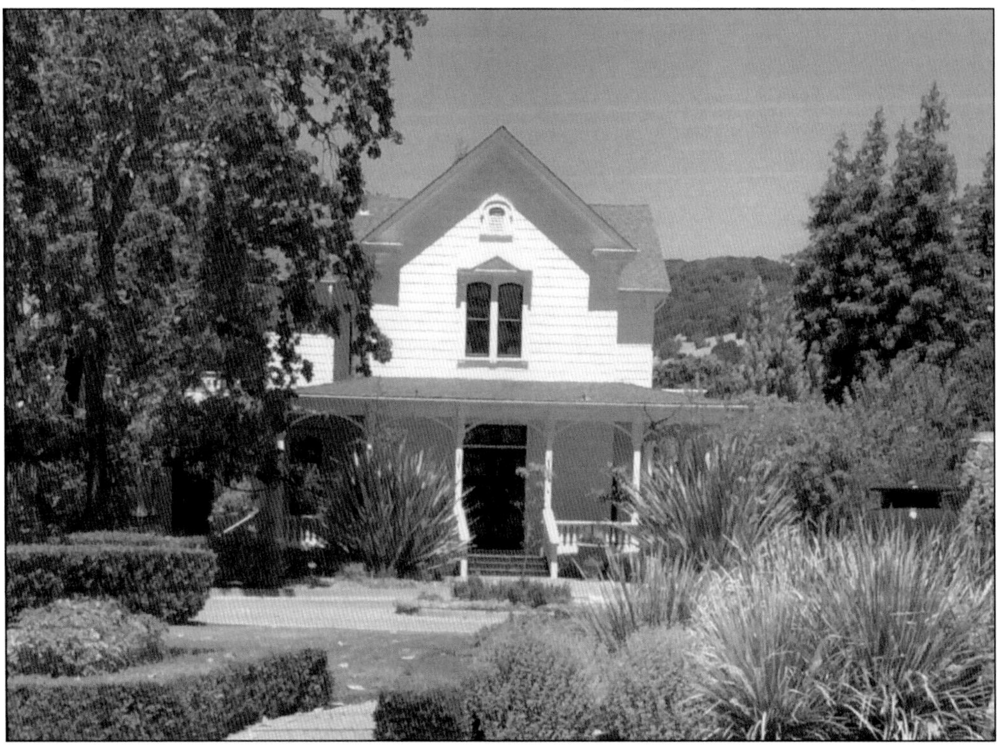

Seen here in an early portrait from a family collection, James Cooper has become part of the valley's school lore. In September 1856, his boys were severely disciplined by teacher H.N. Graham. When Cooper confronted Graham, the man drew a knife and stabbed Cooper to death. While the record of the trial was preserved, the name of the school was not. (Courtesy SVHS.)

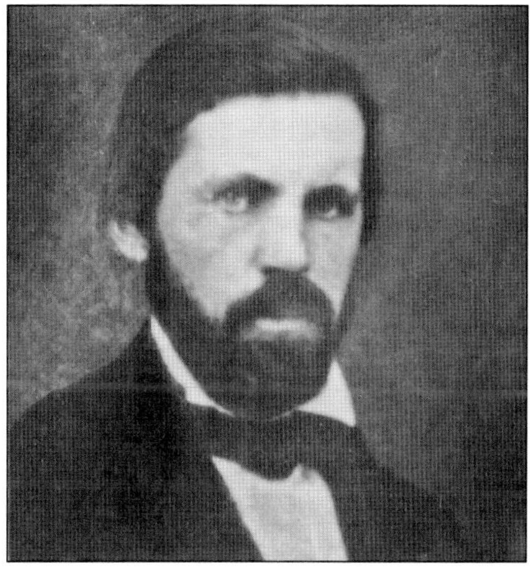

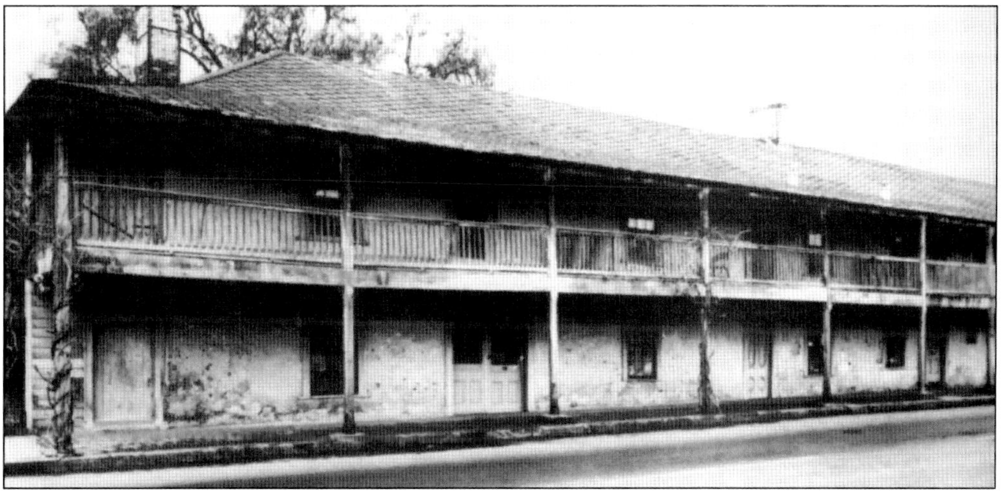

James Cooper and partner Thomas Spriggs built the Blue Wing Inn by expanding an earlier adobe structure around 1849. Cooper was the father of five educated children. Sons Tom and John were born in the Blue Wing, and daughters Barbara, Emma, and Janet were most likely born on the Coopers' ranch just out of town. (Courtesy SIT.)

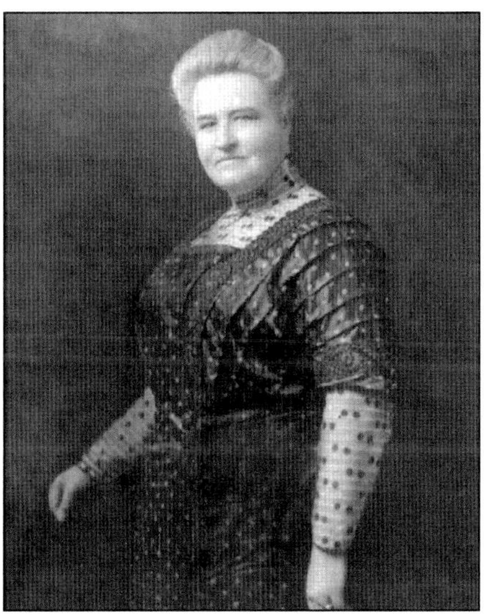

The Napa Ladies Seminary, established about 15 miles from Sonoma in 1860, was a fashionable establishment where some of Sonoma's families sent their daughters. Emma Cooper attended school there. She is seen here in her later years as Mrs. James R. McDonald. She met her husband while attending the school, which was operated by his relatives, and married him in 1879. (Courtesy SVHS.)

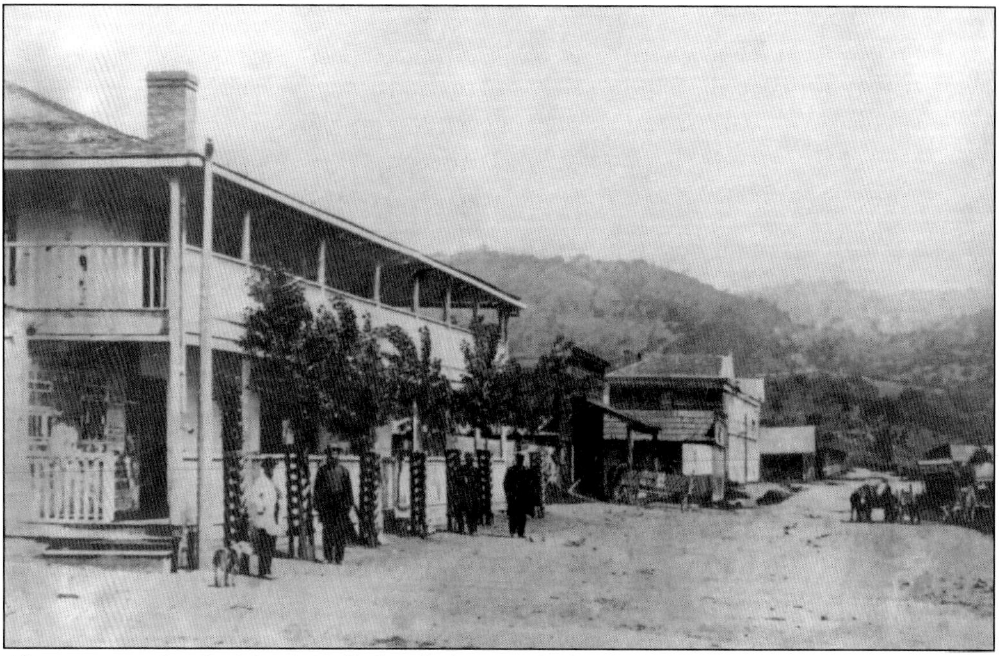

About a year after St. Mary's Hall closed, the Cumberland Presbyterian school opened a block away, in the Salvador Vallejo Adobe on the corner of First Street West and West Spain Street. It was called the Sonoma Academy. The operators connected two buildings and added a second floor, creating rooms for boarders. In 1861, the school's name was changed to Cumberland College. It is the El Dorado Hotel today. (Courtesy SVHS.)

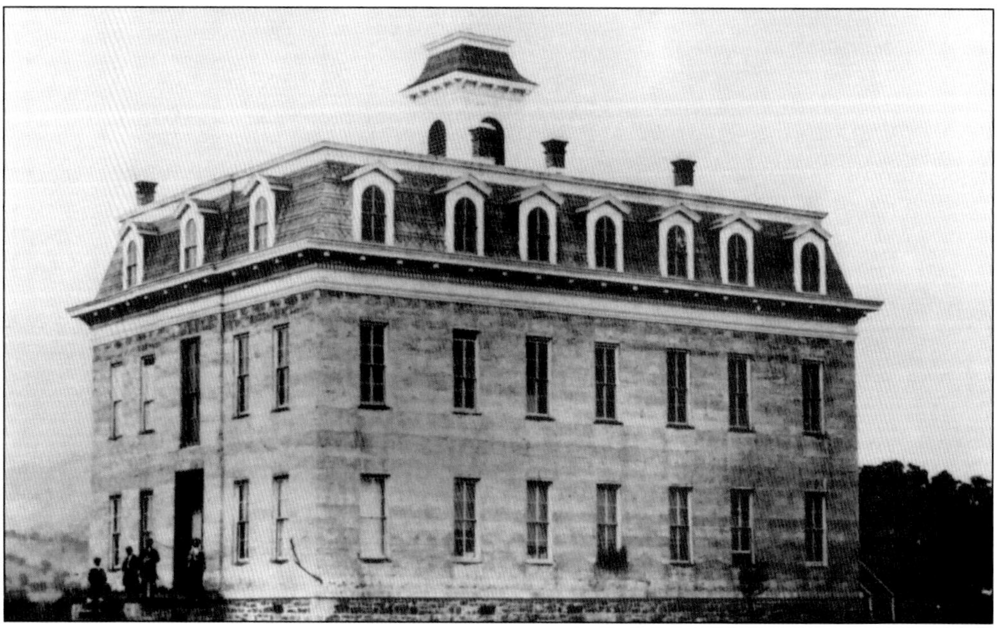

With a coed student body of about 100, a new Cumberland College building was constructed in 1864 on Broadway, on the northeast corner of Broadway and MacArthur Street. The three-story building featured a mansard roof, a cupola, and a full basement. It closed in 1873, ostensibly due to a lack of students. (Courtesy SVHS.)

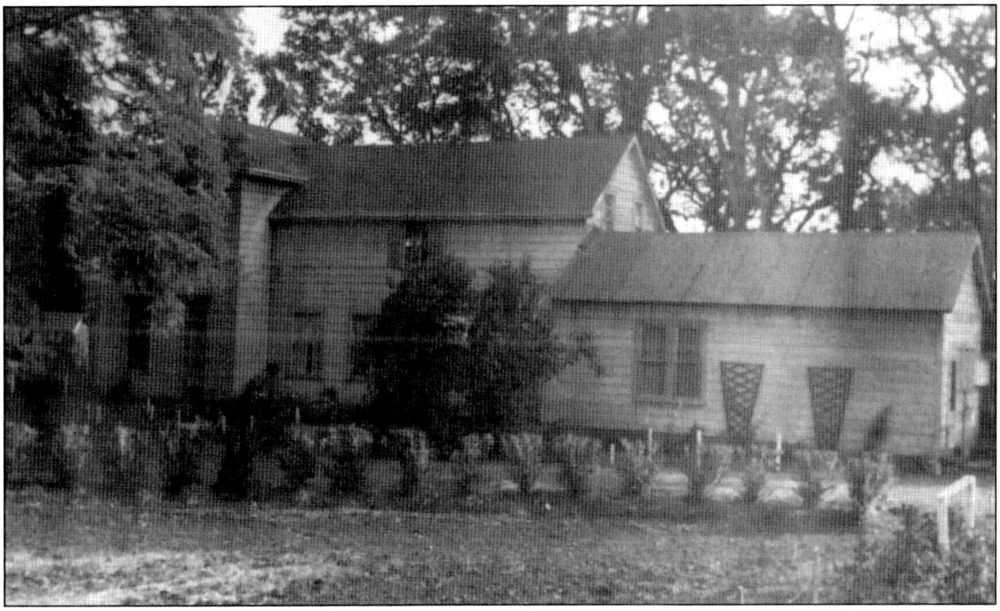

A third private school in the Sonoma area was the Locust Grove School, located at the embarcadero on lower Broadway and next to Sonoma Creek. According to *Schools and Scows in Sonoma Valley*, a third private school in the Sonoma area was the Locust Grove school, located at the embarcadero on lower Broadway next to Sonoma Creek. Founded by Mr. and Mrs. C.W. Lubeck, it was a "preparatory and boarding school of splendid reputation," functioning at full steam by 1880. It was a boys' school but had some functions that included girls. (Courtesy SVHS.)

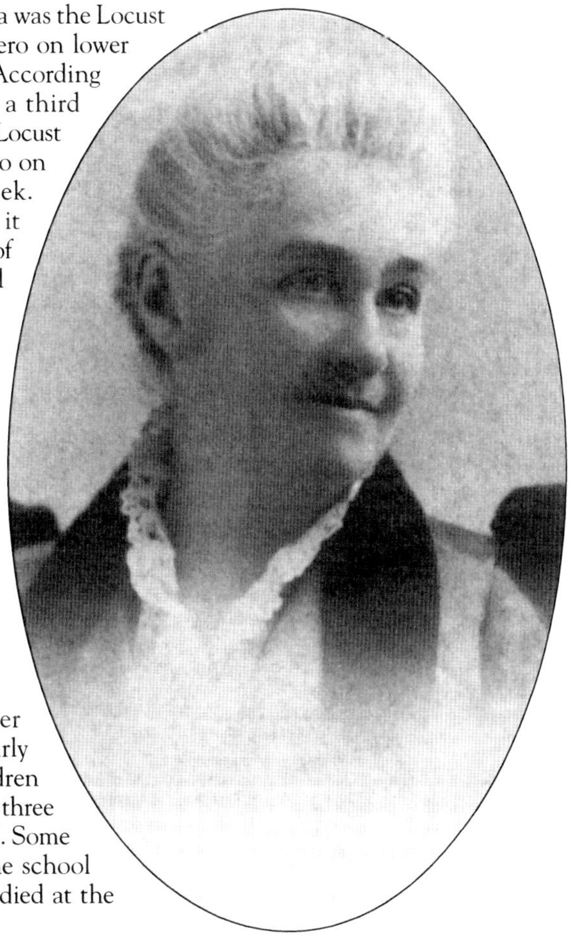

Amelia Lubeck, called "Auntie" by her students, began taking in orphans as early as 1869, when her late sister's eight children needed a home. When a neighbor died, her three children came to live at the school as well. Some of these girls were trained to teach. The school operated until 1909, when Mrs. Lubeck died at the age of 78. (Courtesy SVHS.)

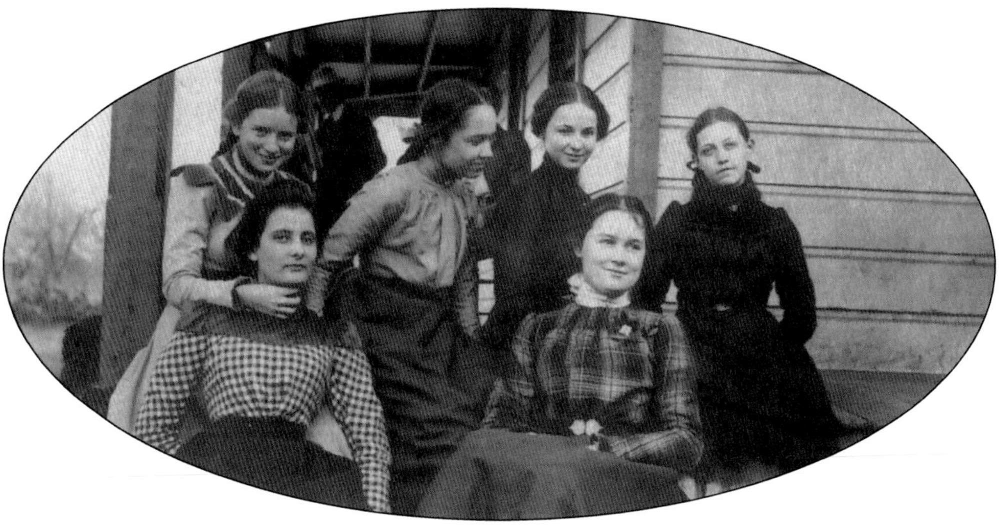

A group is shown on the porch of a Locust Grove building. Della Pauli (back row, second from left) and sister Ethel (front row, right) helped run this private school for many years. Their father, C.T. Pauli, owned a general merchandise store in Sonoma, on the south side of the plaza. (Courtesy SVHS.)

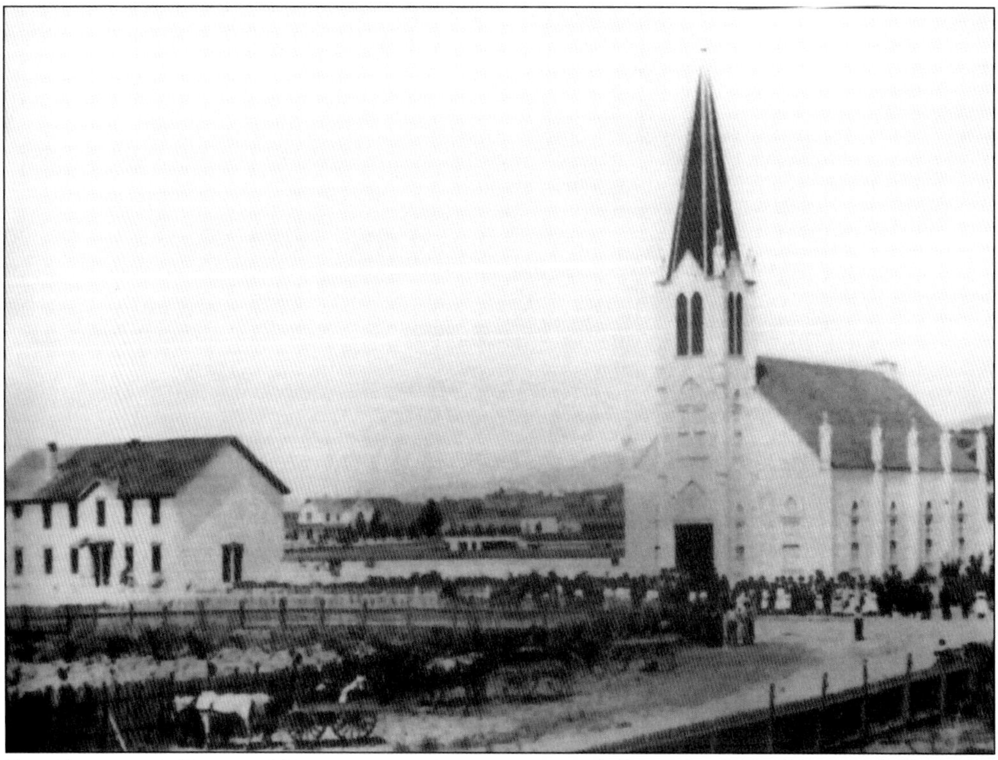

San Francisco's Sisters of Presentation Convent opened this school (building at left) in the 1880s. The Presentation Convent School was known for its music, entertainments, and lavish graduation ceremonies. It was located next to St. Francis Parish on West Napa Street and closed in 1917. A new St. Francis School opened in 1945, and a new Presentation School formed in 1997. (Courtesy SVHS.)

In 1853, Sonoma became one of three towns in the county designated to open a public school. Serving on the committee was D.O. Shattuck, county supervisor of Sonoma, pictured here with his wife. No districts were formed until 1857, when, in response to petitions by Sonoma Township trustees, four were allowed for the area: Ash Springs, Watmaugh, Dunbar, and Sonoma. (Courtesy SIT.)

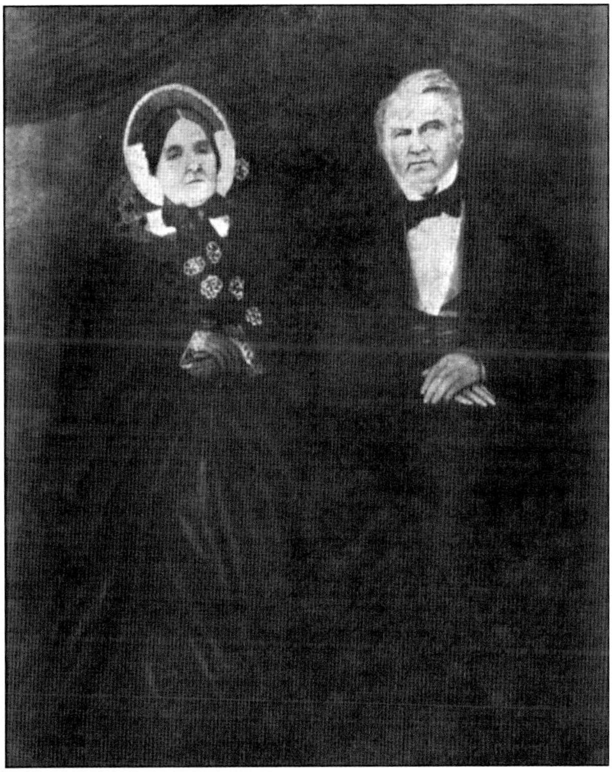

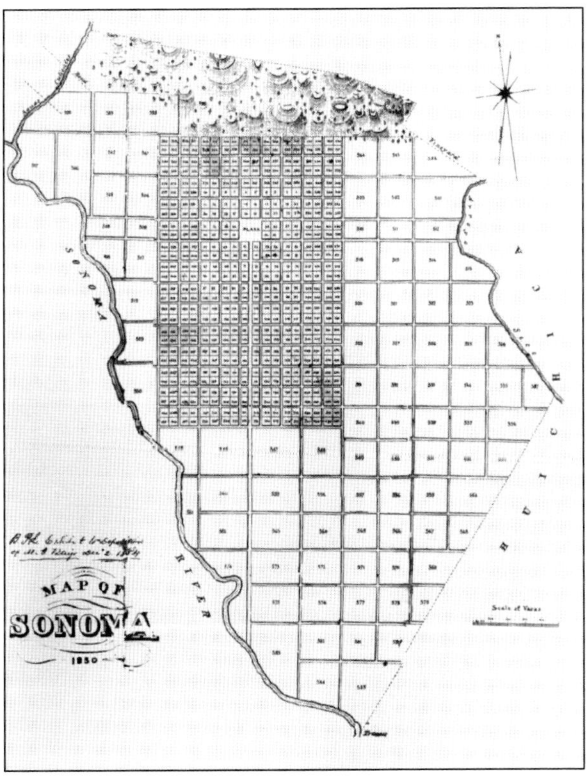

The site chosen for the new Sonoma schoolhouse was Lot 39 of the old township map, which bordered East Napa Street. According to some accounts, it was purchased from John Lewis for $400. Jesse Prestwood, a longtime principal, stated that it was purchased from E. Janssens for $600. The official county records show the seller as E.W. Hanssens. Handwritten discrepancies aside, a handsome wooden schoolhouse was open by 1869. (Courtesy David Goodison.)

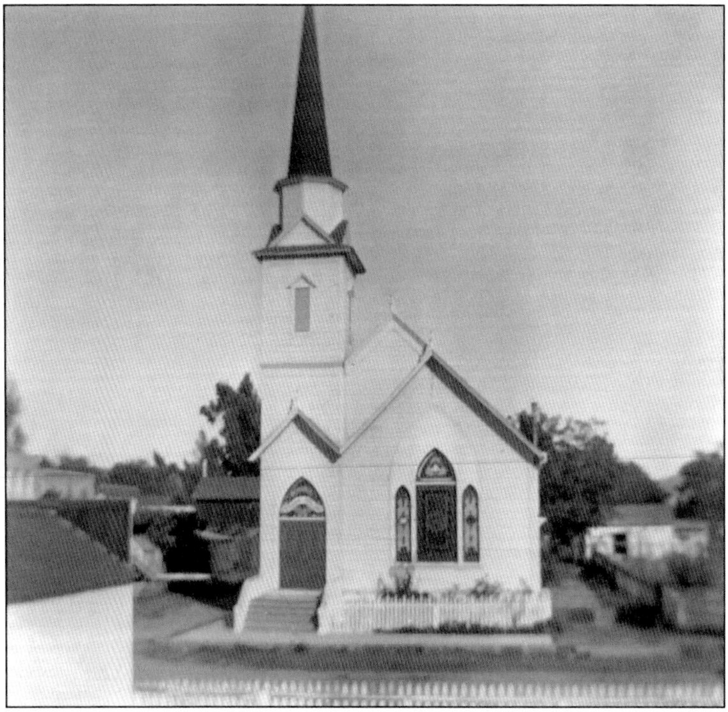

Children were first housed in the Methodist Episcopal church, which was located just across the creek. The church held the first public school classes and continued instruction from 1857 to 1869. In its first year of operation, it had an enrollment of 22 and an average daily attendance of 13—jumping to 69 the second year. The building was relocated to First Street East, where it was later sold to a Baptist congregation. (Courtesy SVHS.)

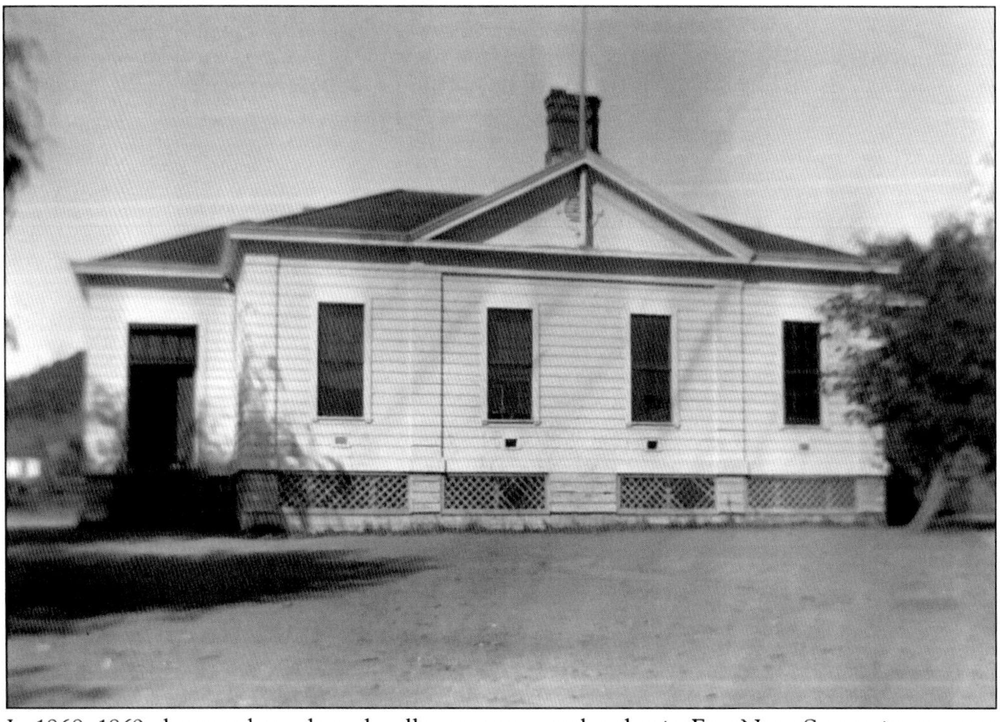

In 1868–1869, the grand wooden schoolhouse was completed at its East Napa Street site at a cost of $6,500. Made to house the Sonoma Grammar School District's primary-grade children, it was designed by a San Francisco architect and located in approximately the center of the lot—providing lots of room for outdoor activities. (Courtesy SVHS.)

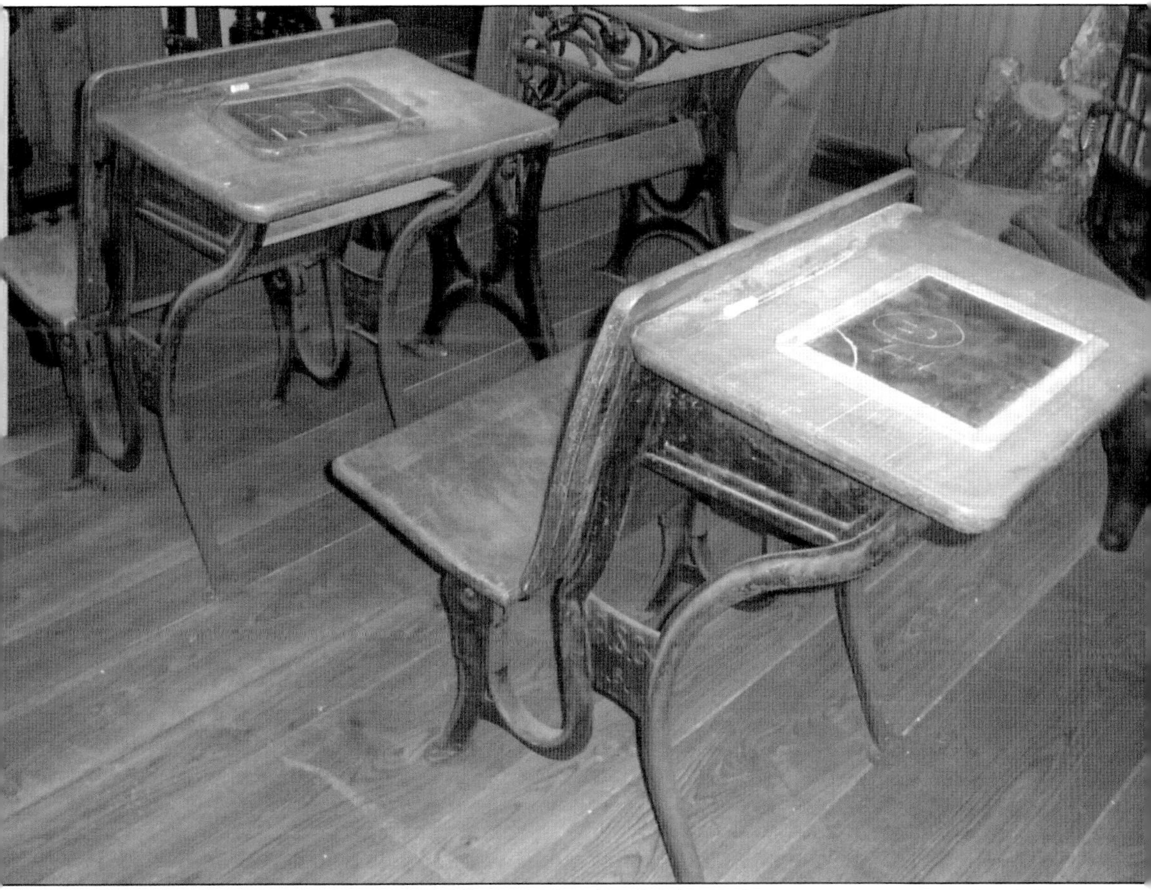

Desks are part of the capital expenses for any school. Schools run by private groups in early adobes often only had benches, but the "modern" school houses of the Sonoma Valley were equipped with desks that looked much like these. Slates and chalk were also standard in early classrooms, as were blackboards on walls. (Courtesy SVHS.)

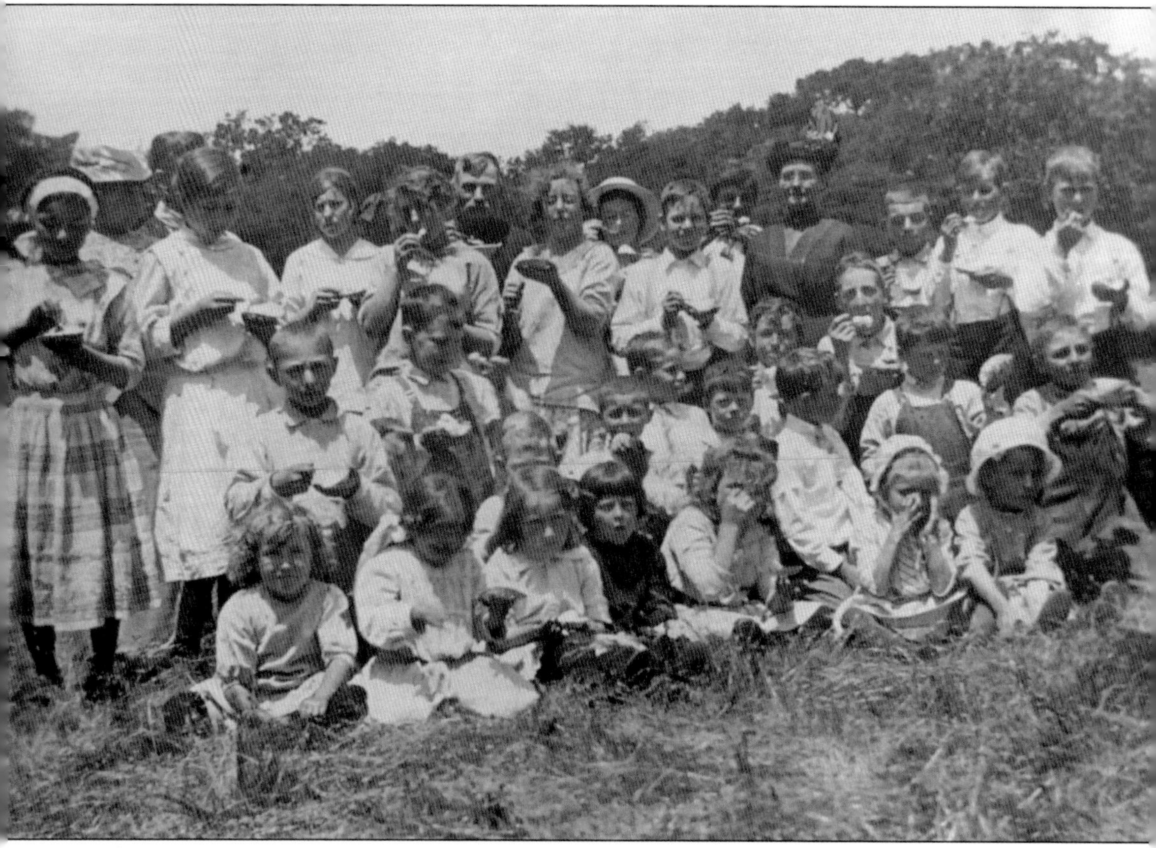

While most country schools did not have formal athletic facilities, children enjoyed the outdoors. These children from Watmaugh School—one the first schools authorized, but not established until around 1870—are on a picnic. The Watmaugh Schoolhouse survived many years, was moved several times, and eventually became part of El Verano School in 1947. (Courtesy SVHS.)

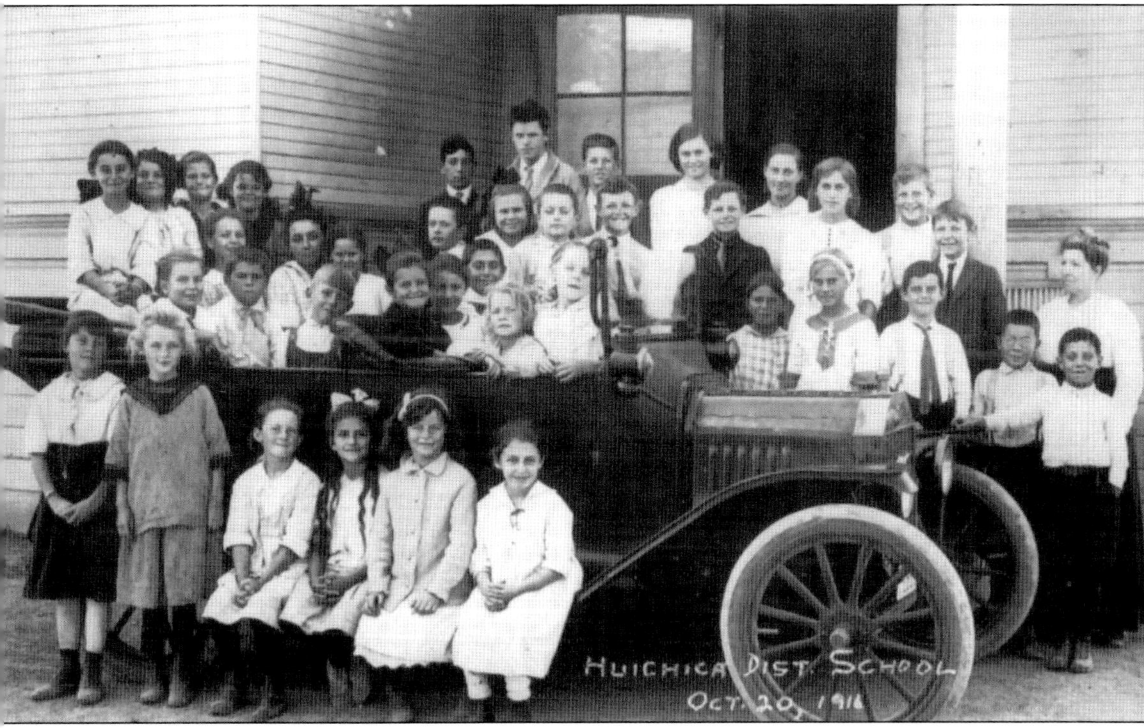

Another early school was the Huichica School, located east of town. It had a fine wooden pavilion, which was relocated to Sonoma's Depot Park when the school closed. The school building is still standing and can be seen south of Napa Road in Vineburg. It is a private residence today. (Courtesy SVHS.)

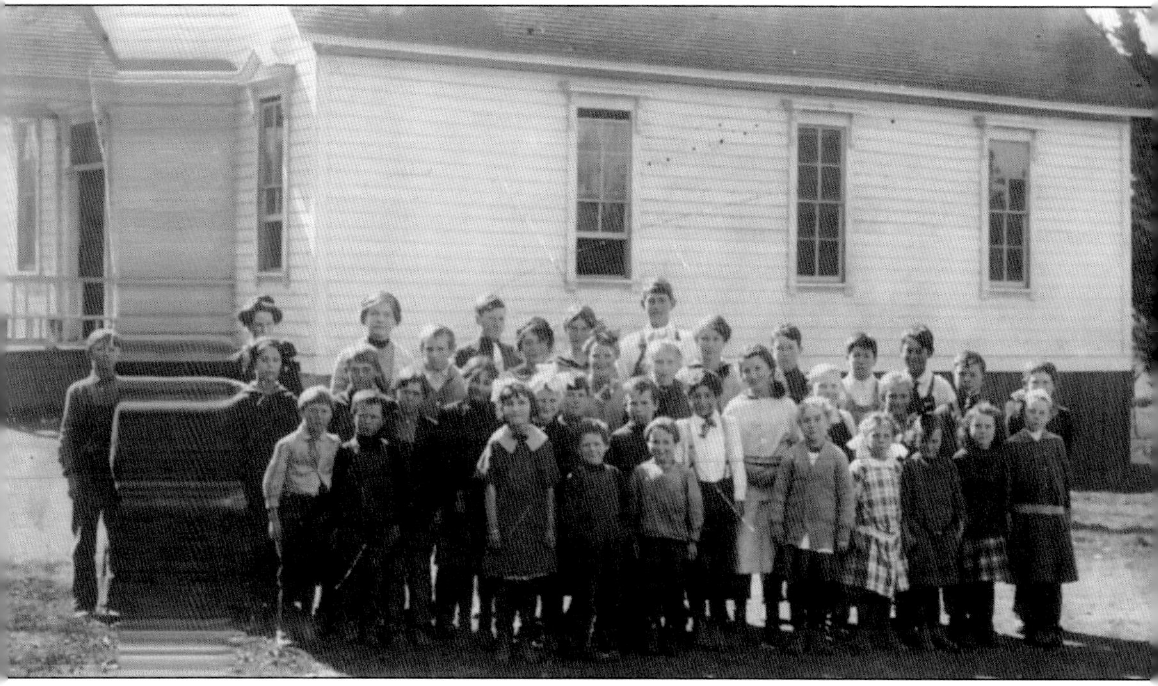

San Luis School, in Schellville, was founded in the 1880s and was one of several schools in Sonoma Valley. Other schools were formed at various times, including Glen Ellen, El Verano, Tule Vista, Enterprise, Flowery, Harvey, and Summit Joint School at Los Guilicos. Ash Springs, later called Oak Grove, only lasted a year. Most had one or two rooms and served all grades. (Courtesy SVHS.)

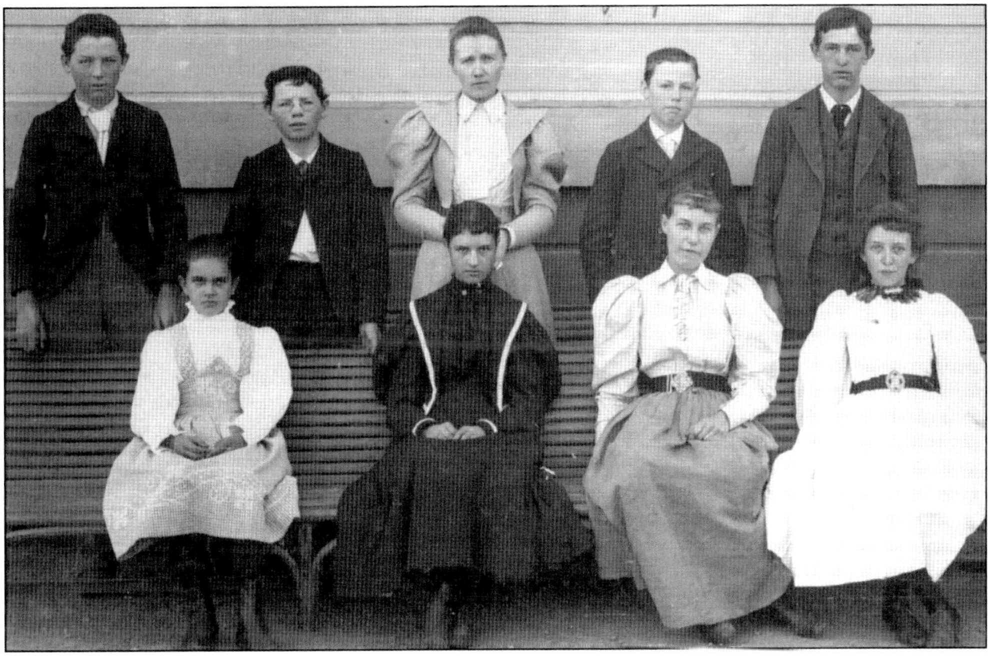

Sonoma Grammar School's attendance rose steadily, but mostly in the lower grades. This photograph of the 1896 seventh- and eighth-grade class includes, from left to right (first row), Doris Clewe, Maude Thompkins, Lydia Culbertson, and Grace Trudgen; (second row) Jim Burke, Fred Burke, teacher Miss Gingery, Will Schuman, and Bert Jones. (Courtesy SVHS.)

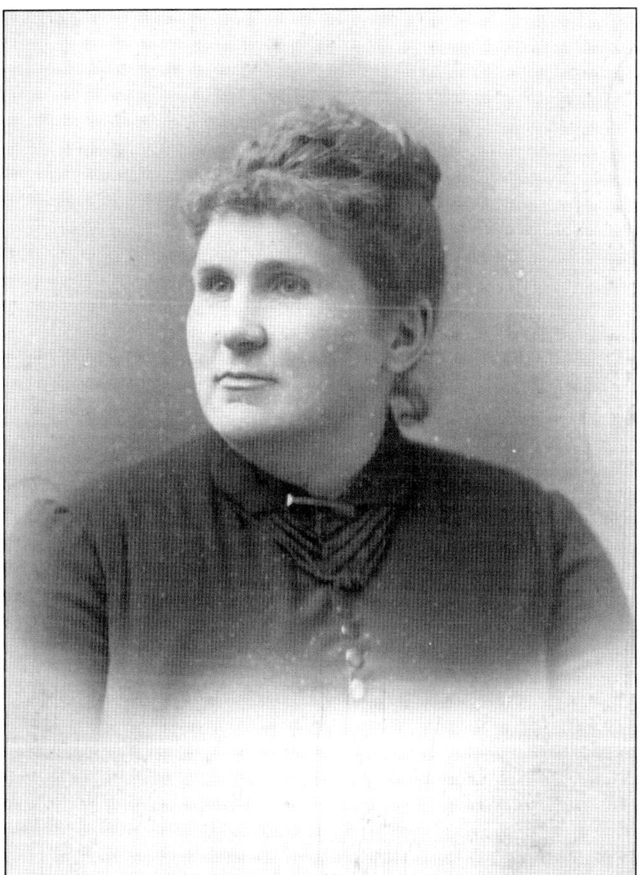

Frances McGaughey Martin, an early teacher in the valley, rose to prominence in the 1880s as the first woman elected to a Sonoma County public office. She served as county superintendent of schools from 1886 to 1892 but is best known as a leader in the women's suffrage movement. She later became a lawyer. (Courtesy SVHS.)

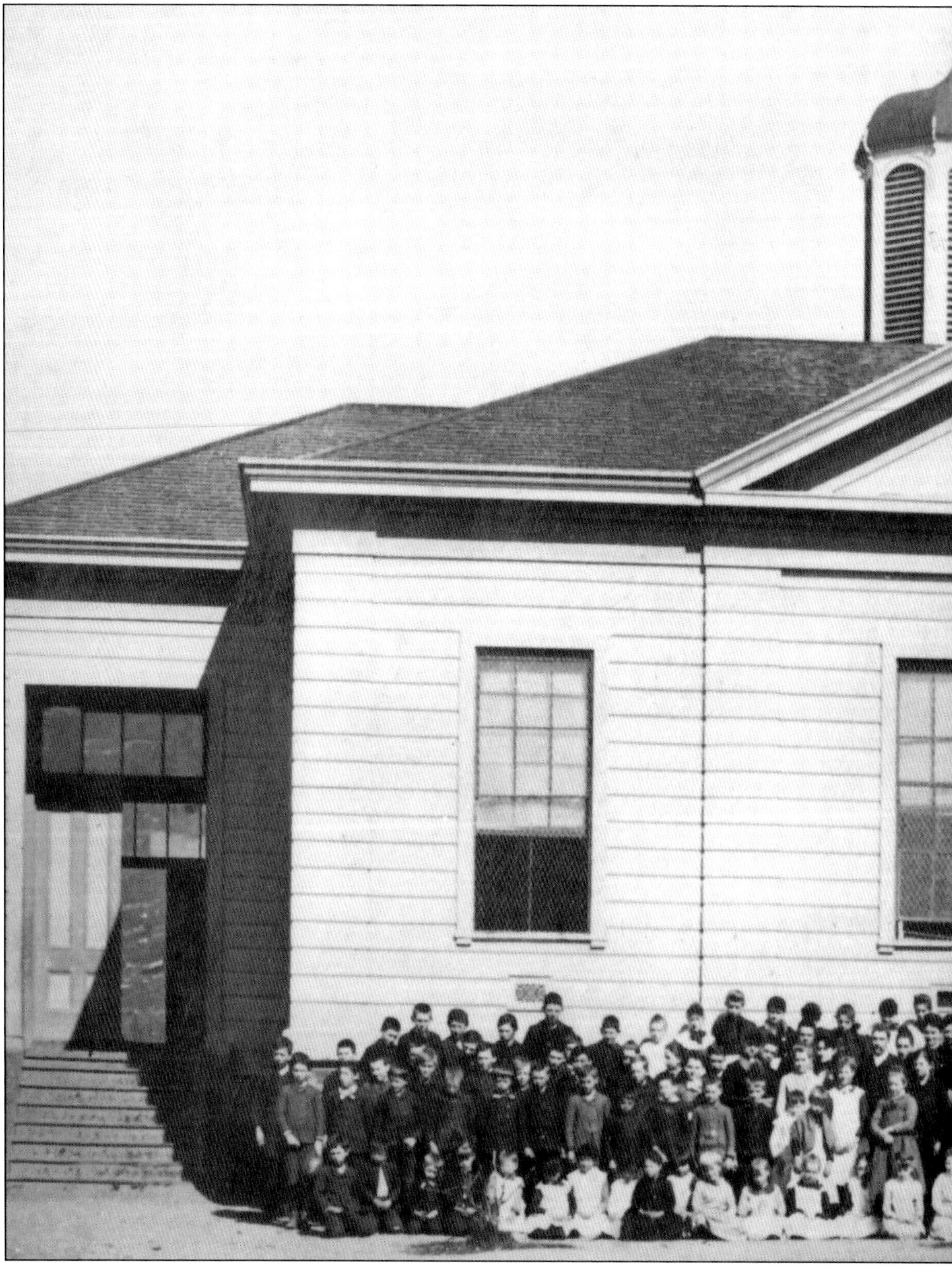

In this 1889 photograph, the Sonoma Grammar School is already starting to show signs of overcrowding. The school was divided into First Primary, Second Primary, Grammar Room, and High School, and a test was required for the latter category. There were approximately 150 students enrolled, but three fourths were in primary grades. Although the architect, described only as being from San Francisco, is unknown, this picture shows a well-designed school building

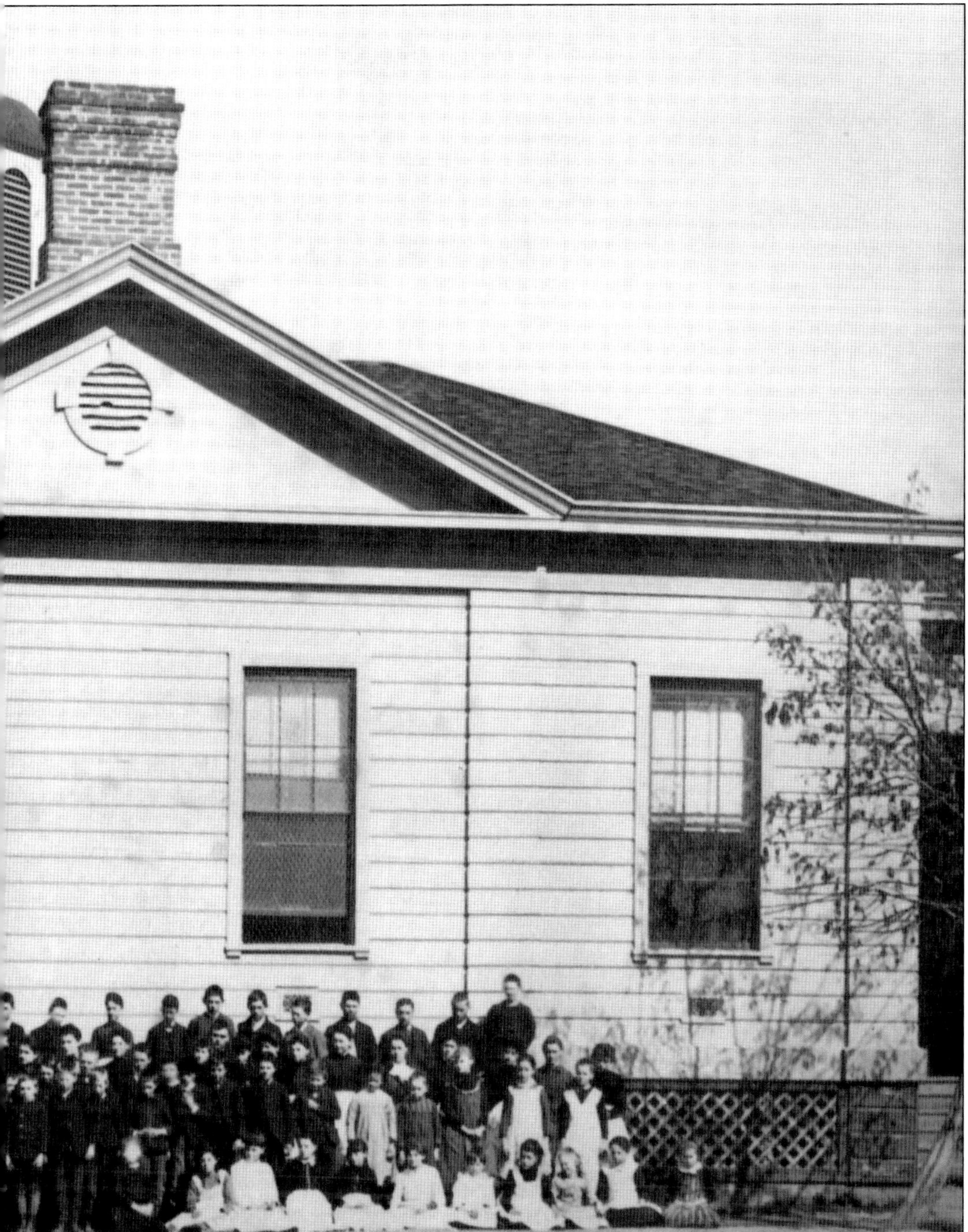

with two entrances—not quite like the other schools scattered throughout the countryside. It also shows what appears to be an enclosed bell. When the new school was under construction in 1915, the incorporation of a bell was the subject of controversy. The bell never made it to the new school, and while its whereabouts are officially unknown, it is thought to be privately owned today. (Courtesy Sonoma League for Historic Preservation.)

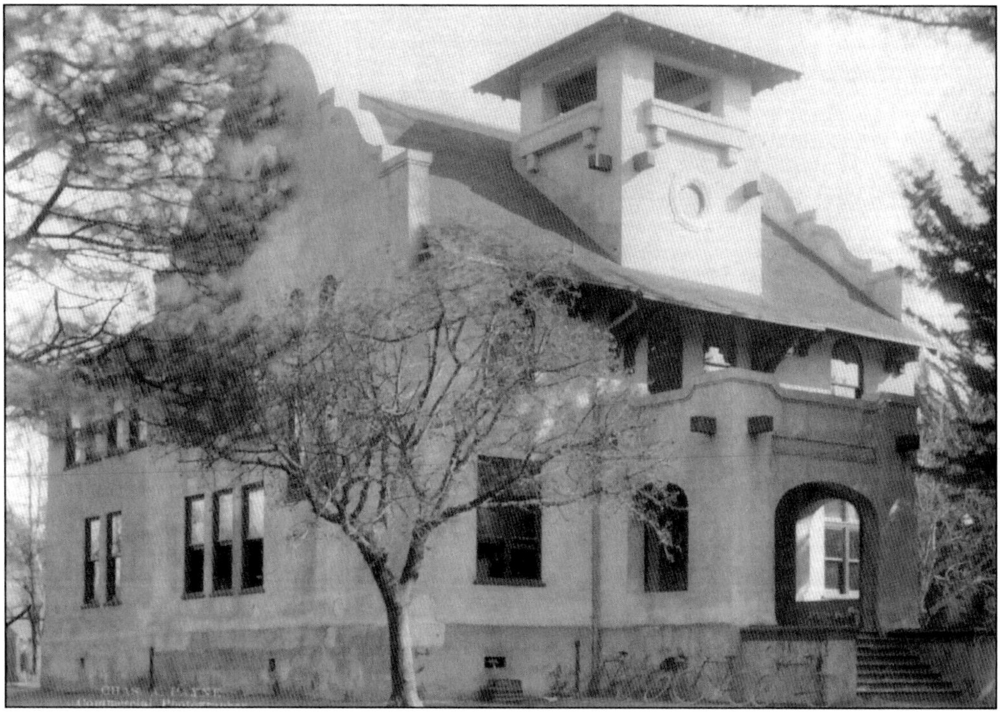

While money was technically not provided for high schools, Sonoma had already graduated five high school classes by calling them something else. In 1890, a bill was adopted by the state legislature allowing high schools to be separate entities. The first Sonoma High School campus was the vacant Cumberland College building. When it was damaged in the 1906 earthquake, this building replaced it. (Courtesy SVHS.)

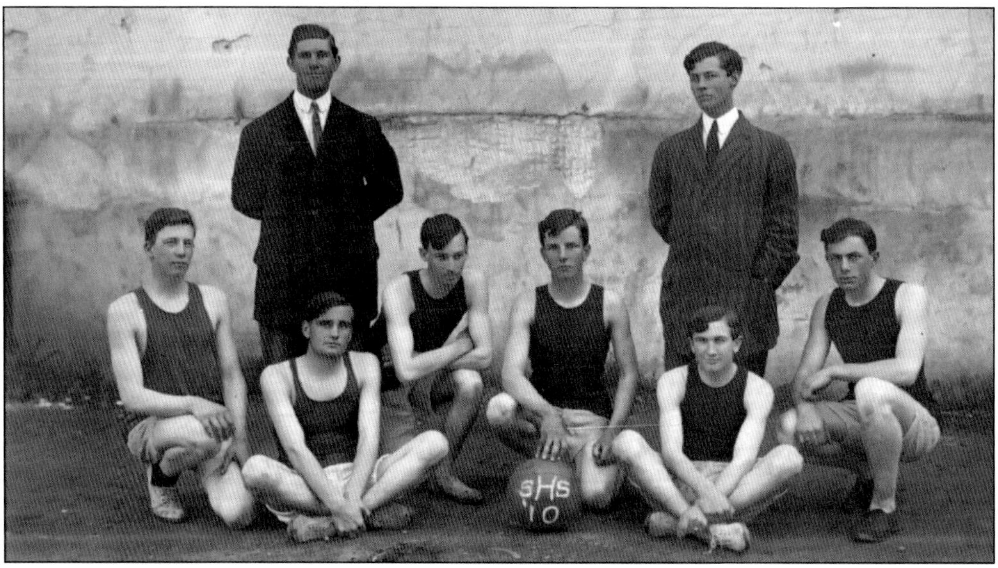

Sports teams, already operating out of the grammar school, continued interschool play when students moved to the high school. This basketball team photograph includes, from left to right, (first row) players R. Wagner, E. Poppe, R. Cooper, O. Dresel, E. Clements, and H. Lutgens; (second row) coaches Ben Greely and Don Campbell. (Courtesy Robert Parmelee.)

The grammar school was near the center of town, but many of its early students lived in outlying areas and either walked or rode a horse to school. The girl on this horse is on her way to school, carrying a lunch pail that closely resembles one in the Depot Museum. (Courtesy SVHS.)

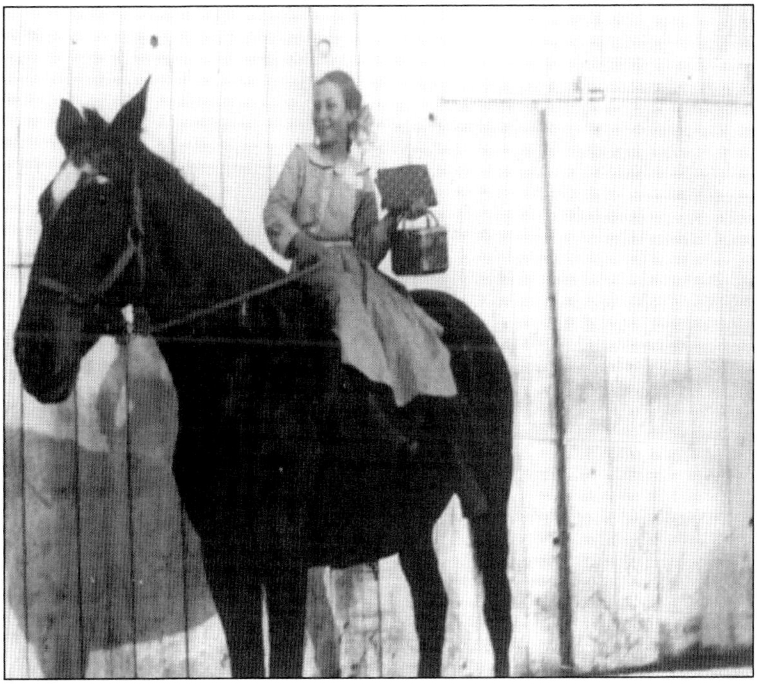

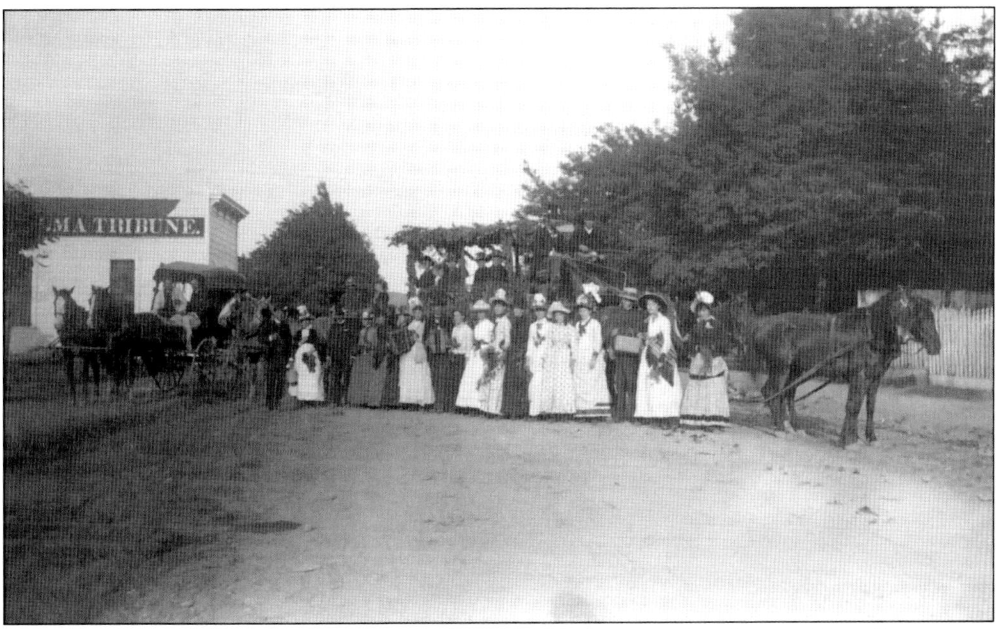

Sonoma families have always loved a parade. This parade unit is lined up on Napa Street, near the school. The 1846 raising of the Bear Flag over Sonoma Plaza was a grand reason to have a celebration, and the people lining up to ride or walk here were probably celebrating the 50th anniversary of the event—though an earlier parade was held for the 41st. The *Sonoma Tribune*, an early newspaper, became the *Index-Tribune* in 1899. (Courtesy SVHS.)

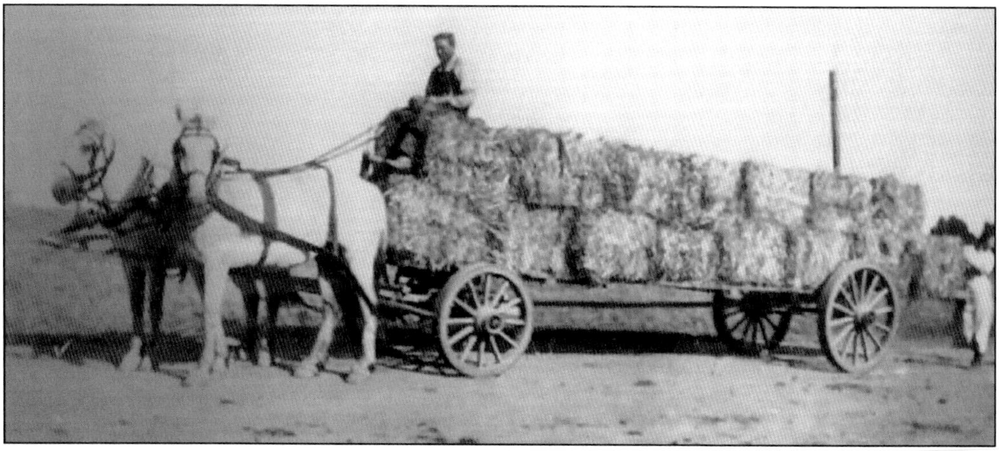

Most children who lived on farms worked with their parents, especially during harvest. Often, the school year was timed around the planting or harvest seasons. In addition to turkey farms, Sonoma had vineyards, hay and alfalfa, prunes, and apples. Average daily attendance at school went down once the crops were ready. (Courtesy SVHS.)

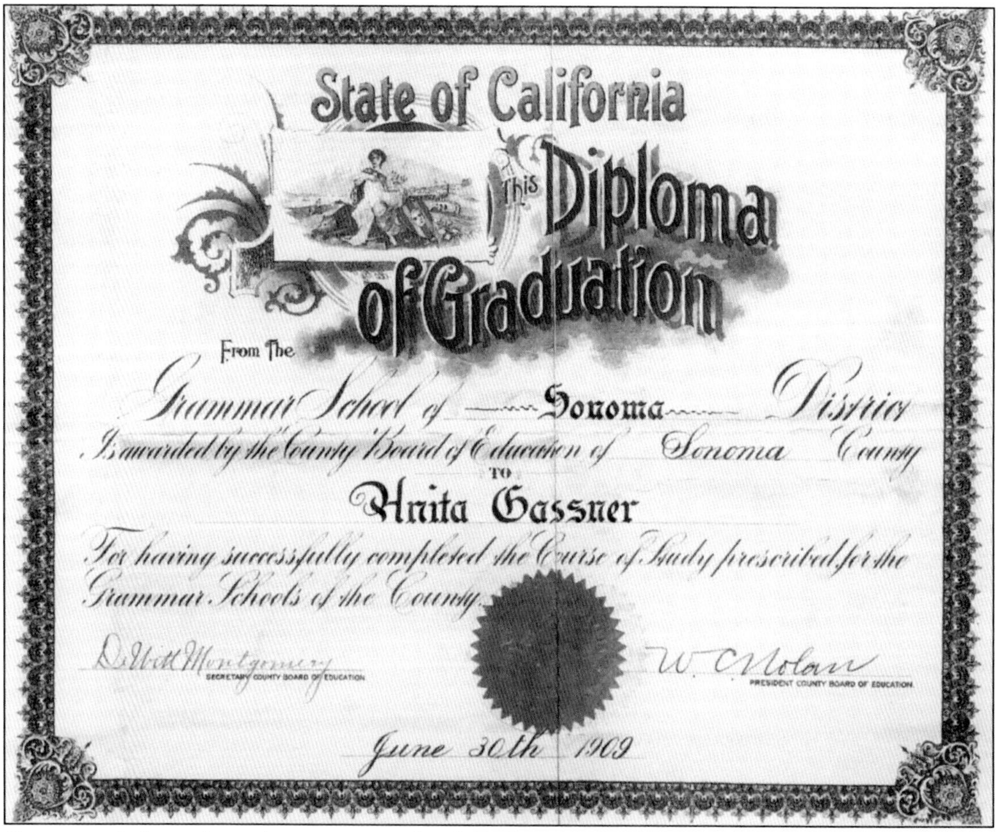

State of California
This Diploma of Graduation
From The Grammar School of Sonoma District
Is awarded by the County Board of Education of Sonoma County
TO
Anita Gassner
For having successfully completed the Course of Study prescribed for the Grammar Schools of the County.
DeWitt Montgomery
Secretary County Board of Education
W. C. Nolan
President County Board of Education
June 30th 1909

Getting a diploma from the grammar school was a momentous occasion, and the flowery script added to its importance. This diploma was for Anita Gassner, who received it in 1909. Diplomas changed in appearance over the years but never lost their status as a symbol of importance—especially for those who experienced hardships just to get an education. (Courtesy Sonoma League for Historic Preservation.)

Two

Sonoma Grammar School: Boom to Depression

In the first quarter of the new century, the look of Sonoma's downtown changed. The 1906 earthquake had damaged the mission, and a devastating fire had consumed most of the buildings on the east side of the plaza. With an expectation of visitors coming after the San Francisco World's Fair in 1915, it was time to give Sonoma a face-lift.

The town was still largely agrarian, although the valley had a large tourist population throughout the year. People came from San Francisco to visit the many hot springs resorts in the area. They could board a train that was loaded onto a ferry and unloaded in Sausalito, where the tracks resumed. Summer was the most popular season, with news of dancing, barbecues, and other outdoor entertainments filling the pages of the local newspaper.

Uneasiness was growing as well. War in Europe dominated the headlines as early as 1914, and although the United States would not enter World War I until 1917, the war was on everyone's mind.

But in 1914, Sonoma had a more pressing problem. With a growing population and a schoolhouse no longer adequate for the number of children filling its classrooms, community leaders decided that it was time to build a new grammar school. When the Sonoma Valley High School District was formed in 1908, some pressure had been taken off of all of the valley schools but not enough to ease overcrowding in Sonoma.

School district trustees decided that a new school should be built. It would be located in front of the old school, on the same site; have all of the modern conveniences; and would be made of brick—a much safer material. In the words of the local newspaper editor, who supported the new school, "Our children will not swelter through the heat in crowded and poorly ventilated rooms or strain their eyes in dimly lit rooms."

The trustees had the land, the will, and after a successful bond election, the money. Little did they know that this school would eventually become a true cultural center—serving the Sonoma community well into the next century.

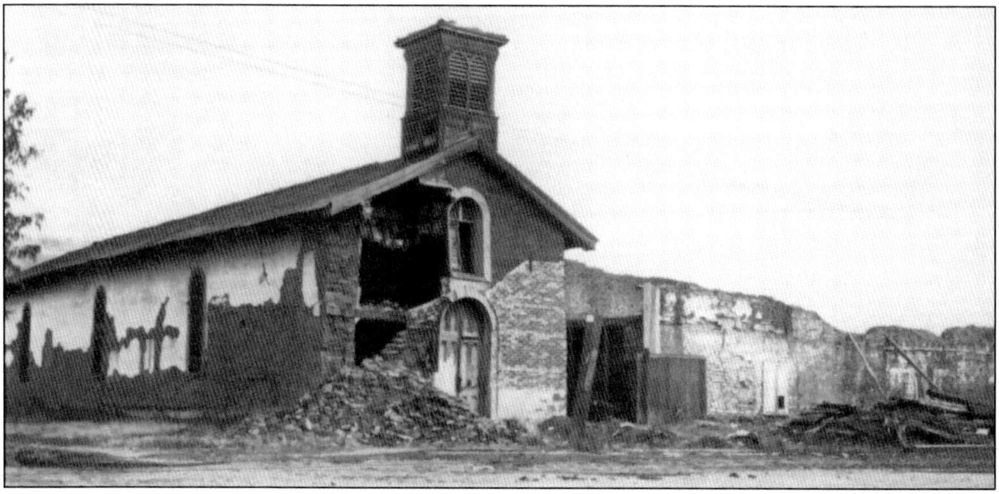

The Great San Francisco Earthquake of 1906 shook and weakened buildings in downtown Sonoma, although the wood-frame school building rode it out with little damage. The mission, made of adobe bricks, eventually lost a wall in 1908. Faced mainly with cracks and chimneys to repair, Sonomans counted themselves lucky but also began to look at their town with a different perspective. In the minds of many, it was time to modernize. (Courtesy SVHS.)

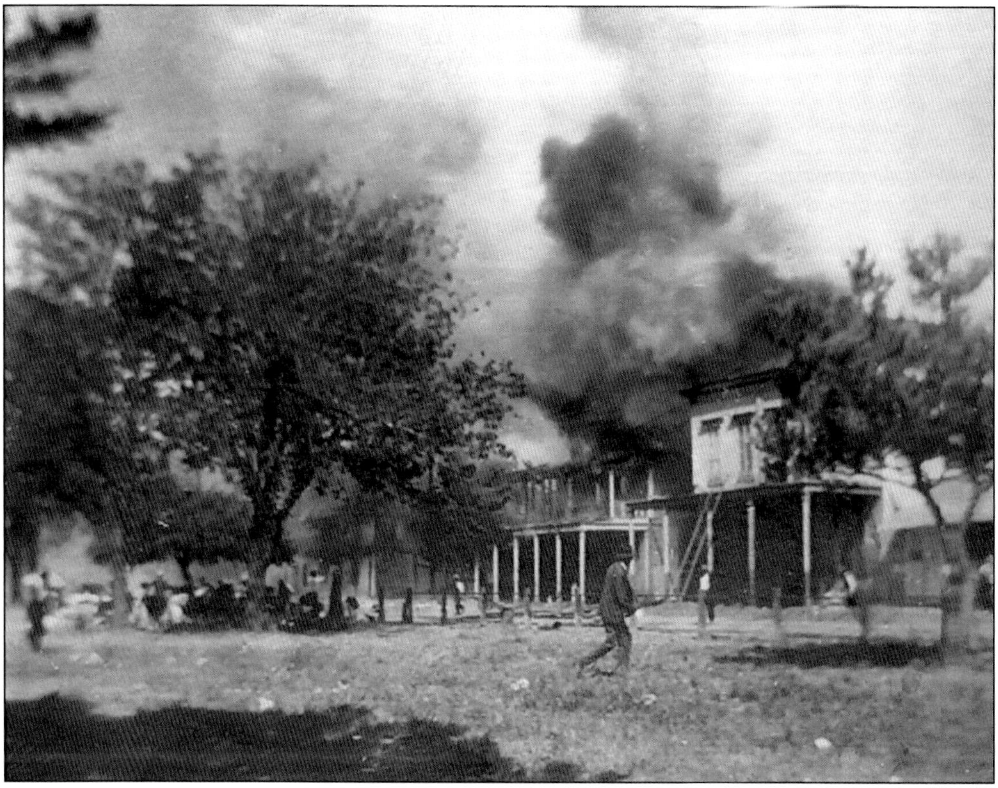

The next tragedy hit closer to home. A block of First Street East was consumed by fire in 1911. While many buildings were made of adobe bricks or quarried stones, others were wooden structures that were completely destroyed when the fire broke out behind them. This brought an uncomfortable awareness of the fragility of the city's wooden schoolhouse. (Courtesy SVHS.)

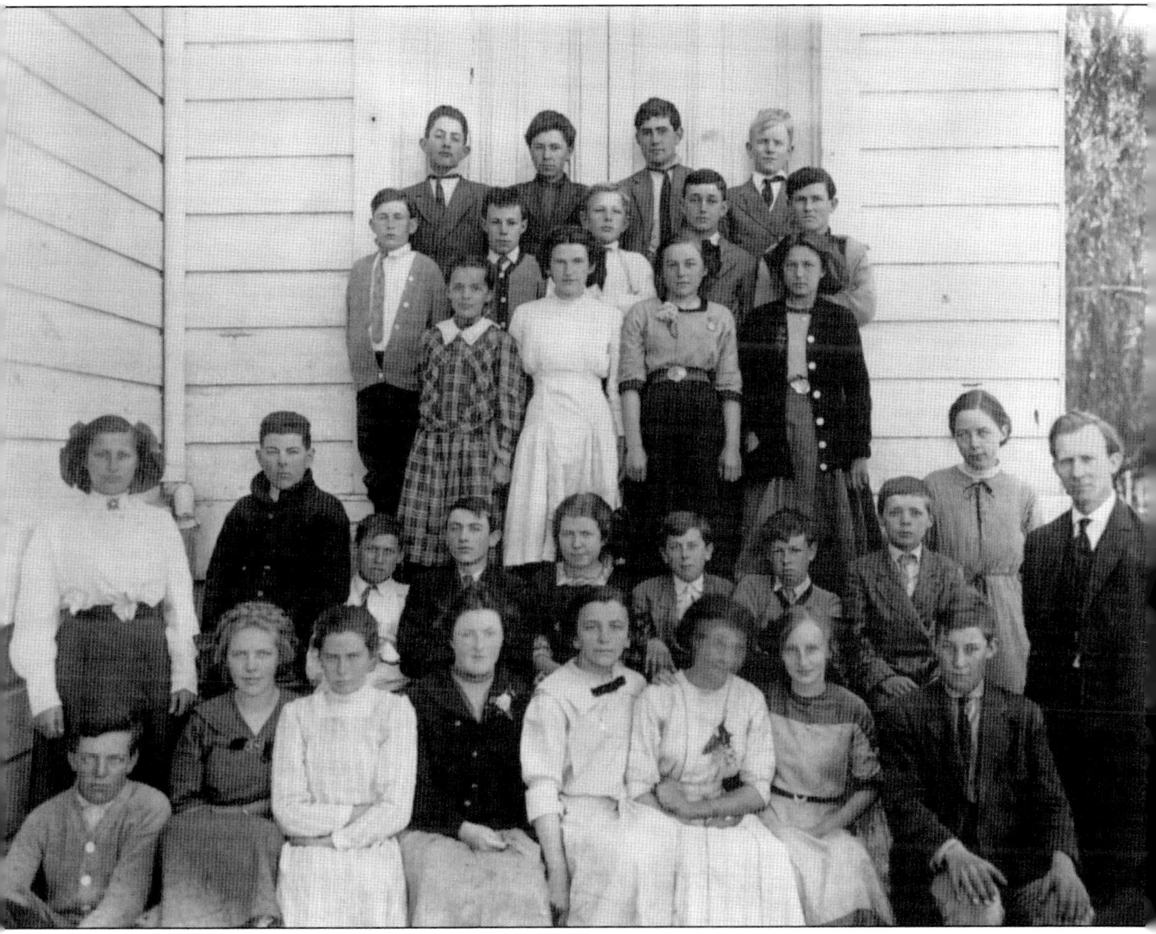

By 1912, the Sonoma Grammar School was growing out of its comfort zone. Although it survived the earthquake of 1906 and the fire of 1911, the building still had only four classrooms to house eight grades. The board of trustees began discussing the possibility of a new, larger school. Seventh and eighth graders that year are seen here, listed from left to right: (first row) Carl Smith, Dorothy Dobble, Eugenie Froment, Sadie Dunbar, Dorothy Breitenback, Julie Carriger, Etta Rassmussen, Roy Nelson, and their young teacher, Jesse Prestwood; (second row) Julia Marioni, Joe McMullin, Henry Palmer, Edward Pauli, Alice Trudgen, Gusie Alber, Sidney Cameron, Fred Heggie, and Elma Bill; (third row) Amy Heggie, Alma Cooper, Edith Luhis, and Martha Luhis; (fourth row) Elmer Rambo, Russell Prestwood, Bunker Dresel, Louis Maffei, and Clayton Darling; (fifth row) Eddic Gothe, Willie Perry, Ray Gottenburg, and John Duhring. The descendants of many of these students still reside in Sonoma. (Courtesy SVHS.)

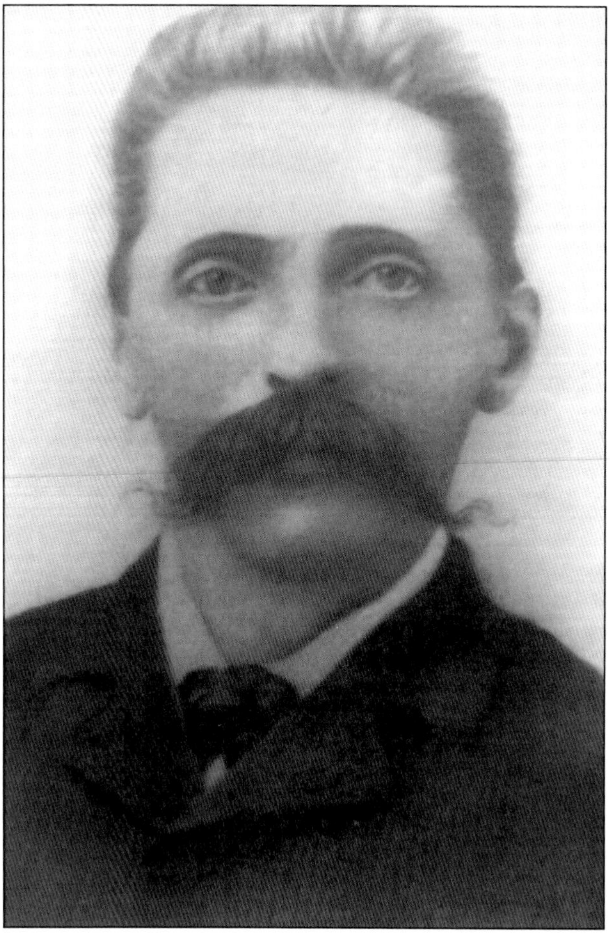

An election was held in 1914 asking voters to pass bonds to build a new school. Supporting the measure was *Sonoma Index-Tribune* editor Harry Granice. On March 21, he wrote, "It is the duty of every voter to support the bonds in order that a deplorable, even criminal, condition can be remedied." In the end, the $30,000 bond issue passed by 56 votes. (Courtesy SIT.)

Adolph Charles Lutgens of San Francisco was selected to be the architect for the new school. He must have been following in the footsteps of his parents, who moved to Sonoma in 1862 and later built the Union Hotel (pictured). One of seven children, Adolph grew up in Sonoma and most likely attended the old grammar school. He studied architecture and designed many buildings in San Francisco. (Courtesy SVHS.)

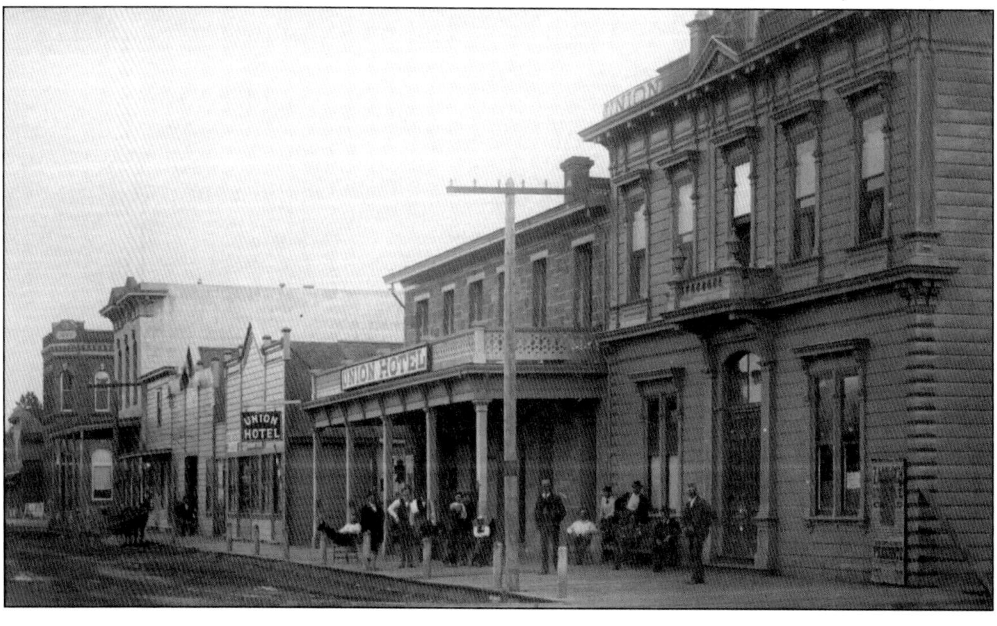

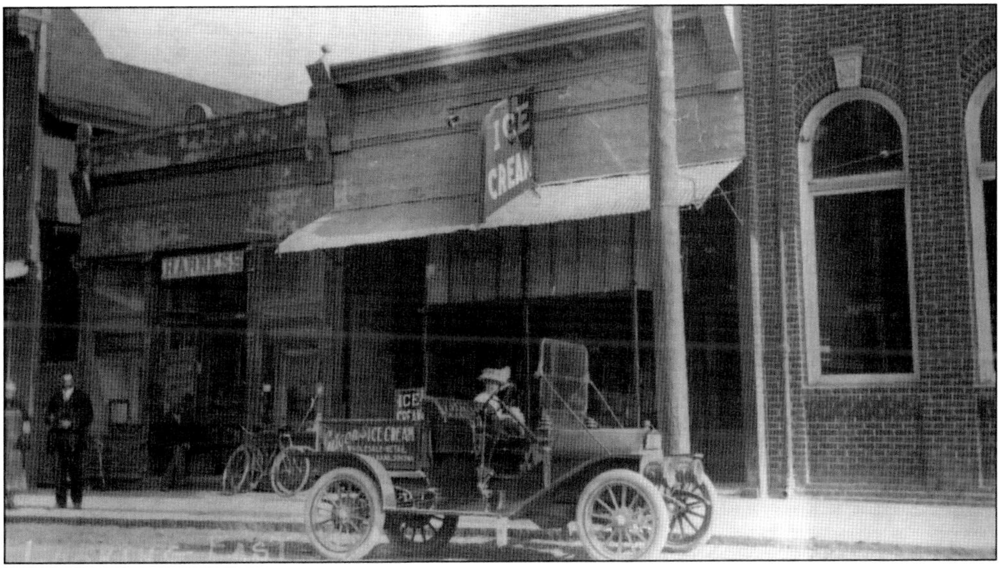

Some of the Lutgens family remained in Sonoma. In 1903, Lizzie Lutgens opened an ice cream and candy store on East Napa Street, on the east side of the bank that occupied the corner of East Napa Street and Broadway. Her son Artie's Studebaker is noted in the picture, parked in front of his mother's store. (Courtesy SVHS.)

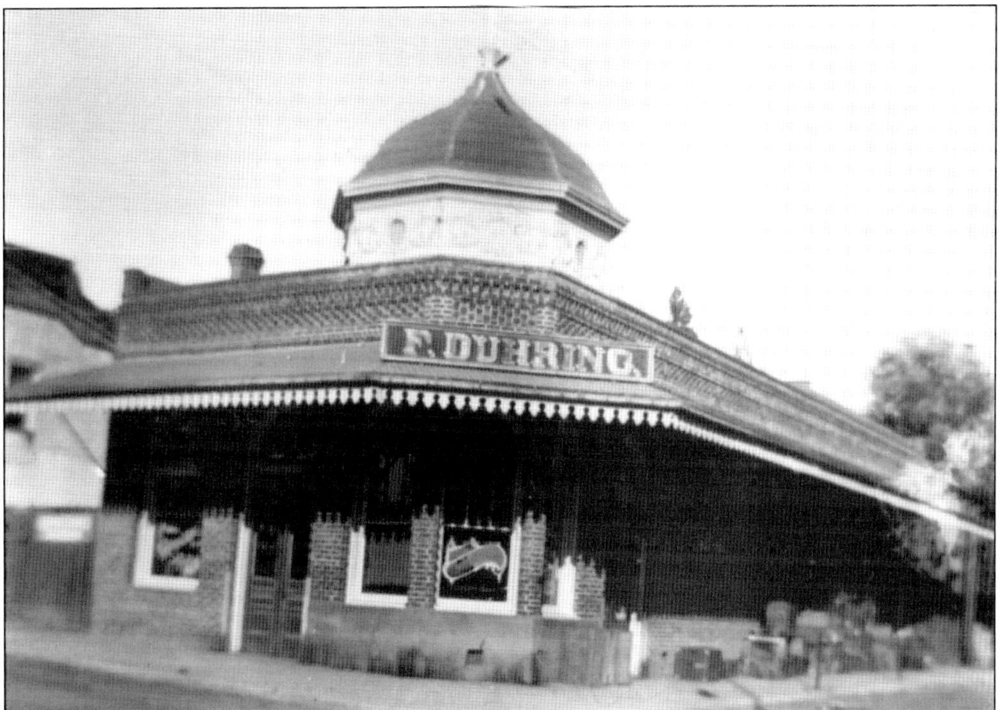

The Fred T. Duhring Building was most likely Adolph Lutgens's first architectural project in Sonoma. Built in 1891, it stood on the northeast corner of Napa Street and First Street East and escaped the 1911 fire that destroyed other buildings. In 1990, its luck ran out when a fire damaged much of it. It was rebuilt and still stands today. (Courtesy SVHS.)

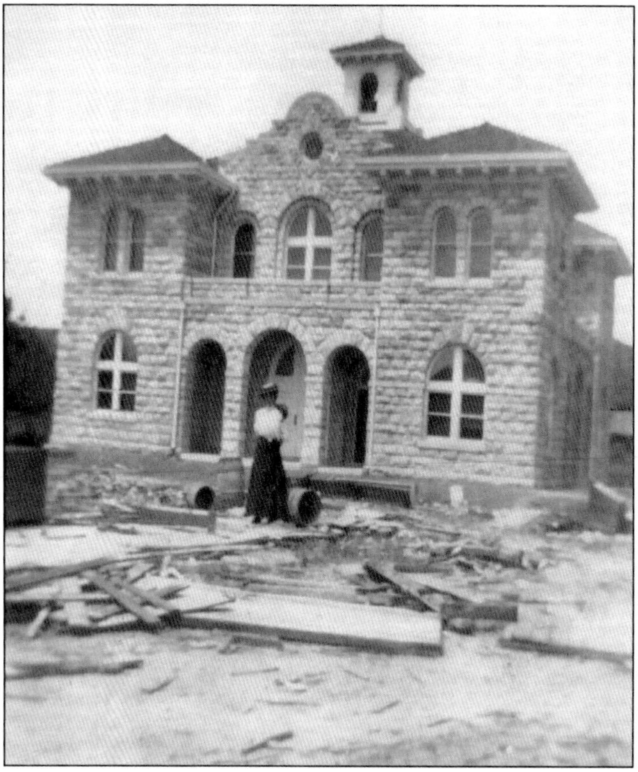

The most prominent building designed by Adolph Lutgens was the Sonoma City Hall. After a $10,000 bond issue was passed, construction started in 1906. The San Francisco Earthquake halted construction, as workmen could make more money in the big city. Built in the center of the Sonoma Plaza, the edifice lay unfinished for over a year. When workmen returned, the city trustees had to rebid the job and get a new contractor. Construction began again in late summer, and work was finally completed in 1908. The building, whose original cost ended up being nearly $16,000, is still in use today. These photographs show that, even unfinished, it had its attraction for the many tourists who visited the city. (Both, courtesy SVHS.)

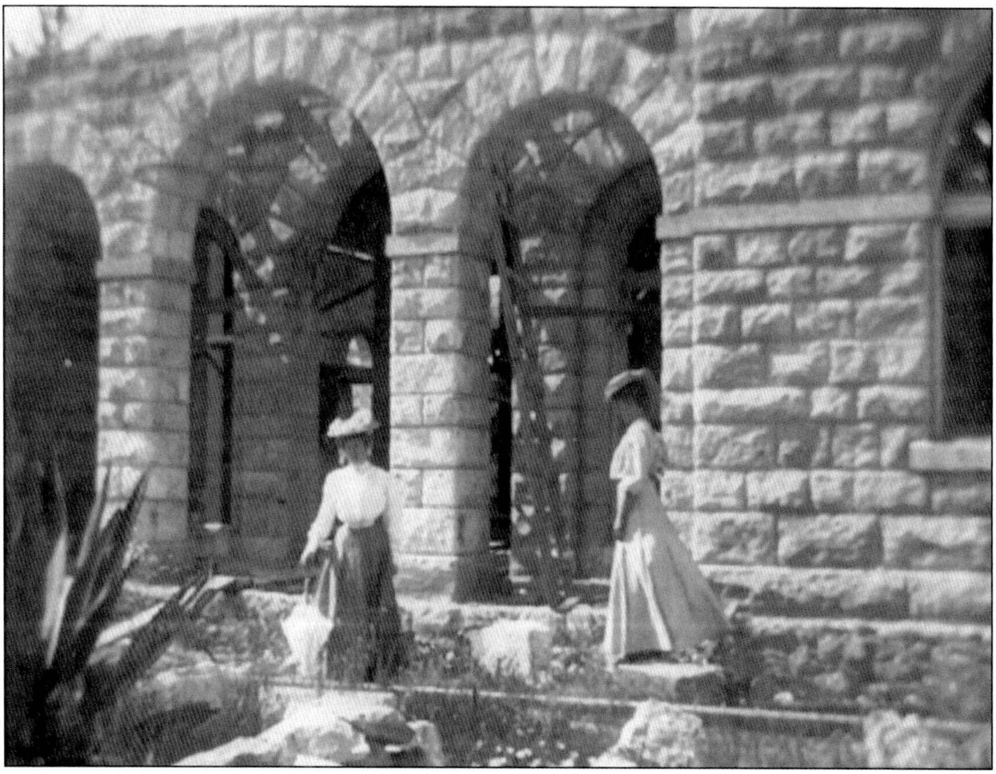

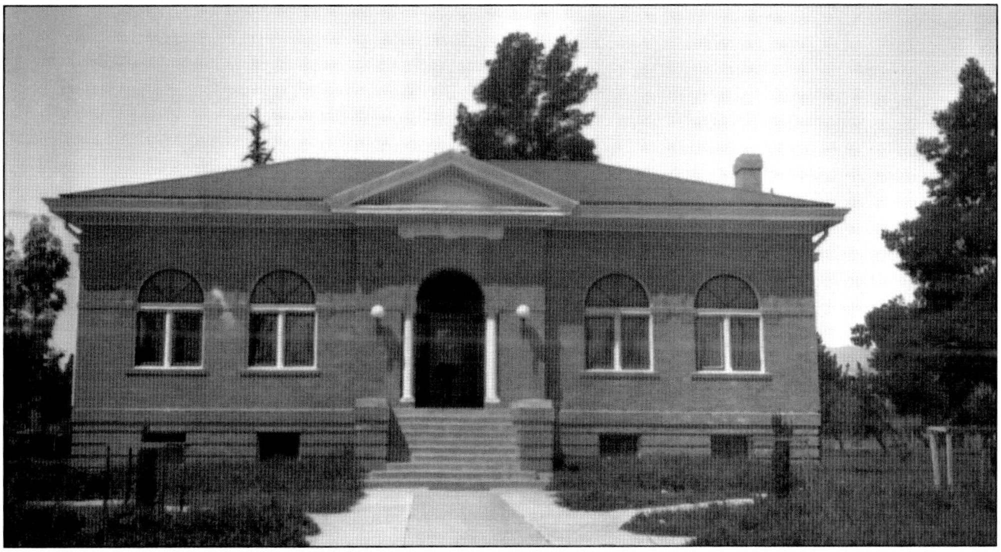

Lutgens's third downtown building was the Carnegie Library, built on the plaza in 1913. It was constructed at a cost of $6,600 and was funded largely by a grant from the Carnegie Foundation, which was requested by the Sonoma Woman's Club. A new library was built in 1978, but the building still houses the visitors' bureau and several city offices. (Courtesy SVHS.)

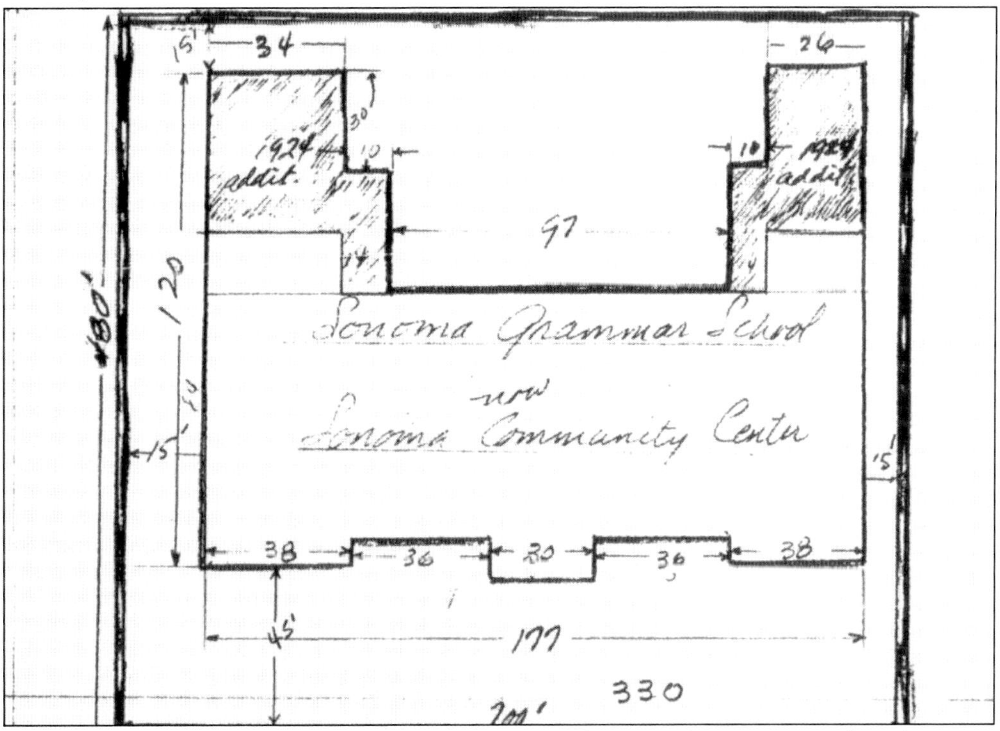

The architect's plan for the school was far-reaching. With roomy classrooms—each with its own cloakroom—a modern principal's office, and an auditorium for assemblies and other school events, the building would be the pride of the community. There was room to build it close to East Napa Street, and as the old school was situated near the center of the lot, classes could continue until its completion. (Courtesy SCC.)

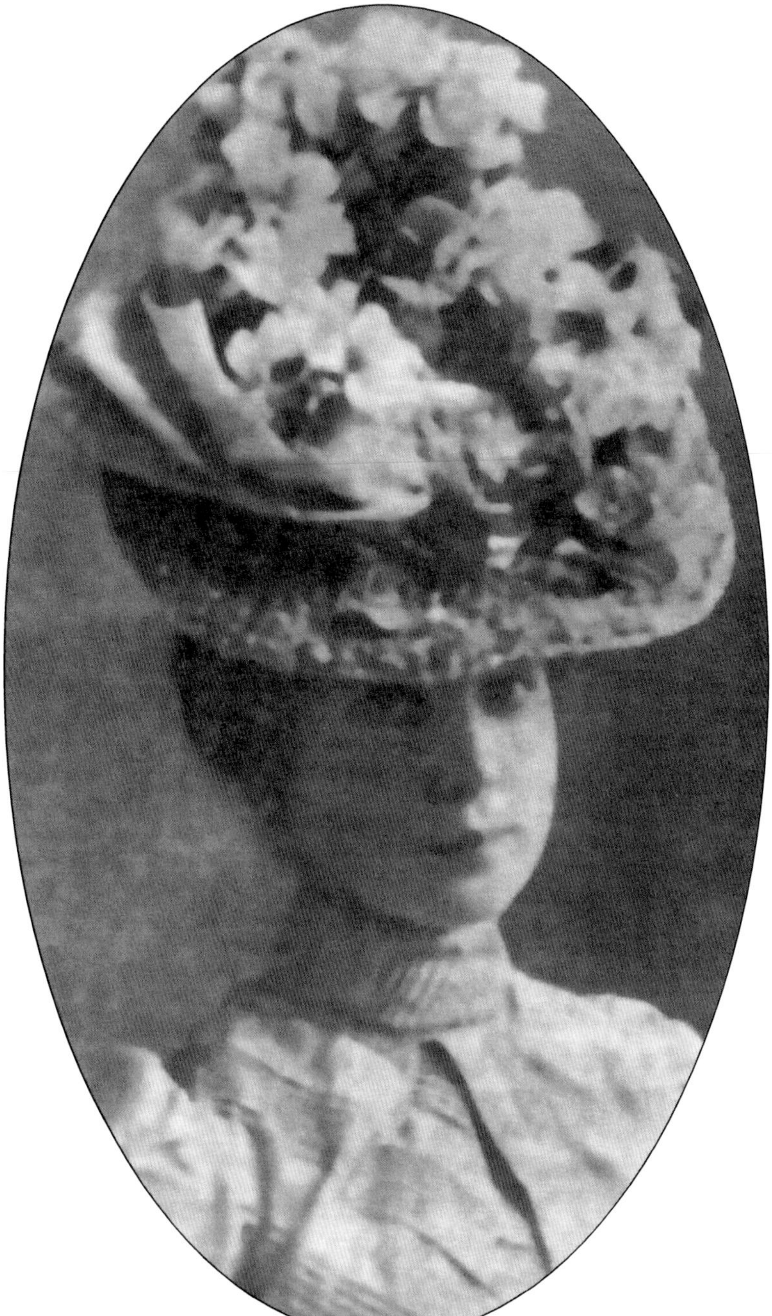

Progress reports on the construction of the grammar school were given in the local paper. Celeste Granice Murphy, shown here as a young woman, took over from her father as editor of the local paper when he became ill. She reported on the school's progress all during 1915. In an editorial dated February 19, 1916, she said, "The coming into possession of the magnificent new Grammar School building is a proud moment for us and one that is shared by the entire valley. It marks a new epoch in the progress of our citizenship and is a forerunner of greater public work and more pronounced pride in the upbuilding of the future." (Courtesy SIT.)

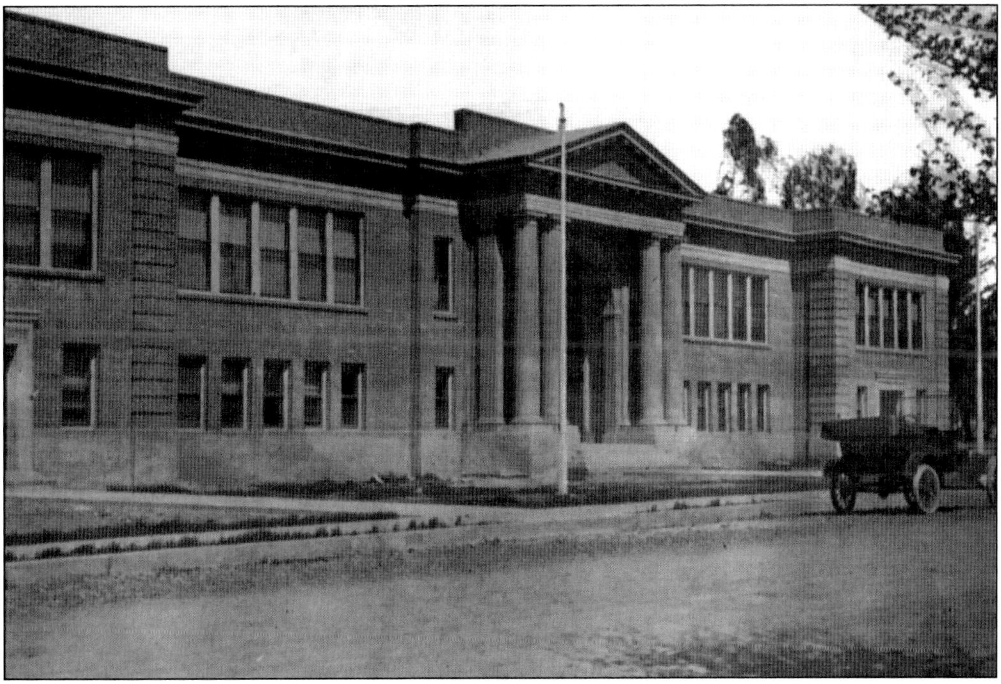

Sonoma Grammar School was dedicated in May 1916. Dr. A.M. Thomson, president of the board of trustees, presided at the ceremony where the Native Sons of the Golden West presented a Bear Flag and the Moose Social Club presented an American flag to the school. Enrollment for the coming year was estimated at 160 students and growing. (Courtesy SVHS.)

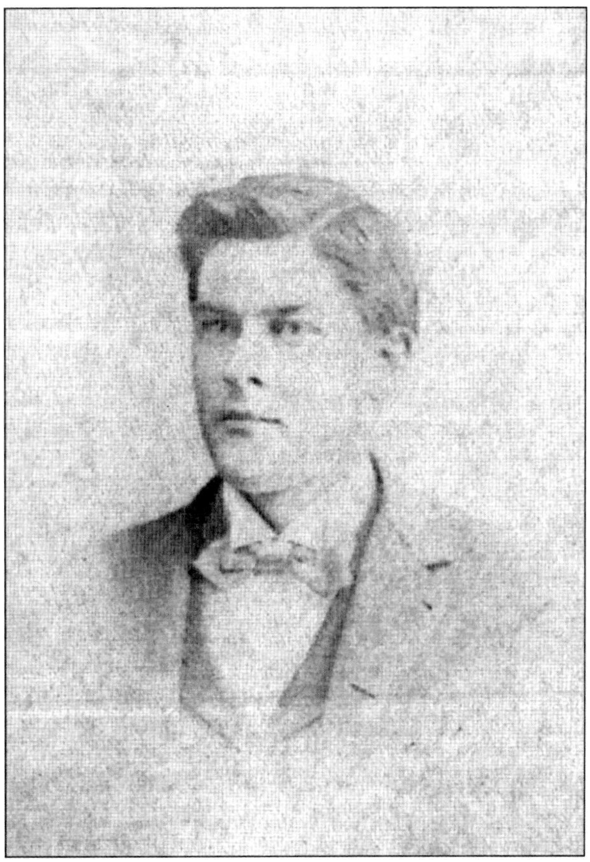

Dr. Allen M. Thomson, who married Anita Emparan, a granddaughter of General Vallejo, was a prominent citizen and took on many projects in town. He and Anita eloped, despite the objections of her mother, Luisa. They eventually moved back to town, where Thomson had a busy practice and was an early advocate for a community hospital, as well as good schools. (Courtesy SVHS.)

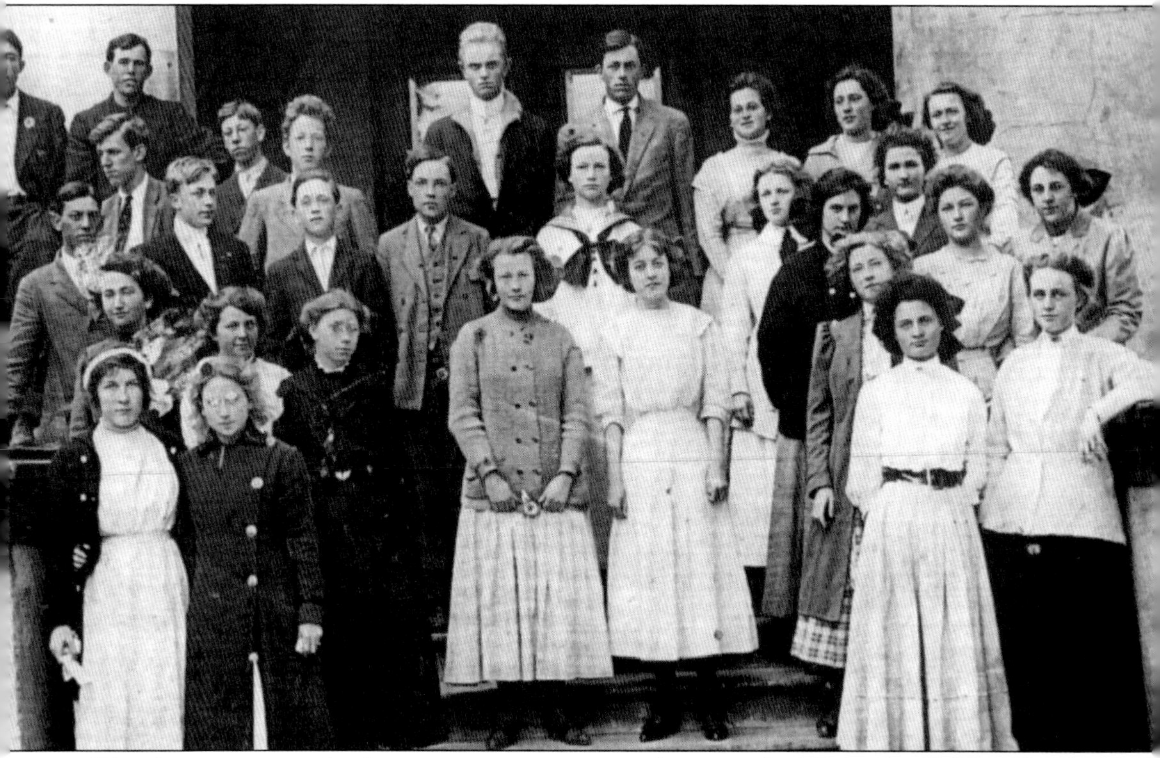

Edna Cooper—pictured at front row, center, in a grey jacket—was the fifth teacher to be employed. A high school student when this photograph was taken, she was the granddaughter of Blue Wing Inn owner James Cooper. "The fifth teacher will do away with overcrowding and give the children the advantage of more attention," said the local newspaper. She remained at the school until it closed. (Courtesy Robert Parmelee.)

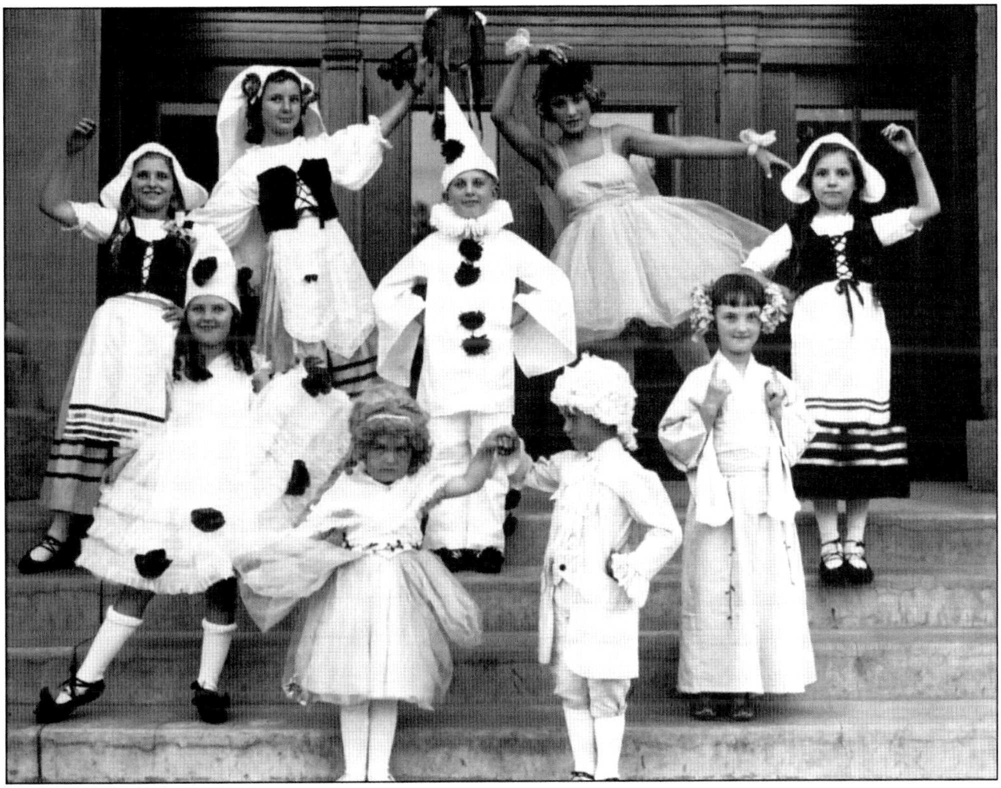

The grammar school thrived and became a popular place for entertainments and independent classes. Miss Tamara Lawb's Ballet School gave many performances in the auditorium—its beautiful floors perfect for dance. The above performance, given on June 21, 1921, after school ended, also had a dance until the wee hours of the morning. Seen at left in the first row is June Picetti Shepard, who became one of Sonoma's honorary *alcaldesas*—an award granted to those who have a lifetime of exemplary public service. The dancer at third row, center, is Jerry Casson, who would be a prominent advocate for saving the grammar school building when its use as a public school ended in 1949. The program at right for Lawb's event lists the names of several other people who grew up in Sonoma and continued to live here. (Both, courtesy SVHS.)

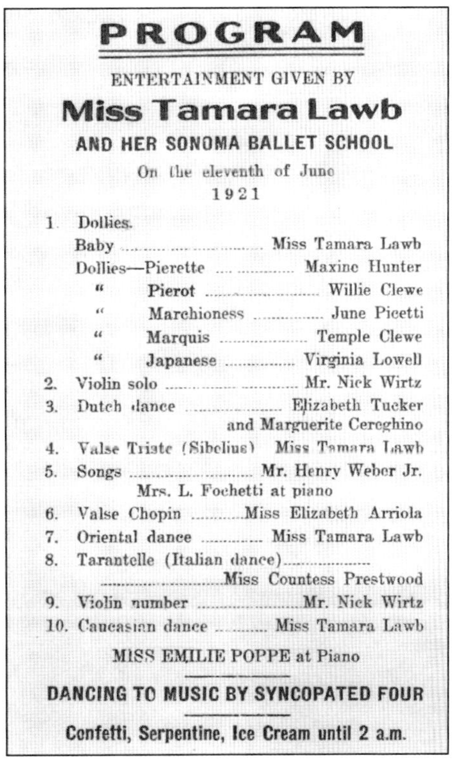

PROGRAM

ENTERTAINMENT GIVEN BY

Miss Tamara Lawb

AND HER SONOMA BALLET SCHOOL

On the eleventh of June
1921

1. Dollies.
   Baby .... Miss Tamara Lawb
   Dollies—Pierette .... Maxine Hunter
   " Pierot .... Willie Clewe
   " Marchioness .... June Picetti
   " Marquis .... Temple Clewe
   " Japanese .... Virginia Lowell
2. Violin solo .... Mr. Nick Wirtz
3. Dutch dance .... Elizabeth Tucker and Marguerite Cereghino
4. Valse Triste (Sibelius) Miss Tamara Lawb
5. Songs .... Mr. Henry Weber Jr. Mrs. L. Fochetti at piano
6. Valse Chopin .... Miss Elizabeth Arriola
7. Oriental dance .... Miss Tamara Lawb
8. Tarantelle (Italian dance) .... Miss Countess Prestwood
9. Violin number .... Mr. Nick Wirtz
10. Caucasian dance .... Miss Tamara Lawb

MISS EMILIE POPPE at Piano

DANCING TO MUSIC BY SYNCOPATED FOUR

Confetti, Serpentine, Ice Cream until 2 a.m.

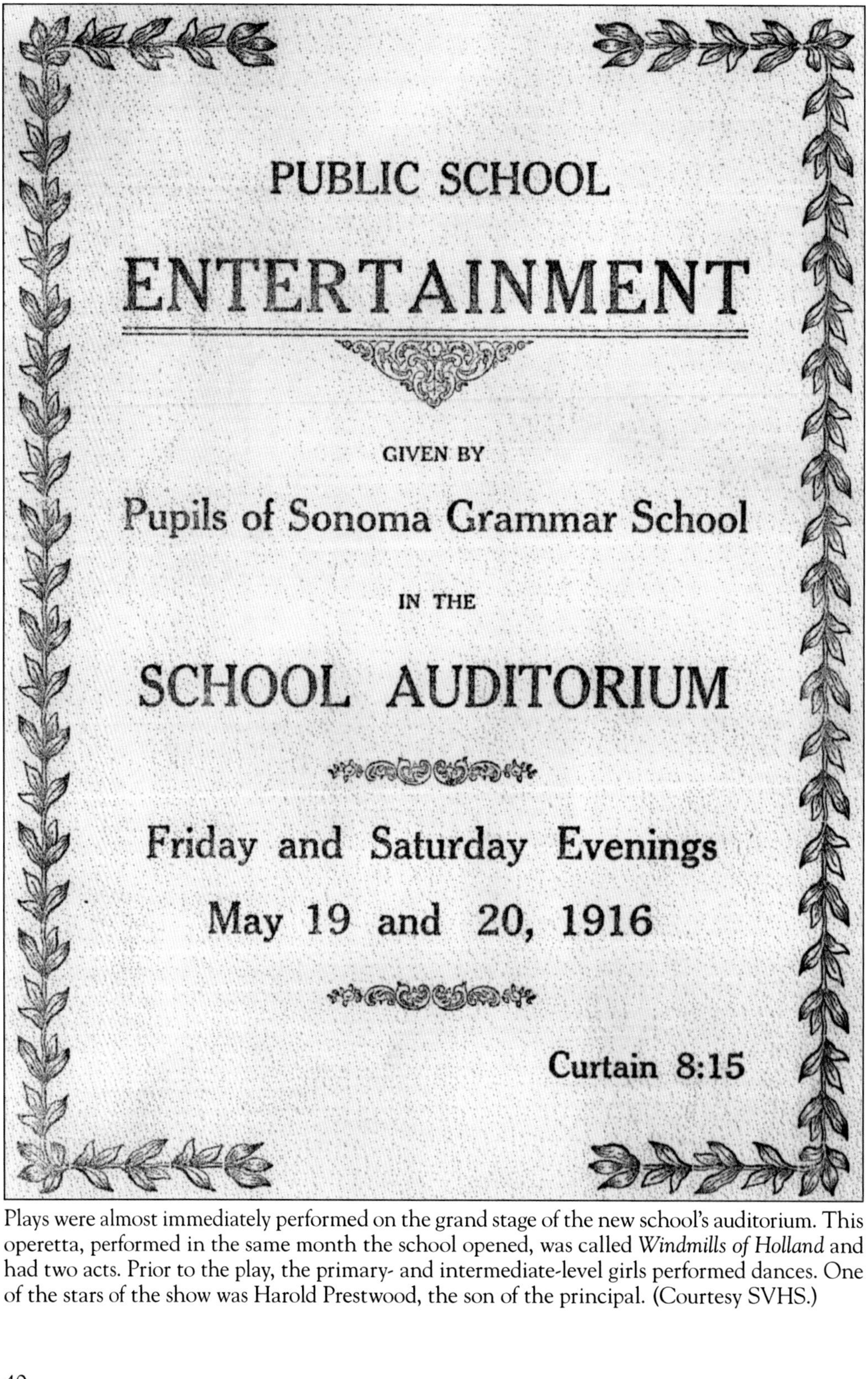

Plays were almost immediately performed on the grand stage of the new school's auditorium. This operetta, performed in the same month the school opened, was called *Windmills of Holland* and had two acts. Prior to the play, the primary- and intermediate-level girls performed dances. One of the stars of the show was Harold Prestwood, the son of the principal. (Courtesy SVHS.)

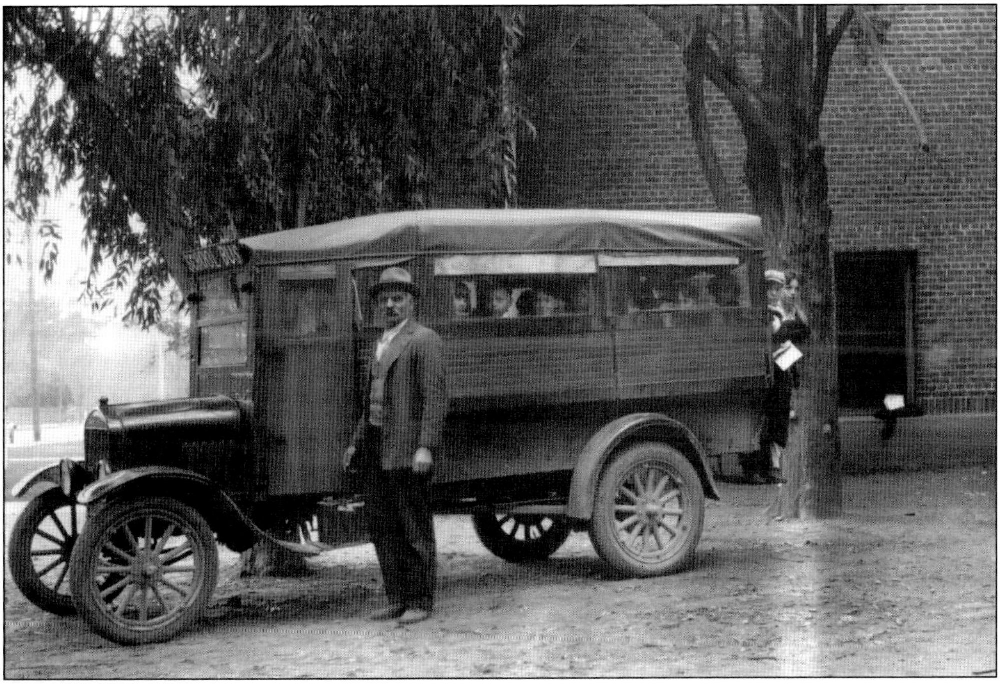

Bus service was a luxury, but the grammar school had a bus as early as 1923. Frederick Schmidt began driving his daughter to school and gradually added so many neighbors' children that he had to modify a Ford truck to create the bus. In later years, an additional bus was added with a second route. (Courtesy SVHS.)

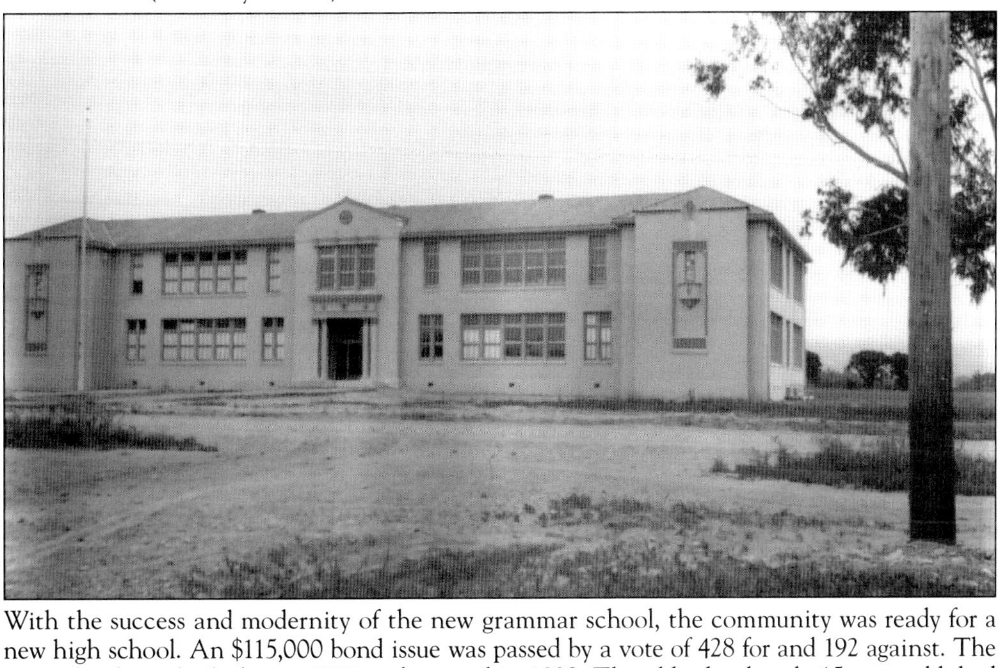

With the success and modernity of the new grammar school, the community was ready for a new high school. An $115,000 bond issue was passed by a vote of 428 for and 192 against. The new school was built during 1922 and opened in 1923. The old school, only 15 years old, had "wretched heating, poor ventilation, defective plumbing, and crumbling walls," according to the local newspaper. (Courtesy SVHS.)

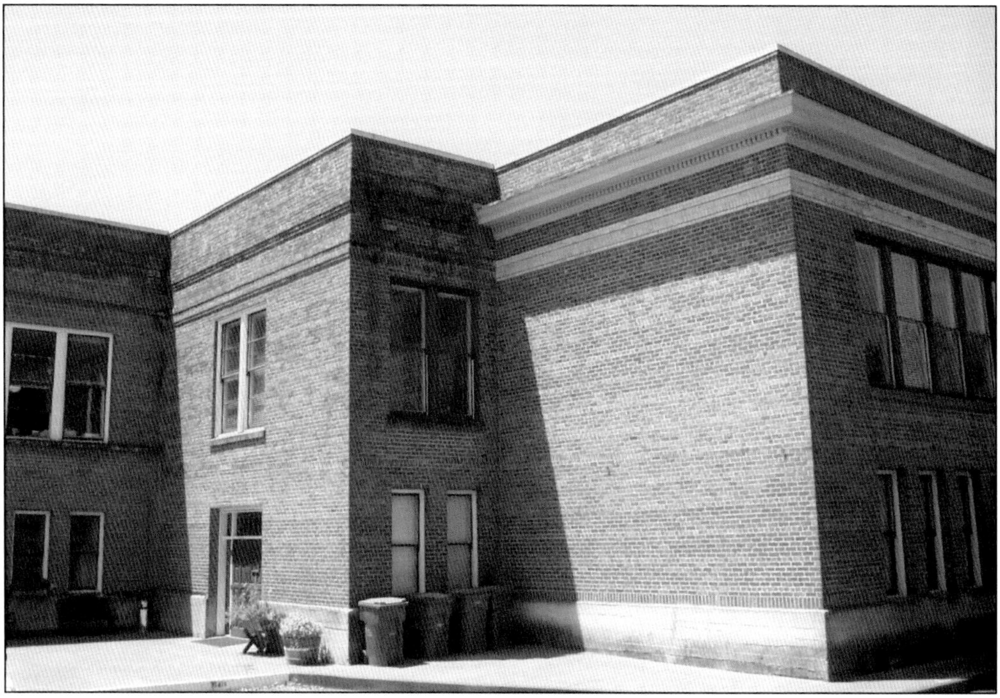

Sonoma experienced growing pains in the 1920s, and the school population began to feel cramped. In 1923, two wings were added to the back of the grammar school, adding large rooms at top and bottom. The detail running along the upper edge of the walls shows the distinctive difference between the original and the addition, although it may have once matched. (Author's Collection.)

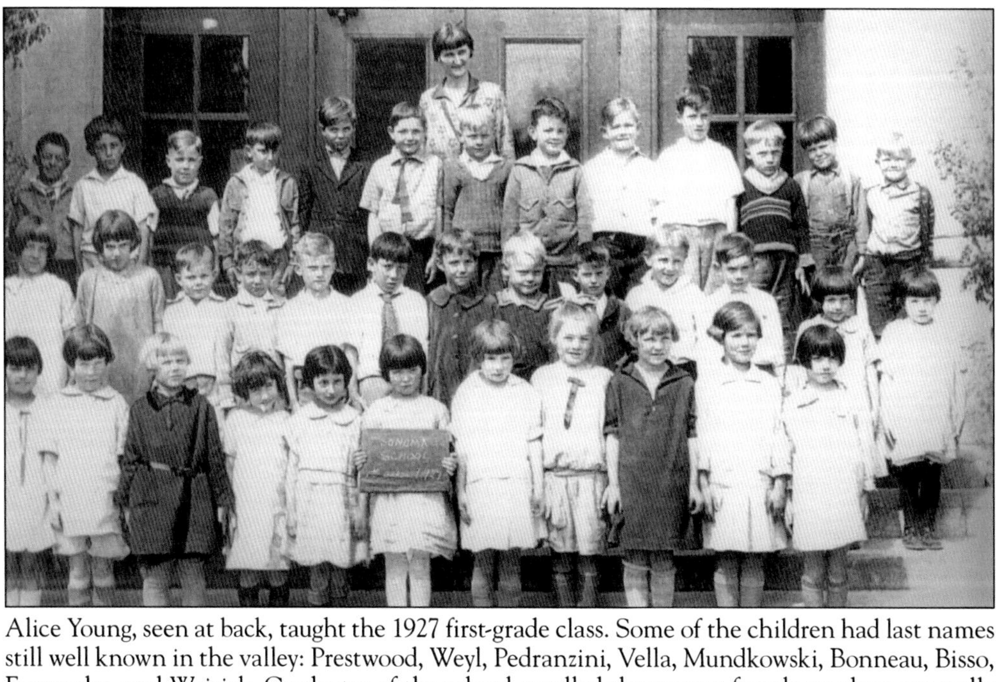

Alice Young, seen at back, taught the 1927 first-grade class. Some of the children had last names still well known in the valley: Prestwood, Weyl, Pedranzini, Vella, Mundkowski, Bonneau, Bisso, Fernandez, and Weirick. Graduates of the school recalled that young female teachers generally resigned once they were married. (Courtesy SVHS.)

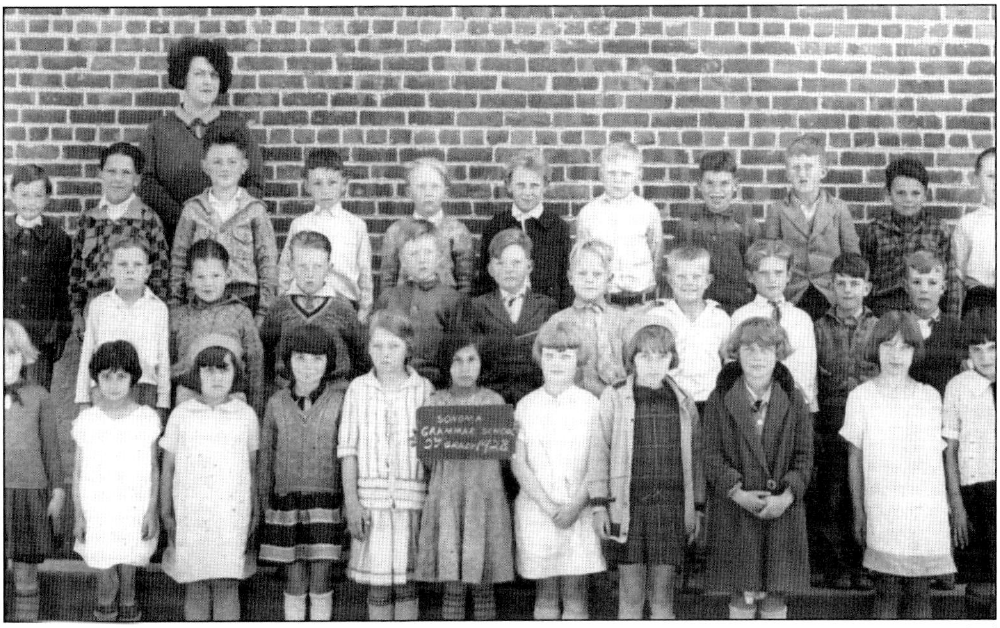

Zolita Bates, seen at back, taught second grade in 1928. She knew the space well, having attended the same school as a student. She remained in the community for her entire life and had a long career as a teacher. Her grandmother Nancy Bones Patton Adler was a survivor of the ill-fated Donner Party. (Courtesy SVHS.)

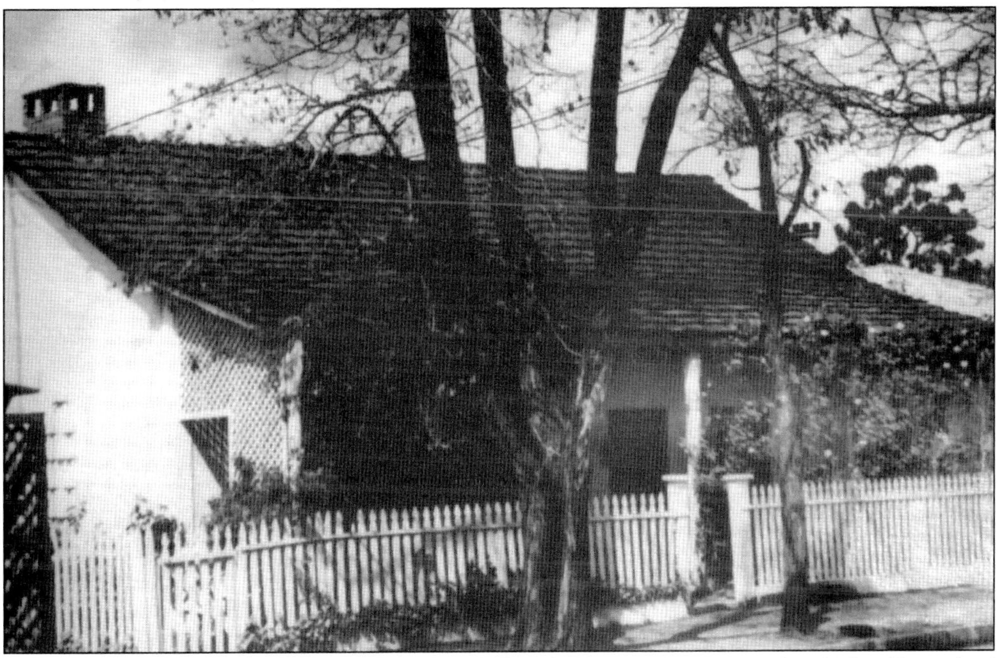

Many of the unmarried schoolteachers boarded with prominent citizens, but Zolita Bates had her own home. She restored the Nash-Patton Adobe on First Street East in 1931. Built in 1837, the building had been the home of her grandmother Nancy Bones Patton Adler, who lived in the building after her 1848 marriage to Lewis Adler, a merchant in San Francisco and Sonoma. (Courtesy SVHS.)

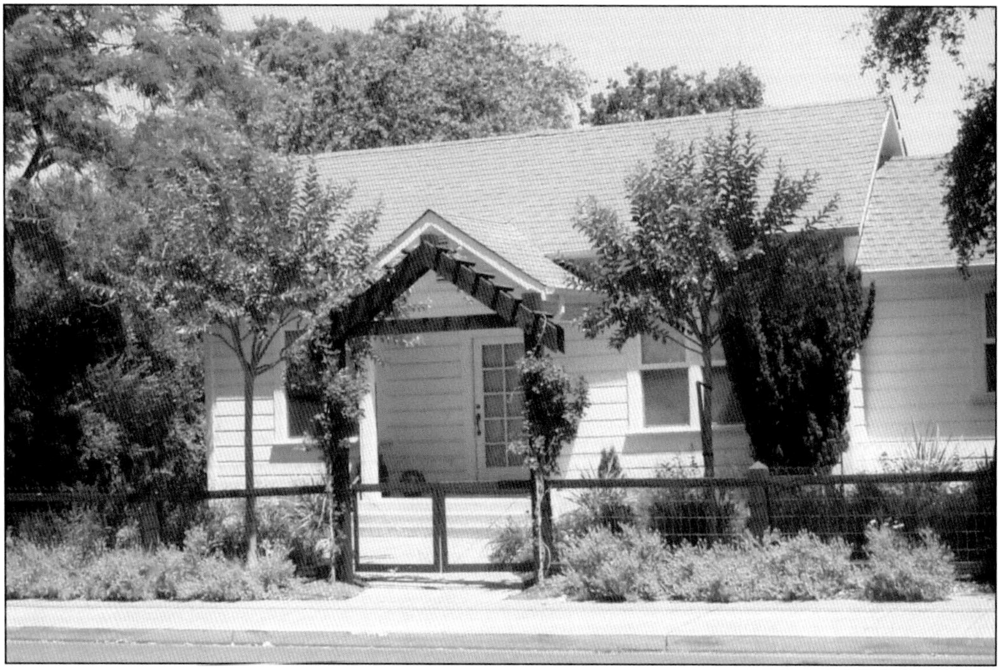

Principal Jesse Prestwood lived next to the school for many years. The house he occupied longest, now fully remodeled, changed gradually over the years but still exists. On the west side of the brick building, the modest wood home—in many ways similar to the original schoolhouse—must have given him a sense of belonging, even when he was not with his students. (Author's Collection.)

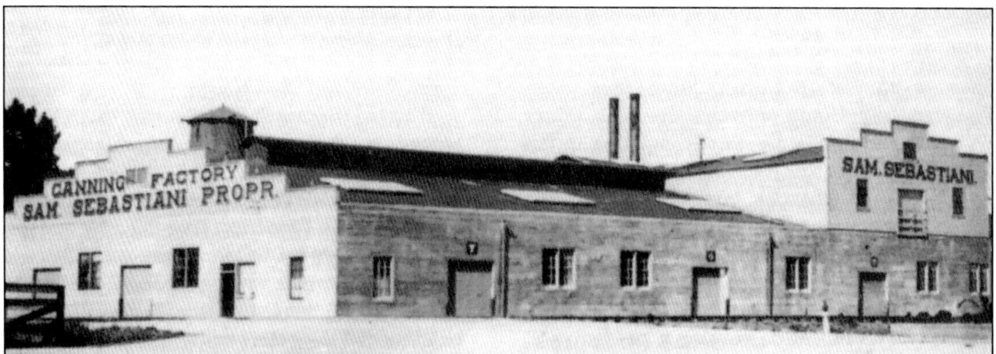

Sonoma Valley, with its flourishing viticulture and tourist trades, was thrown off balance when Prohibition became law. Although his winery—a few blocks from the school—continued to make sacramental and medicinal wine, local winemaker Samuele Sebastiani converted it to a cannery and put many people to work during the Great Depression. That included teens old enough for after-school jobs. (Courtesy SVHS.)

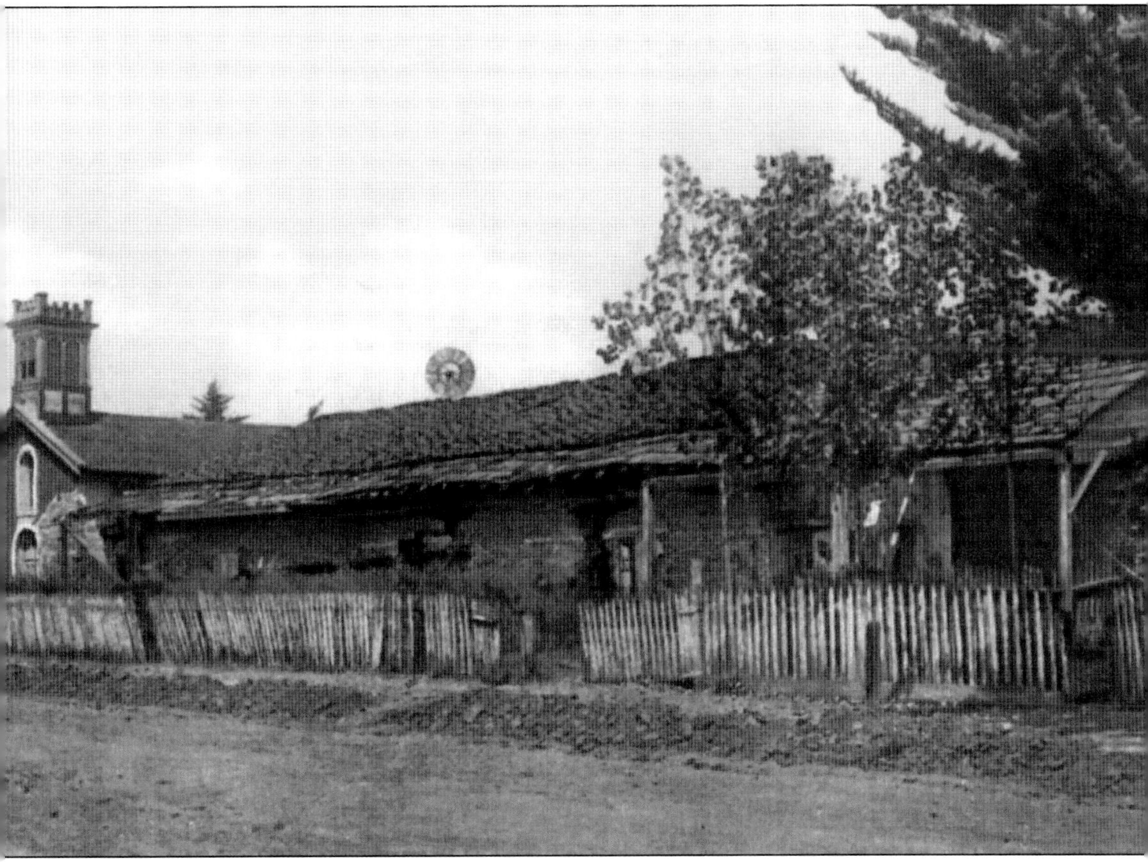

Sonoma is a place where history can be found around every corner, and even after the crash of 1929, tourists continued to visit. By 1930, the mission had been repaired, and when children studied California's history in the fourth grade, they could reach out and touch its mud brick surface on the way to school. (Courtesy SVHS.)

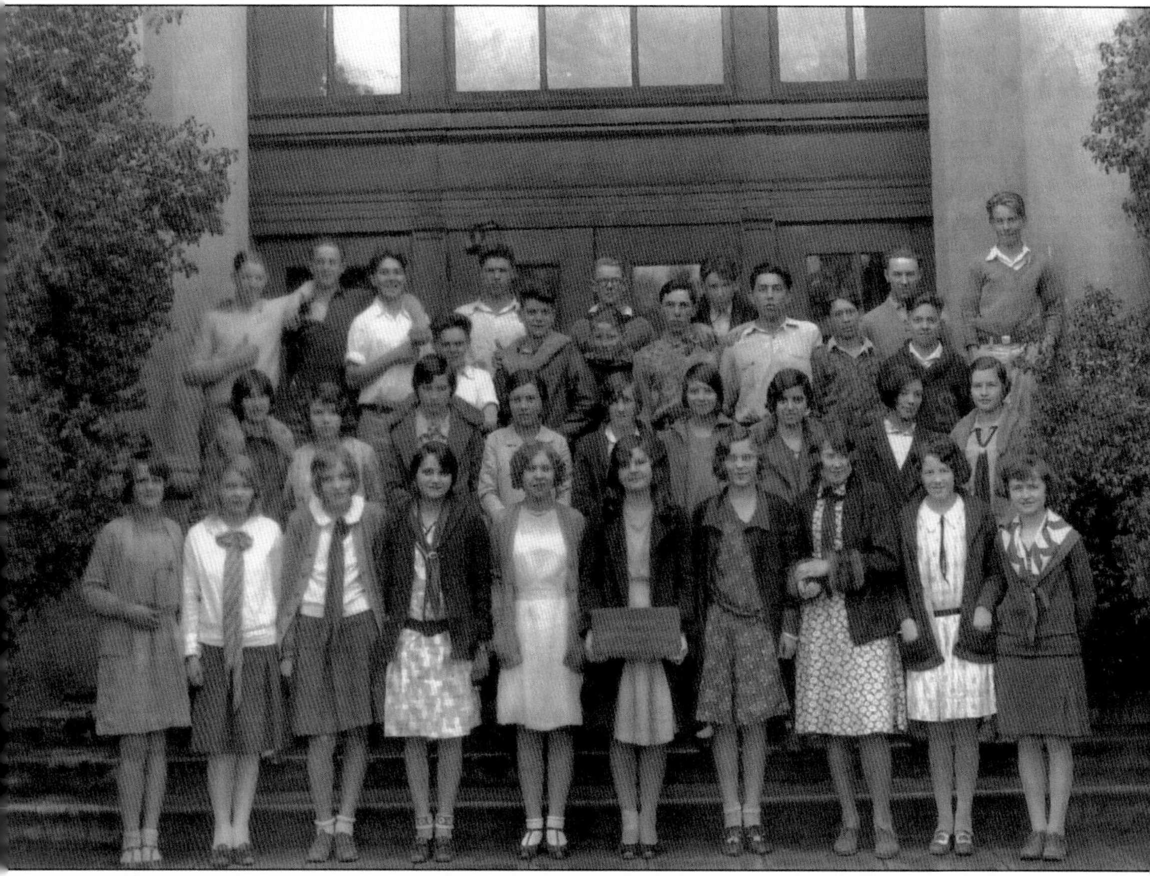

As the school year ended in 1930, the eighth-grade class stood proudly in front of the auditorium doors, knowing they would soon walk across the stage in front of parents and friends. Looking forward to high school, many reflected the optimism of their parents and did not realize that, even in a rural place like Sonoma, the Great Depression would soon become a reality. (Courtesy SVHS.)

Three

War, Recovery, and Closure

The Great Depression descended on Sonoma not with an aura of gloom but with the hope of a better future. Secure in its rural cocoon, Sonoma Valley went on about its business, relatively untouched by the economic ruin felt in the rest of the country. Yet an undercurrent of apprehension was never far away.

Government programs created jobs, paved roads, improved sewers, and made improvements to Sonoma Plaza, but locals did their share too—forming a relief committee that supplied people with groceries, medical care, and emergency aid. Local winery owner Samuele Sebastiani set about building homes and many public facilities that entertained families and provided safe environments for youngsters during their non-school hours. When Prohibition was repealed, the local wine industry was revived and Sonoma got back on its feet.

As 1940 approached, there was prosperity in the air and new concern for the allies who had already entered into the war in Europe.

Everything changed on December 7, 1941, when the United States was attacked at Pearl Harbor. Sonoma Valley residents rallied and formed committees to do their part: raising funds, rationing, and volunteering. Sonoma Grammar School practiced evacuation drills, and its students learned about what it meant to ration. For them, the war was still far away until their classmate Virginia Matsuyama was taken from her German mother and sent to an internment camp far from Sonoma. Her father, a college professor, had been sent away to a different camp earlier. Through the efforts of principal Jesse Prestwood, Virginia Matsuyama was allowed to return home six weeks later.

When the war ended, the town went back to normal. The local paper reported on the new hospital, a new police and fire facility, and the celebration of the 100th anniversary of the Bear Flag Revolt, which brought the governor to town. But age and new laws were catching up with the stately redbrick edifice on Napa Street, which had long provided the town's elementary-age children with an education and its people with a stage for many community entertainments. The building would remain, but its days as a school would end.

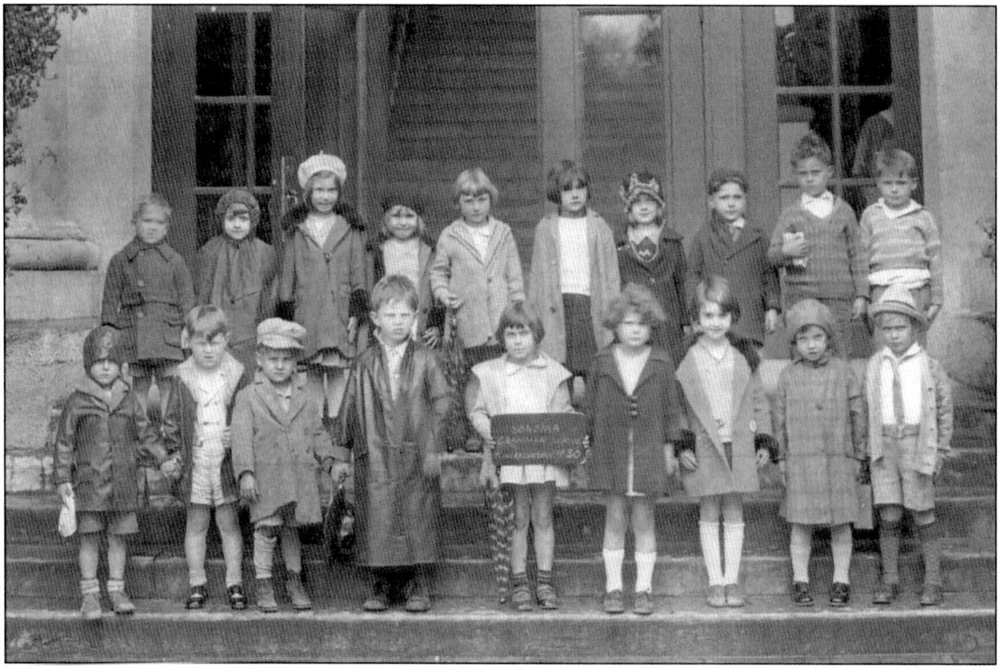

The first kindergarten at the grammar school opened in the fall of 1930. These youngsters gathered on the front steps of the building to have their picture taken, just like the big kids. While their names are preserved, the order in which they appear is not. All the same, there is a Castagnasso, a Grinstead, a Shainsky, a Downey, a Maffei, and a Viviani—all names that still appear in Sonoma today. (Courtesy SVHS.)

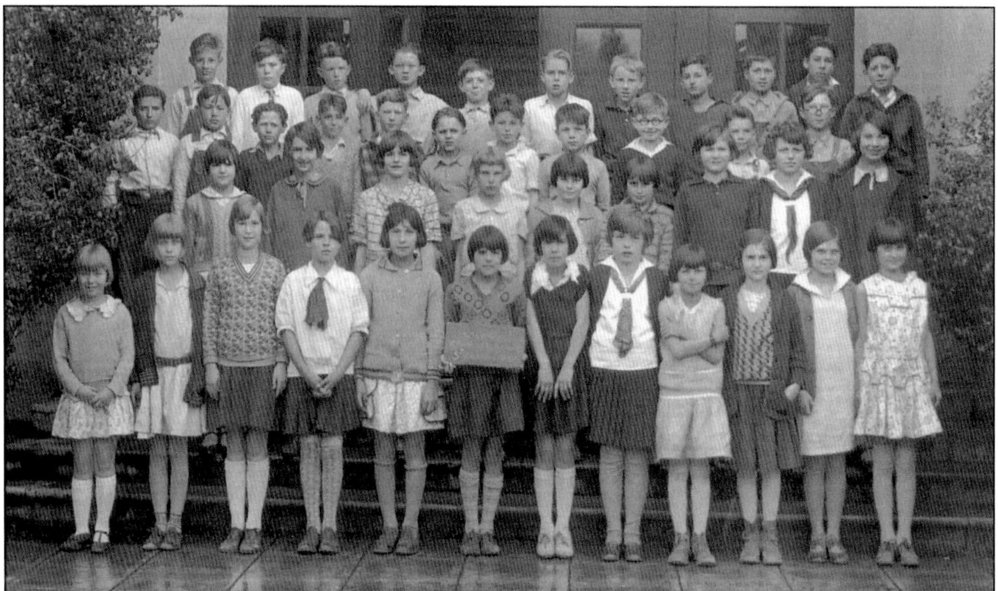

Although she does not appear with her class, Edna Cooper still taught the fifth-grade class in 1930. Her students included Rose Scarafoni Millerick, who is the little girl at far right in the first row. Miss Cooper, a constant at the grammar school, went on to help found the historical society and became Sonoma's first woman planning commissioner. (Courtesy SVHS.)

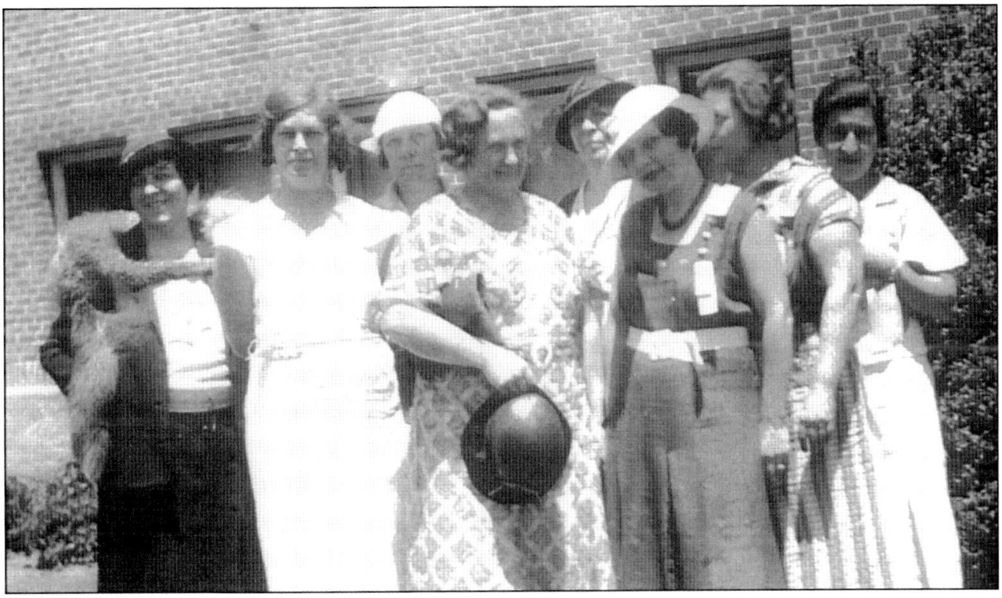

The school had a kitchen, but it did not serve as a cafeteria until these women, known fondly as the lunch ladies, went to war with principal Jesse Prestwood. He supposedly told them, "I'll take care of the school. You take care of your homes." The women won, and a school cafeteria was organized in the early 1930s—despite the principal's initial objections. (Courtesy SVHS.)

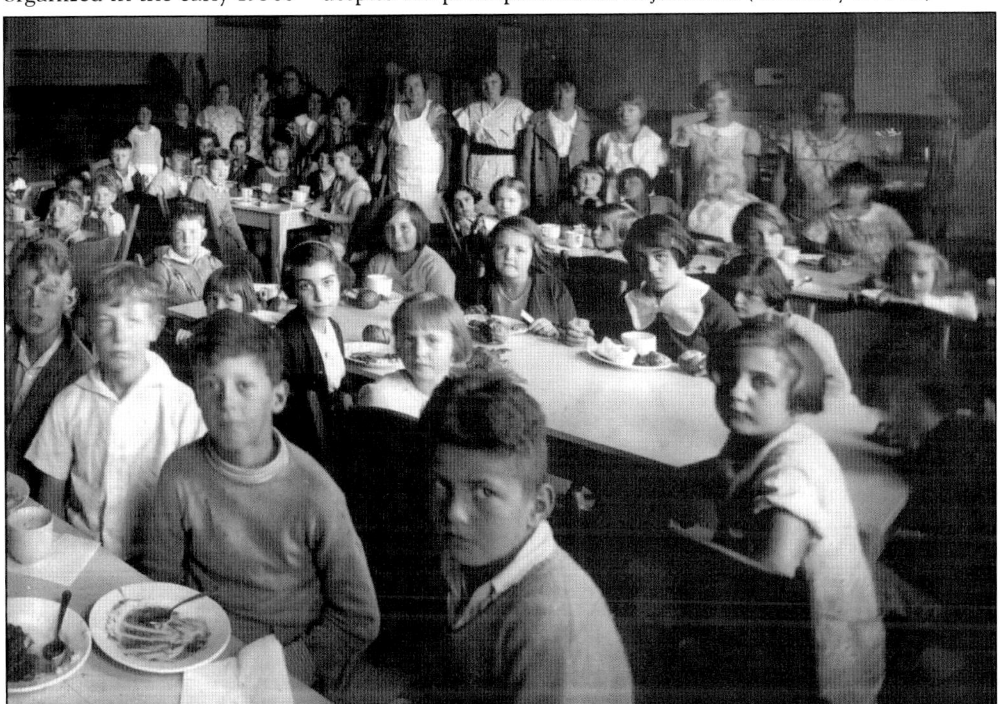

Children enjoyed eating in the cafeteria soon after it opened. The boys in the front row are, from left, John Finnerty, John Cleary, Fred Thomson, and Herman Klebanoff. Others in the picture, who are named but not located, are Helen and Muriel Shainsky, Hugh Grinstead, June Leveroni, and Celia Lambert. Some of the lunch ladies appear at the back of the room. (Courtesy SVHS.)

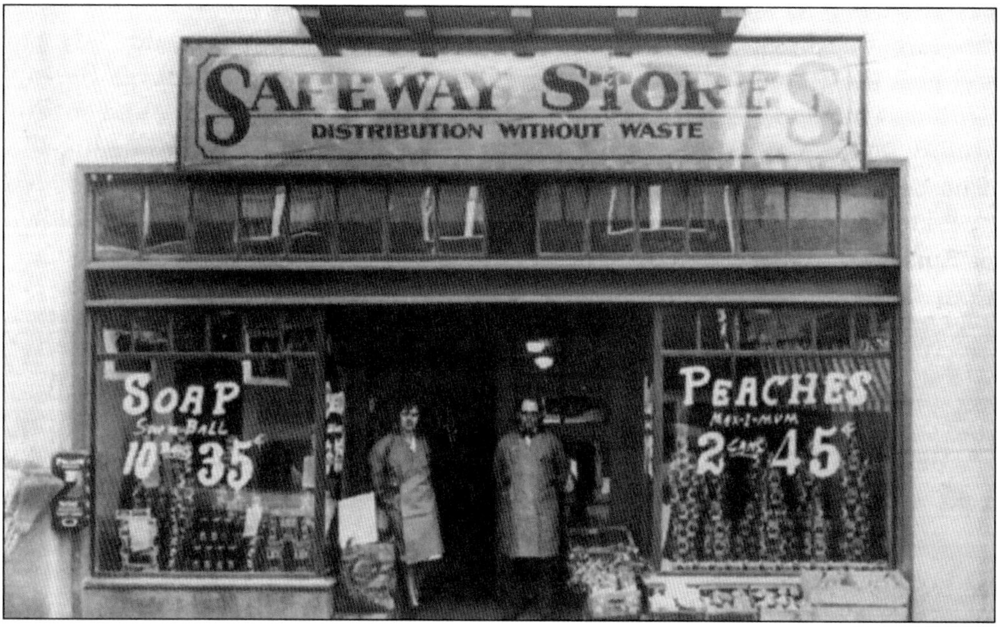

In the 1930s, Sonoma was a town in the throes of the Great Depression. However, tourists continued to come by rail and automobile, and resorts managed to stay open. Sonoma was an agricultural town where people knew each other and lent a hand, and they formed a relief committee to help their neighbors with groceries and utilities. On an optimistic note, some new businesses—like this Safeway—opened in 1930. (Courtesy SIT.)

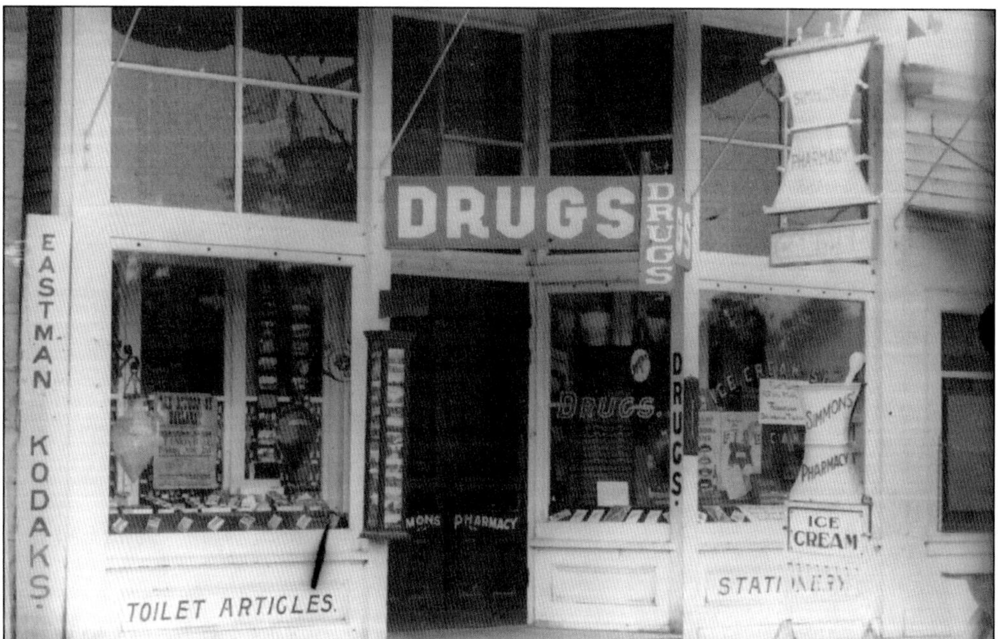

A favorite hangout for the village children was Simmons Pharmacy, which had a soda fountain. Built at 29 East Napa Street in 1903, the building drew locals and visitors and was a fixture until 1986, when it closed its doors. Today the space still exists and is a dress shop. Remnants of its pharmacy days can still be found inside if one looks closely. (Courtesy SVHS.)

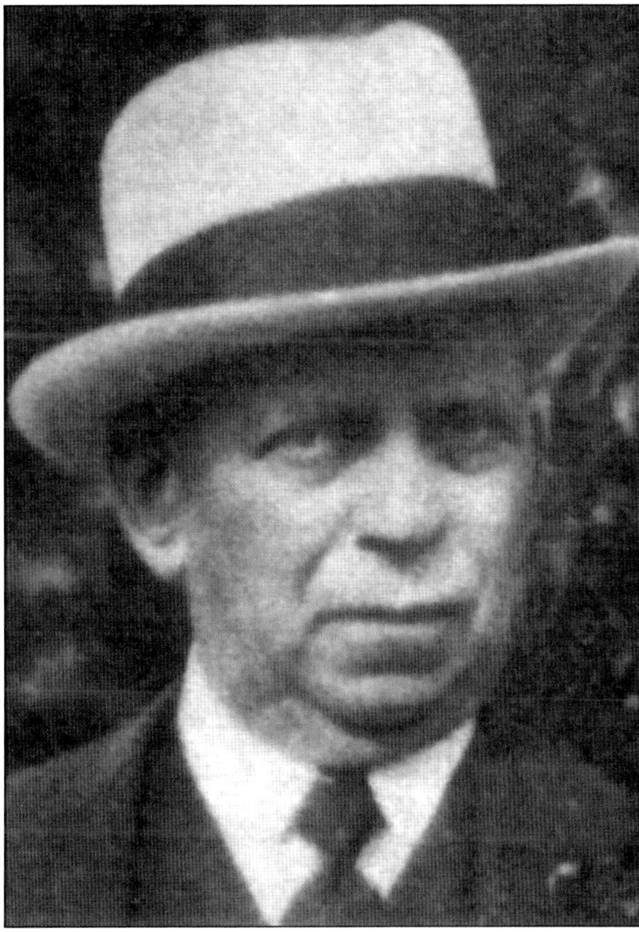

Samuele Sebastiani not only founded a wine business in 1904, he built many amenities in a town recovering from the Great Depression. To the delight of schoolchildren, he furnished the town with public entertainment centers and put people to work in the process. He also built housing, most notably the Craftsman cottages on Fourth Street East and the Sebastiani Apartments (now the Cuneo Apartments) on Spain Street. (Courtesy SIT.)

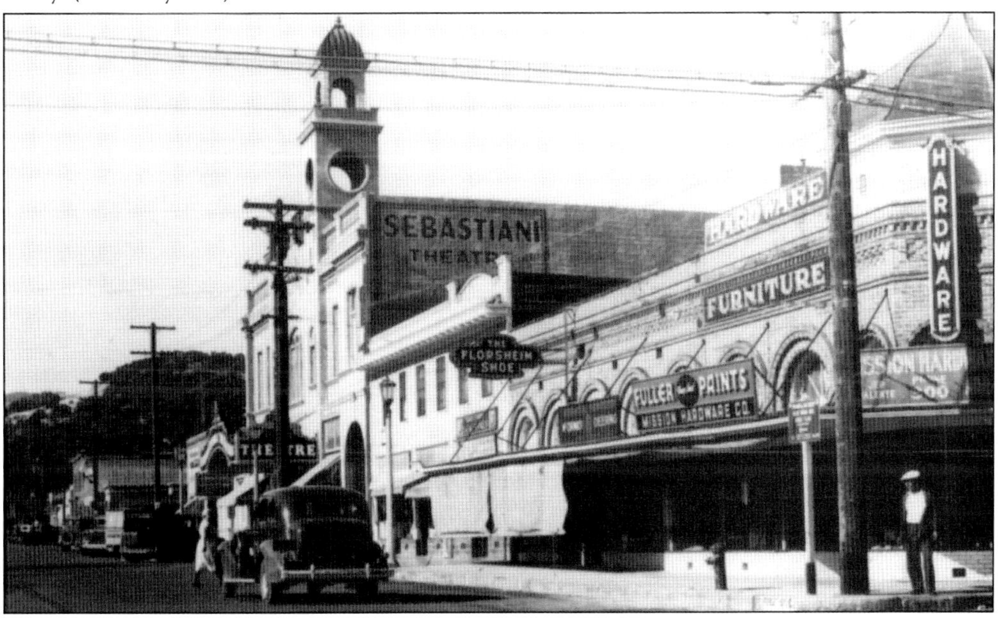

In 1932, Samuele Sebastiani announced plans to build a magnificent new movie theater on First Street East, right across from the plaza. Built in 1933, it opened in 1934 to great fanfare. Its first showing was *Fugitive Lovers*, starring Robert Montgomery. Admission was 30¢. The theater was designed by architect James W. Reid and is still in use today. (Courtesy SIT.)

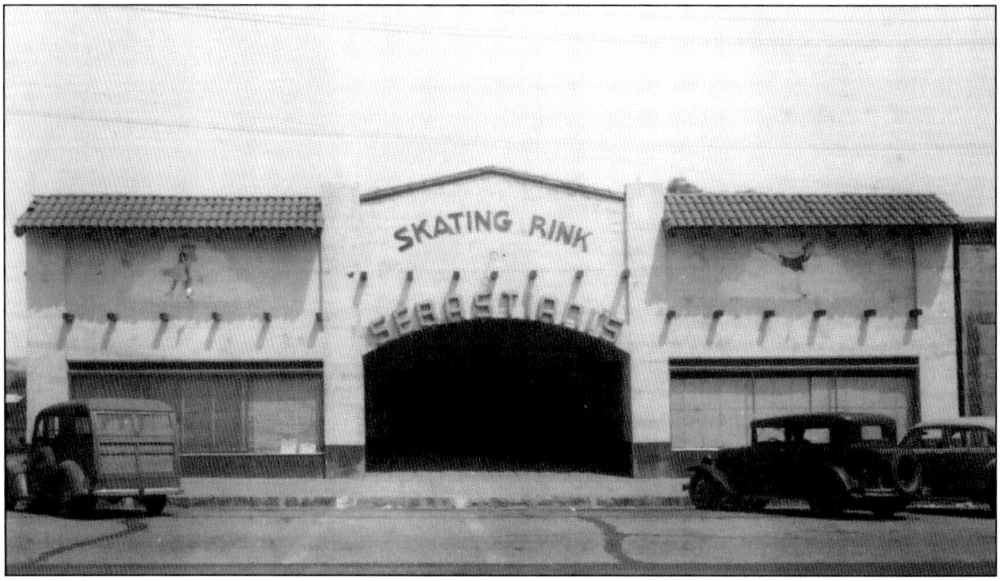

Continuing his projects into the early 1940s, Sebastiani also built a rollertorium and bowling alley—again providing recreational facilities for the town's youth. The skating rink was north of the theater, in what is today the Mercato. The bowling alley, originally planned for the same building, was later built in the 300 block of West Napa Street, along with an auto court and restaurant. (Courtesy SIT.)

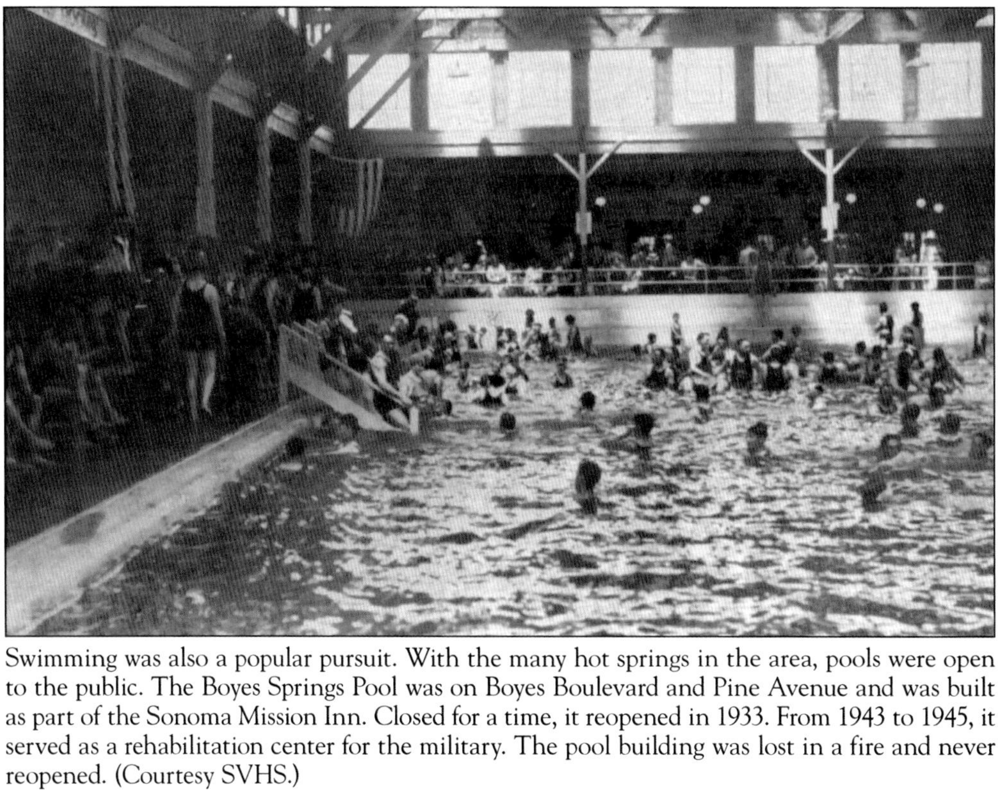

Swimming was also a popular pursuit. With the many hot springs in the area, pools were open to the public. The Boyes Springs Pool was on Boyes Boulevard and Pine Avenue and was built as part of the Sonoma Mission Inn. Closed for a time, it reopened in 1933. From 1943 to 1945, it served as a rehabilitation center for the military. The pool building was lost in a fire and never reopened. (Courtesy SVHS.)

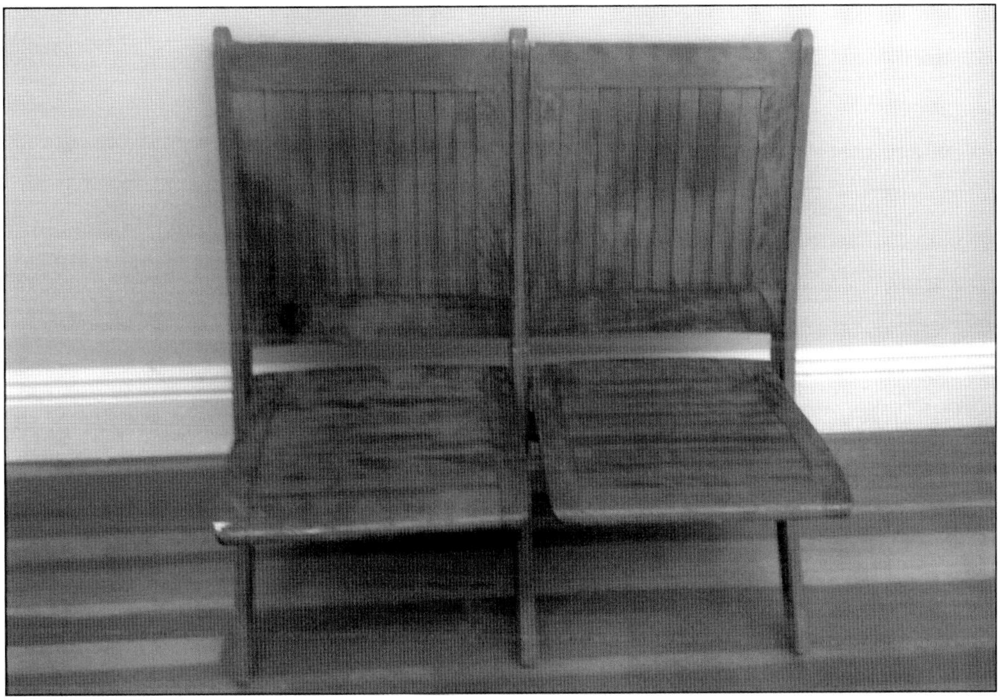

In addition to inter-school sports, students had musical programs, plays, and assemblies right in the grammar school auditorium. Seating was provided on the main floor and in the mezzanine balcony, facing the elevated stage. The hard chairs, used by generations of children, were sometimes removed or pushed back against the walls to make room for dancing. These chairs still survive in the hallways of the building. (Courtesy SCC.)

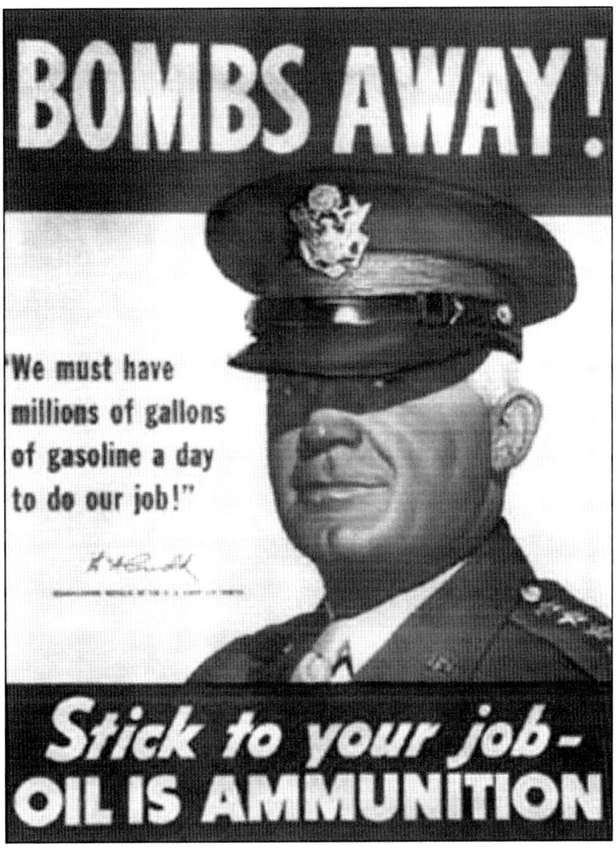

The 1940s came with a dose of anxiety. On December 7, 1941, the Japanese bombed Pearl Harbor, and the news filled newspapers and radio broadcasts. Young men hurried to enlist, and posters urging support of the war effort filled store windows. This one featured Gen. Hap Arnold, who urged conservation of gasoline. He eventually settled in Sonoma. (Courtesy SVHS.)

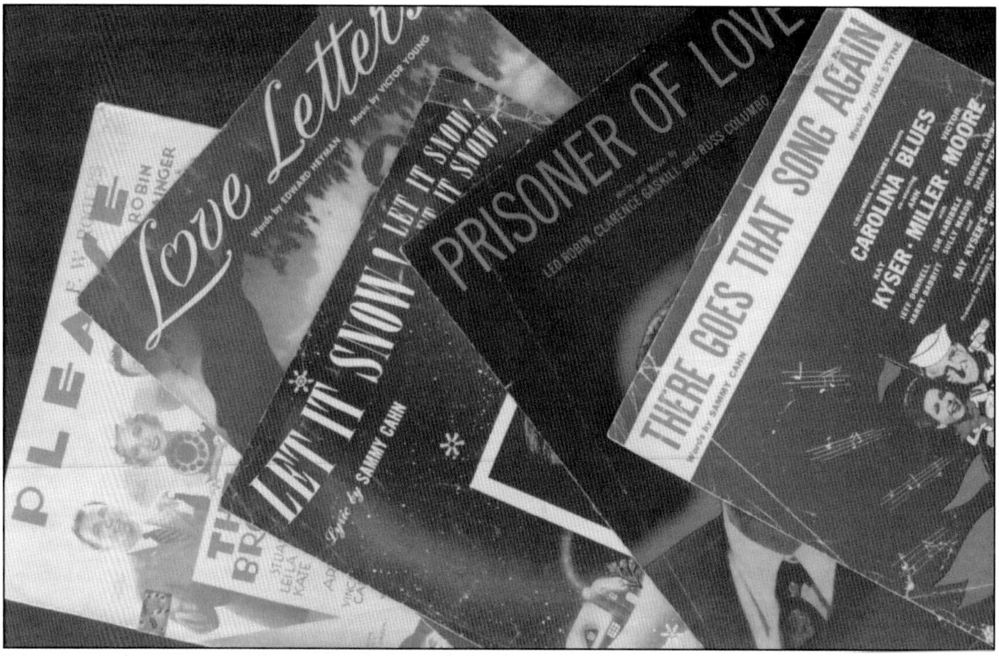

Music was always part of the curriculum, and children who attended school in the 1940s remember singing favorites like the music of Stephen Foster. As the war progressed, new songs filled the airwaves and musical films became popular. The school always had a piano and an array of music, and children were taught to play musical instruments. (Courtesy SCC.)

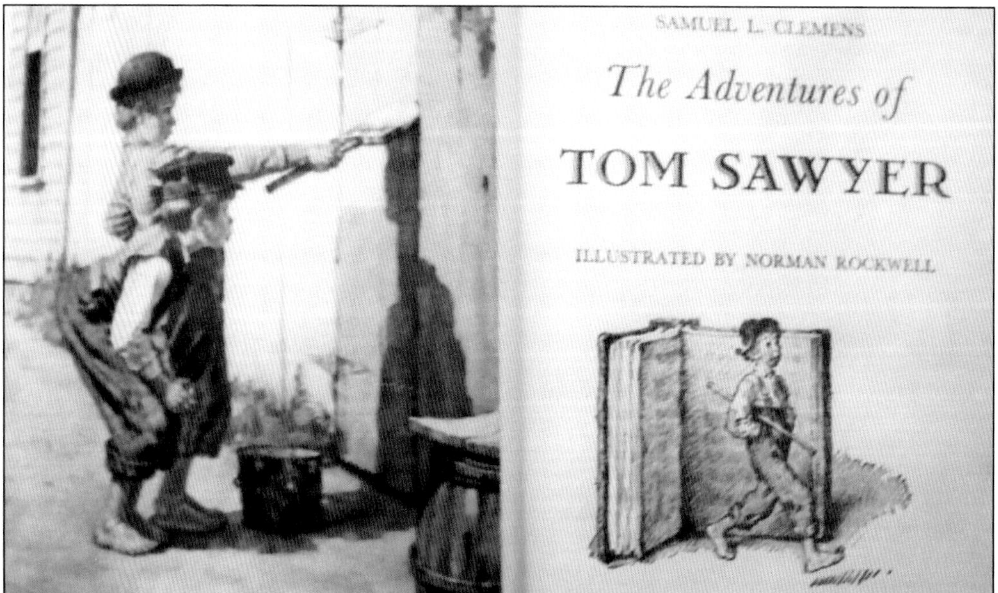

Children also enjoyed popular literature. Rosemarie Carraboches Pedrazini recalled quiet afternoons when teachers read them stories. When she moved to Sonoma at the age of 10, she gave Miss Cooper, her teacher, a copy of *The Adventures of Tom Sawyer*. The teacher read from the book to her class every day. Rosemarie also loved sports and recalled playing baseball behind the building. (Courtesy SVHS.)

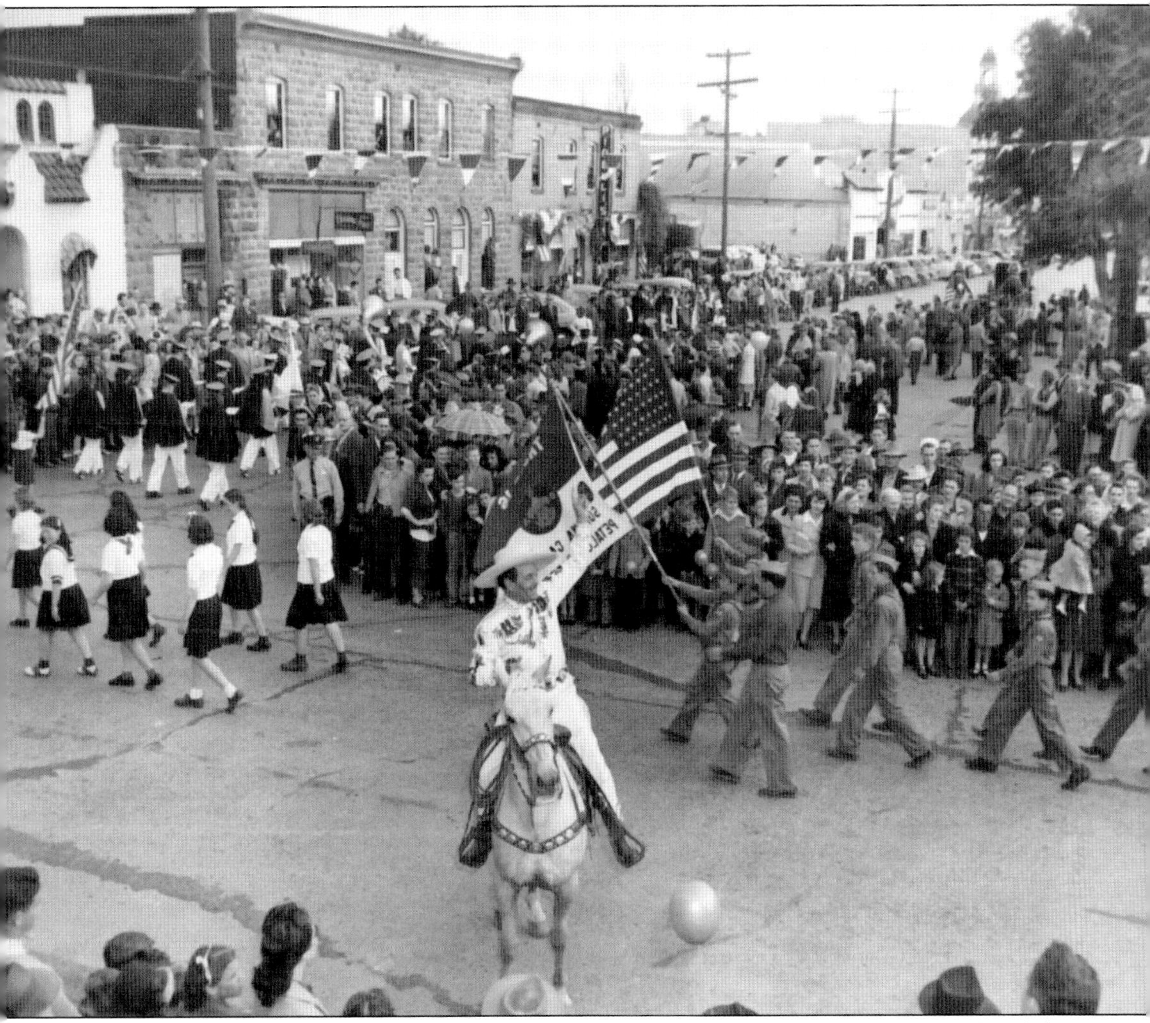

At the end of the war, the town got back to normal. Always fond of parades, children lined the street in 1946 to see actor Leo Carillo during a grand parade to celebrate the 100th anniversary of the raising of the Bear Flag in the plaza. The celebration lasted about a week. California lasted 26 days as a free and independent country. (Courtesy SVHS.)

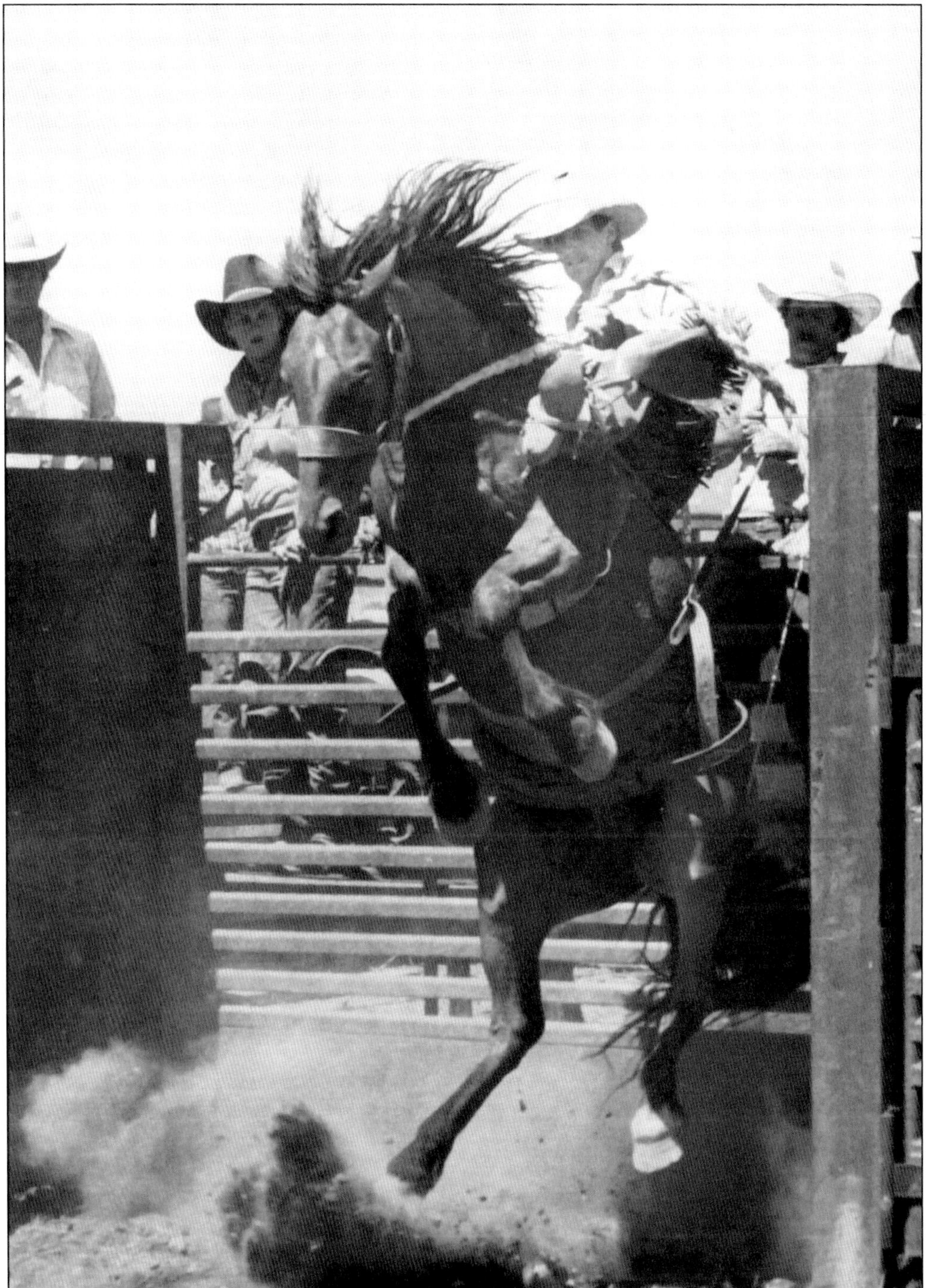

The Wild West held a certain fascination for young boys who lived on ranches. Many dreamed of participating in the annual Sonoma Rodeo, which began in 1929 with an admission fee of $1 that included an "all you can eat" dinner. The rodeo on the Millerick Ranch ended in the 1950s. The tradition was revived for a time, but no rodeos take place in Sonoma today. (Courtesy SIT.)

There were also nature lessons. Because field trips to faraway places were rare in those days, the pupils of the late 1930s and 1940s often took long walks with their teachers to learn the names of flowers and plants and to press them into books like this one, which belonged to Rose Scarafoni Millerick and survives today in the Depot Museum. (Courtesy SVHS.)

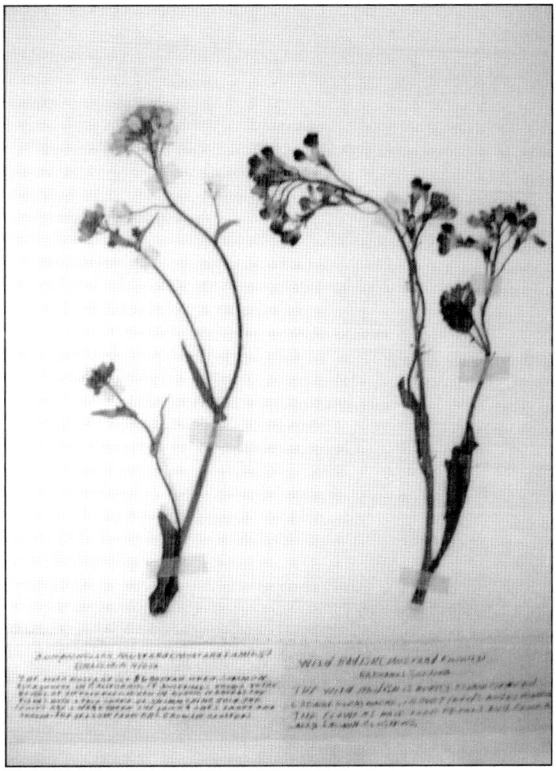

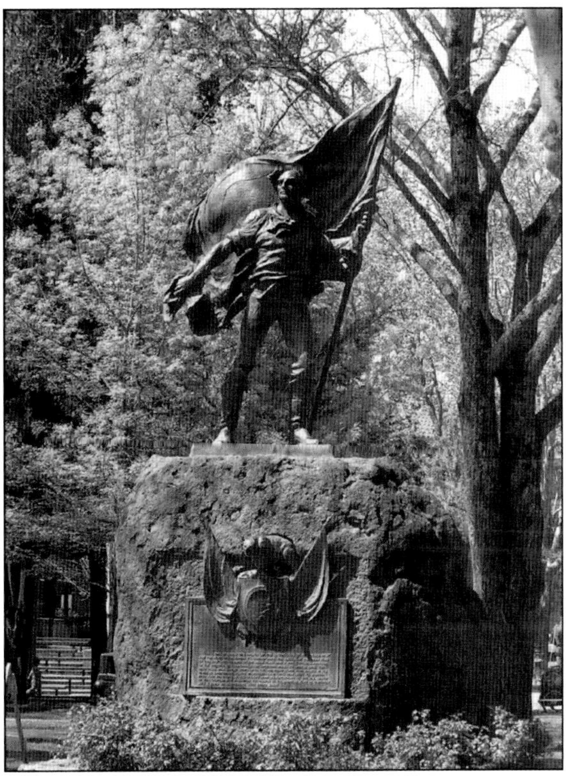

The statue commemorating the raising of the Bear Flag was placed in 1914 and has since been a fixture in the town plaza. It serves as a reminder to visitors and residents alike that Sonoma is California's birthplace. This history lesson was drummed into the heads of children who saw many reminders on field trips taken around town with their teachers—learning their history lessons first hand. (Courtesy David Goodison.)

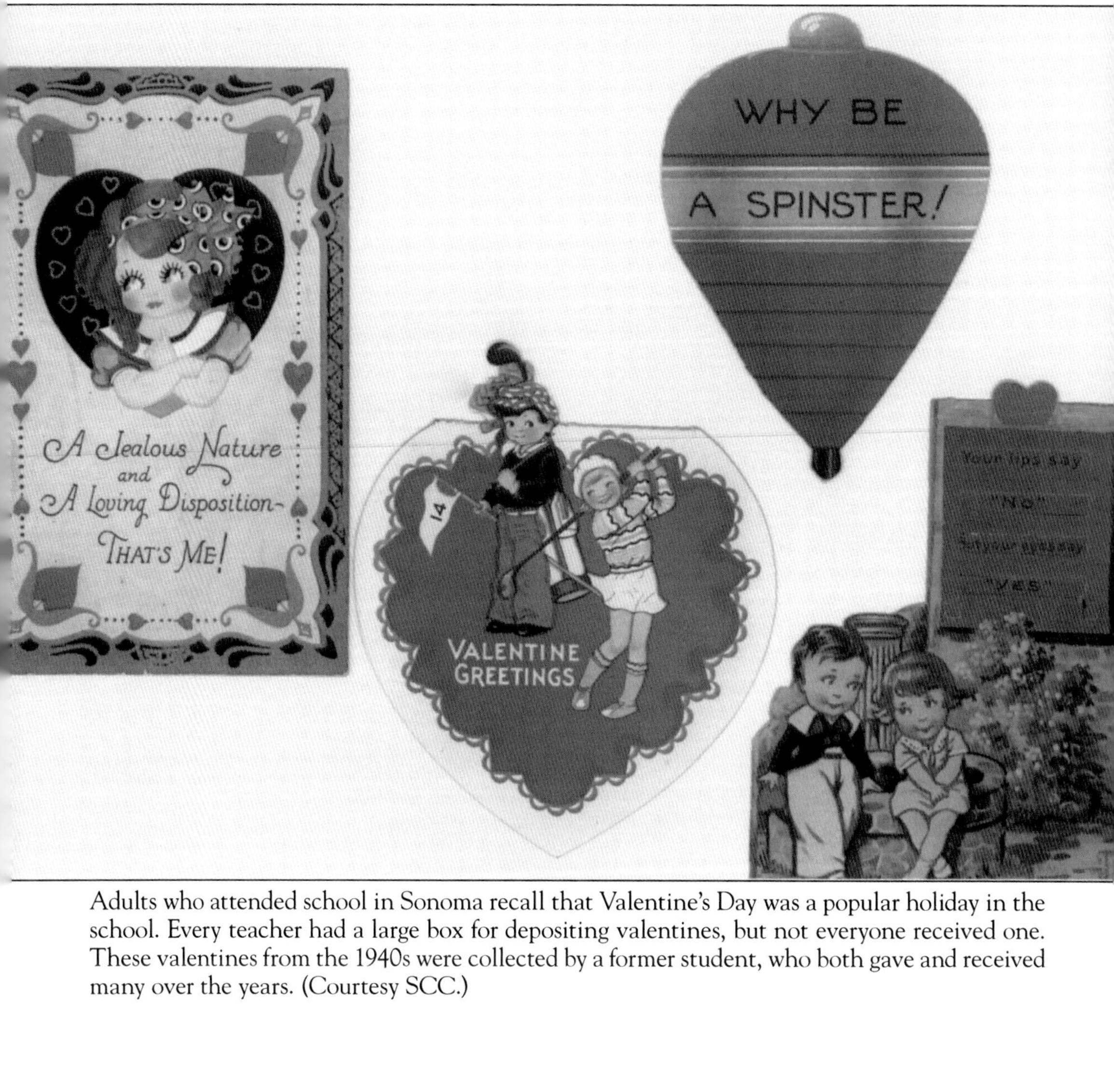

Adults who attended school in Sonoma recall that Valentine's Day was a popular holiday in the school. Every teacher had a large box for depositing valentines, but not everyone received one. These valentines from the 1940s were collected by a former student, who both gave and received many over the years. (Courtesy SCC.)

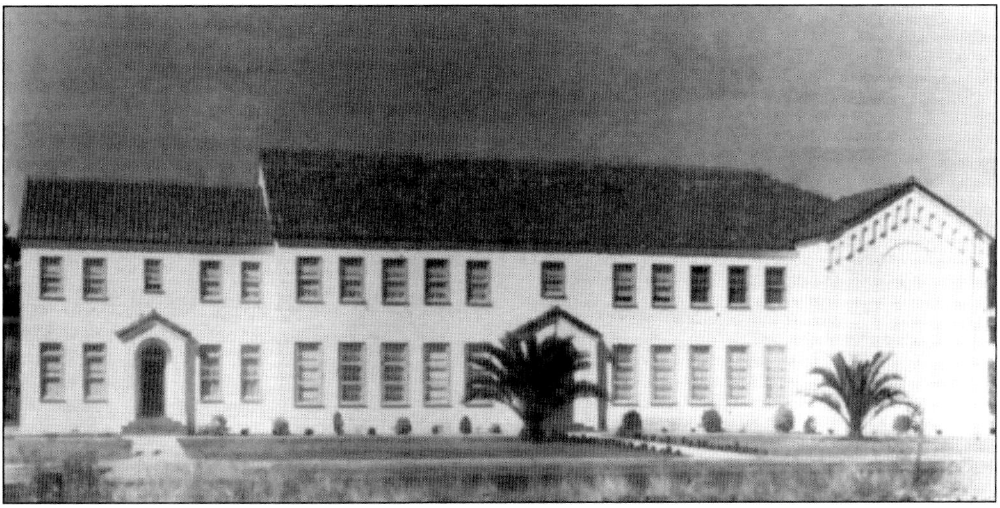

In 1946, a new school opened across town. St. Francis Catholic School was built next to the church of the same name on West Napa Street. The original church school—Presentation—had not been reopened after its 1917 closure. St. Francis still exists, and a new Presentation School has also been built on Broadway south of town. (Courtesy SVHS.)

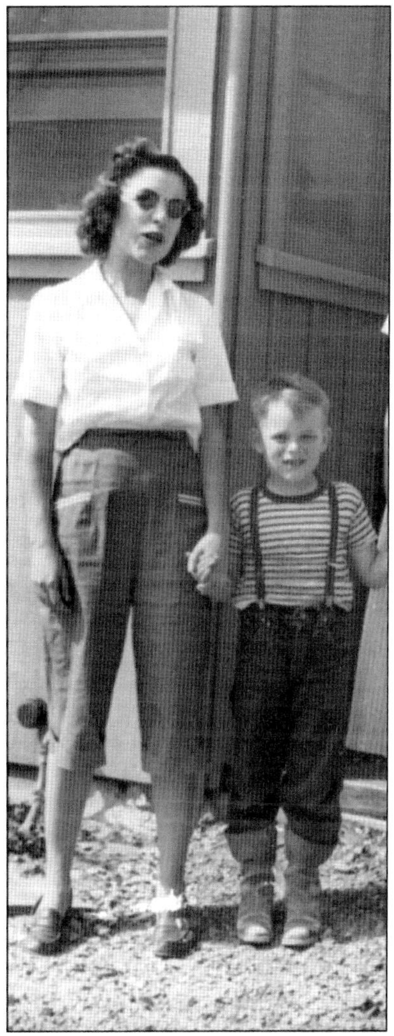

Bill Lynch, shown with his mother, Jean, was part of the last generation of Sonomans to attend school at the Sonoma Grammar School. He grew up to become editor and publisher of the *Sonoma Index-Tribune*, following in the footsteps of his father, Robert Lynch, and great aunt Celeste Granice Murphy. The newspaper was in his family for over 135 years. (Courtesy Bill Lynch.)

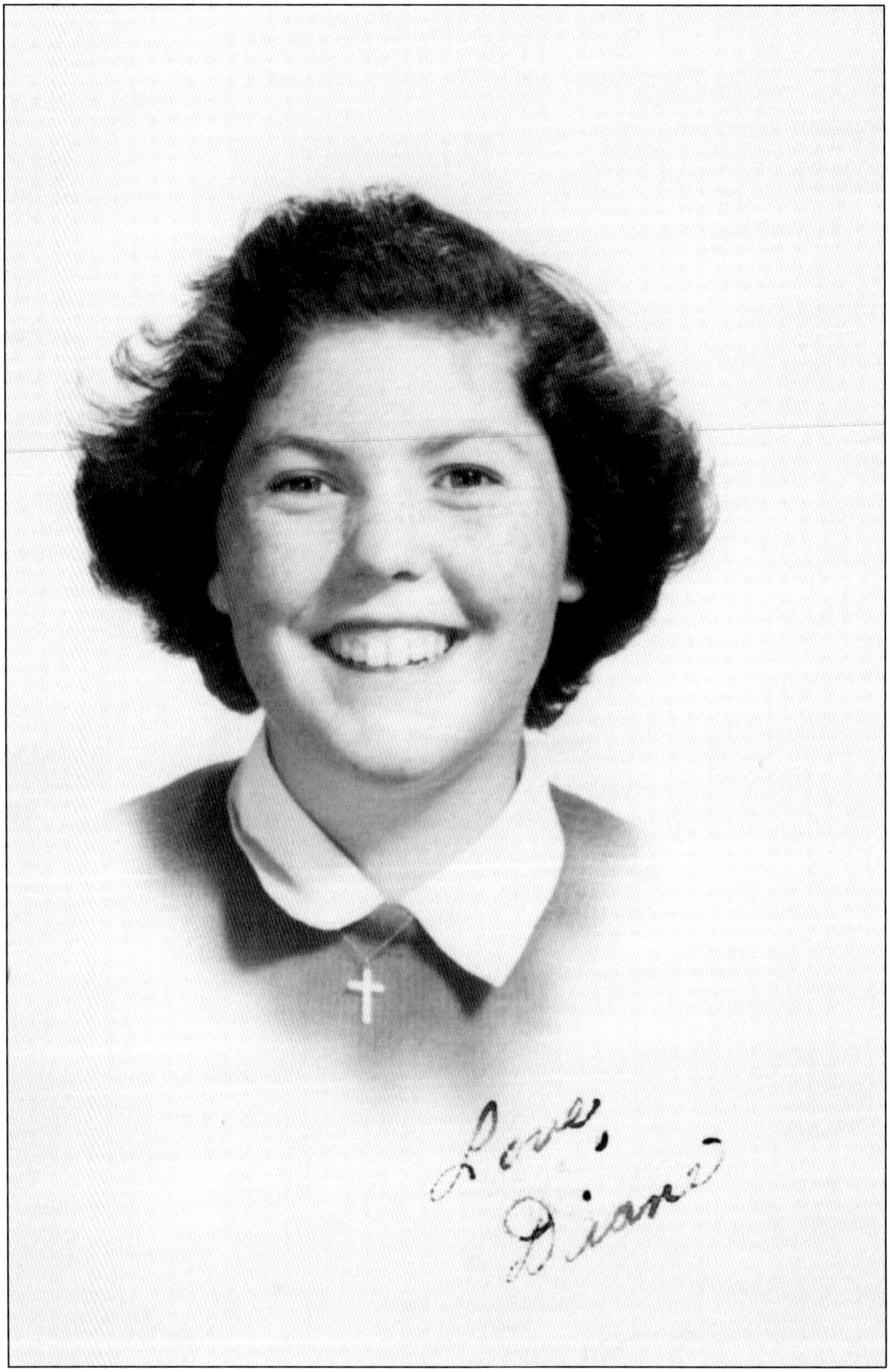

Diane Johnson Mayo, shown in her eighth-grade picture, was in the last class to graduate from the Sonoma Grammar School building. She remembers walking across the stage in the school auditorium to get her diploma in 1948, not realizing it would be the last time for eighth graders to do so. (Courtesy Diane Mayo.)

This report card from the school—showing that Diane Johnson had excellent grades—was signed by the teacher, the principal, and the superintendent of schools. Diane remained in Sonoma Valley, marrying realtor and winery owner Henry Mayo. Both have been great supporters of the Sonoma Community Center over the years. (Courtesy Diane Mayo.)

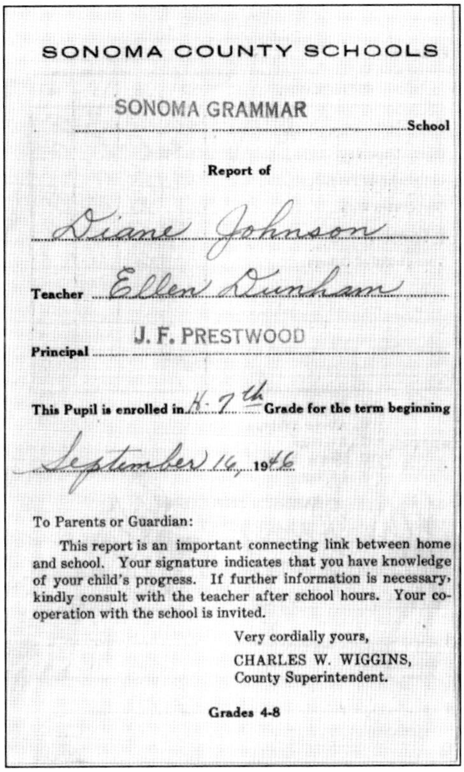

SONOMA COUNTY SCHOOLS

SONOMA GRAMMAR School

Report of

Diane Johnson

Teacher Ellen Dunham

Principal J. F. PRESTWOOD

This Pupil is enrolled in H. 7th Grade for the term beginning

September 16, 1946

To Parents or Guardian:

This report is an important connecting link between home and school. Your signature indicates that you have knowledge of your child's progress. If further information is necessary, kindly consult with the teacher after school hours. Your co-operation with the school is invited.

Very cordially yours,
CHARLES W. WIGGINS,
County Superintendent.

Grades 4-8

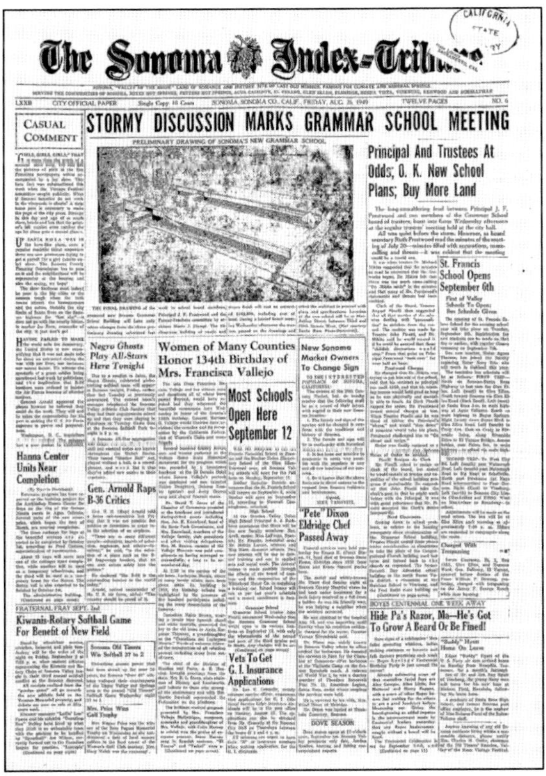

The Sonoma Index-Tribune

CASUAL COMMENT

STORMY DISCUSSION MARKS GRAMMAR SCHOOL MEETING

Principal And Trustees At Odds; O. K. New School Plans; Buy More Land

St. Francis School Opens September 6th

Negro Ghosts Play All-Stars Here Tonight

Women of Many Counties Honor 134th Birthday of Mrs. Francisca Vallejo

New Sonoma Market Owners To Change Sign

Most Schools Open Here September 12

Hanna Center Units Near Completion

Gen. Arnold Raps B-36 Critics

"Pete" Dixon Eldridge Chef Passed Away

Kiwanis-Rotary Softball Game For Benefit of New Field

Vets To Get G. I. Insurance Applications

Hide Pa's Razor, Ma—He's Got To Grow A Beard Or Be Fined!

In 1933, Southern California experienced a severe earthquake that destroyed or damaged over 230 schools. California's Field Act set new standards for public schools and sounded the death knell for Sonoma Grammar School. In 1948, a committee of experts examined the school and deemed it unsafe. The school closed in the middle of the year, despite public outcry. (Courtesy SIT.)

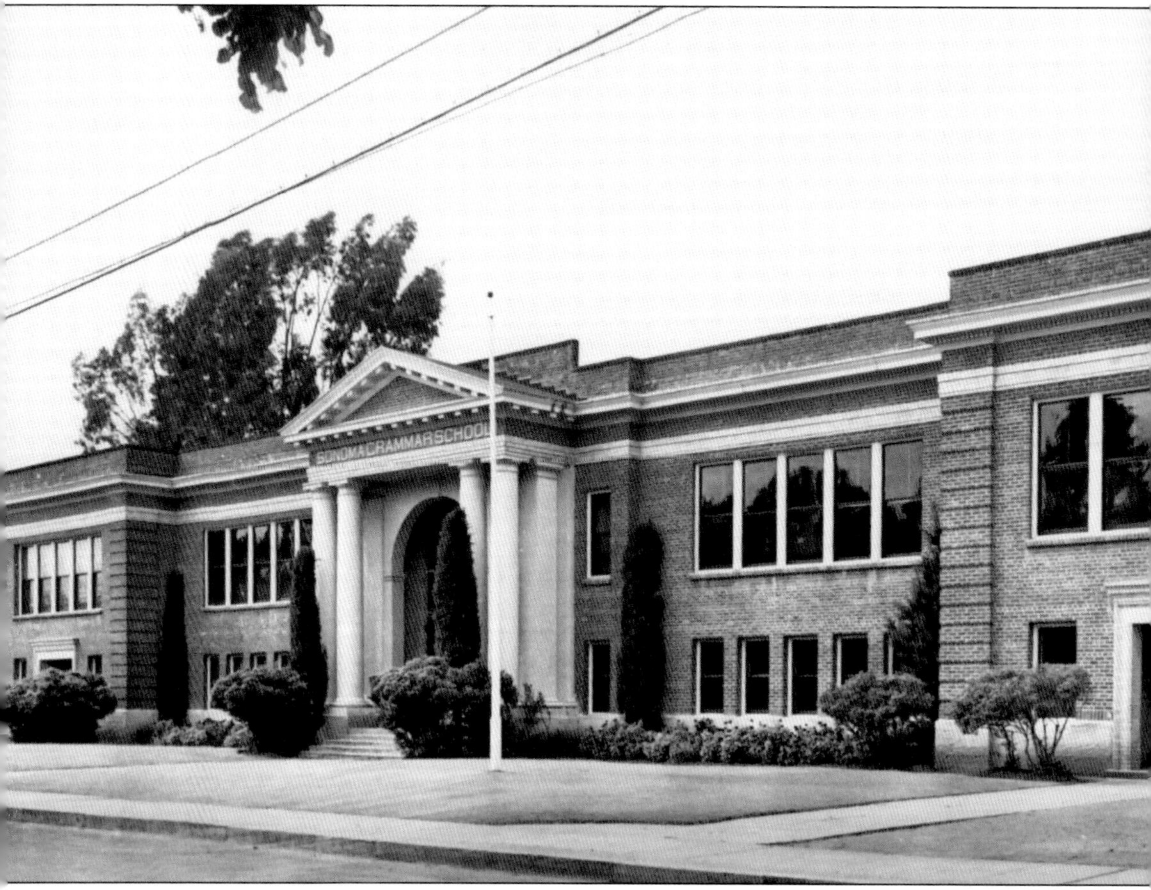

Toward the end of its life as a school, the building had nice landscaping, faced a paved street, and was the pride of the community. Unfortunately, it was made of unreinforced masonry and was starting to feel its years as children filled its classrooms. Sitting empty, the building awaited its fate. Would it be repaired, or would a new school be built elsewhere? The debate continued for the next few years as people took sides—either for or against fixing the building. Both decisions would require money. The board of trustees was divided, but in the end, it was the voters who had the final say. (Courtesy SIT.)

Four

A New Vision for Community Education

As Sonoma Valley settled into its first post–World War II decade, the security of peace and economic stability jump-started growth in a most predictable way: the first members of what would be the baby boom generation reached school age. Caught off guard by the burgeoning throng of children knocking on available school doors, the community scrambled to make sure it could find room for all.

Dr. Carroll Andrews, a progressive physician as much interested in the community's health as that of his patients, suggested that residents take another look at the condemned Sonoma Grammar School to see if it could be resurrected to accommodate the influx of new students. After forming a committee to pursue this possibility, the community received final word from the State of California that the building could not house students until it was retrofitted to meet new earthquake standards—a prohibitively expensive undertaking. And so, the doors finally closed on the building's public school career.

In January 1952, community organizers of the august Vintage Festival Association, led by Dr. Andrews and community activists Dan Ruggles and Jerry Casson, proposed that the old school be used as a center for music, art, and recreation. In a front-page letter to the editor of the *Sonoma Index-Tribune*, Dr. Andrews stirred the community's enthusiasm for this new idea and suggested that it be managed by a permanent nonprofit organization.

He put his money where his mouth was: at an auction held on February 20 at the new Prestwood School, Dr. and Mrs. Andrews entered into a spirited bidding war with Sonoma Winery magnate August Sebastiani—represented during the bidding by his agent realtor Homer Bosse. According to Sonoma's anecdotal legend, the gavel slammed down on the Andrews' successful $28,500 bid after August Sebastiani's wife Sylvia sided with the doctor's vision and called out to her husband, "If the doc really wants it, let him have it!"

On March 12, 1952, Dr. Andrews and the Sonoma School District signed the agreement and the deed was done. And the Sonoma Community Center was delivered to its community.

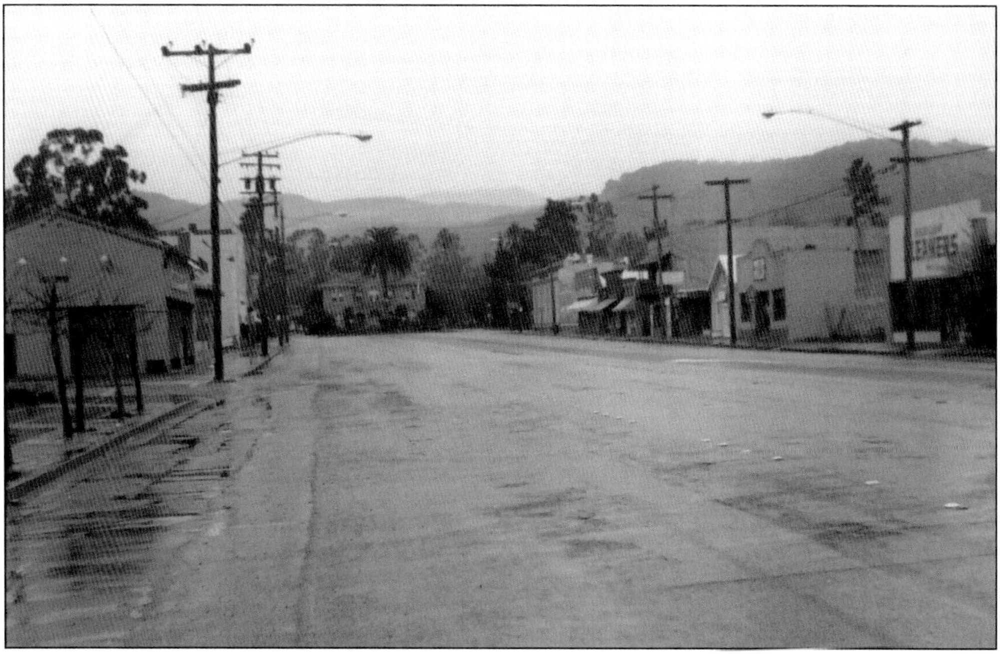

As Sonoma Valley entered the 1950s, residents mirrored small-town citizens across the country as they gave thanks for simple pleasures and families reunited after a long war. Sonomans were happy to return to the slow pace of the valley, as illustrated in this image of Broadway—the main route into the Sonoma Plaza. The photograph was taken on a Sunday at high noon. (Courtesy SVHS.)

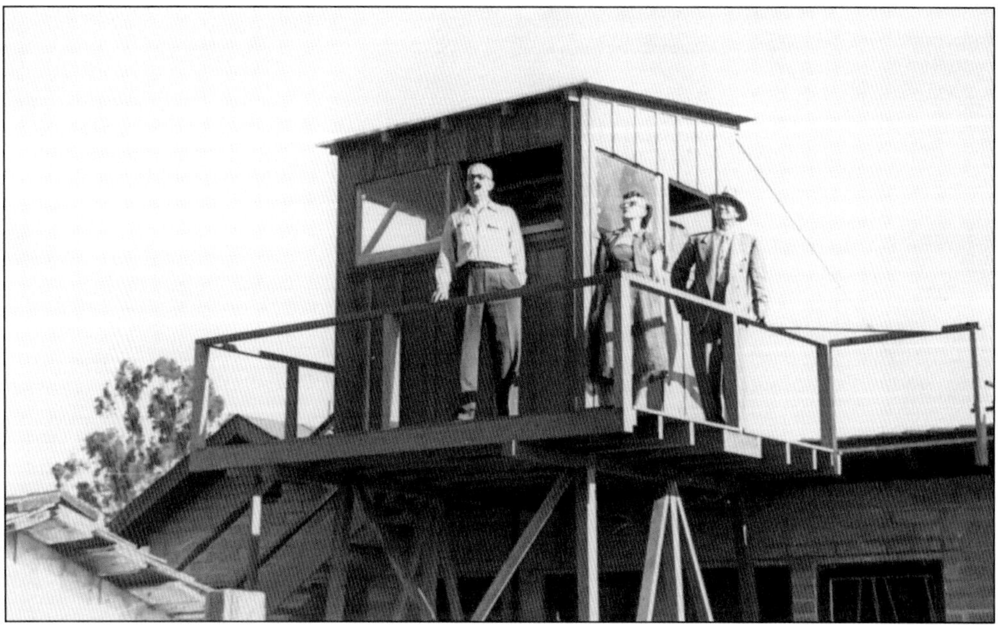

Treasuring the quiet Sonoma life didn't keep community leaders from their civic duties as the federal government touted its new civil defense program and called for community air watch stations. Sonoma's was adjacent to the plaza. Both men and women were recruited as spotters—watching for unidentified hostile planes in the hope that the early detection of a nuclear assault would allow people the necessary time to prepare. (Courtesy SVHS.)

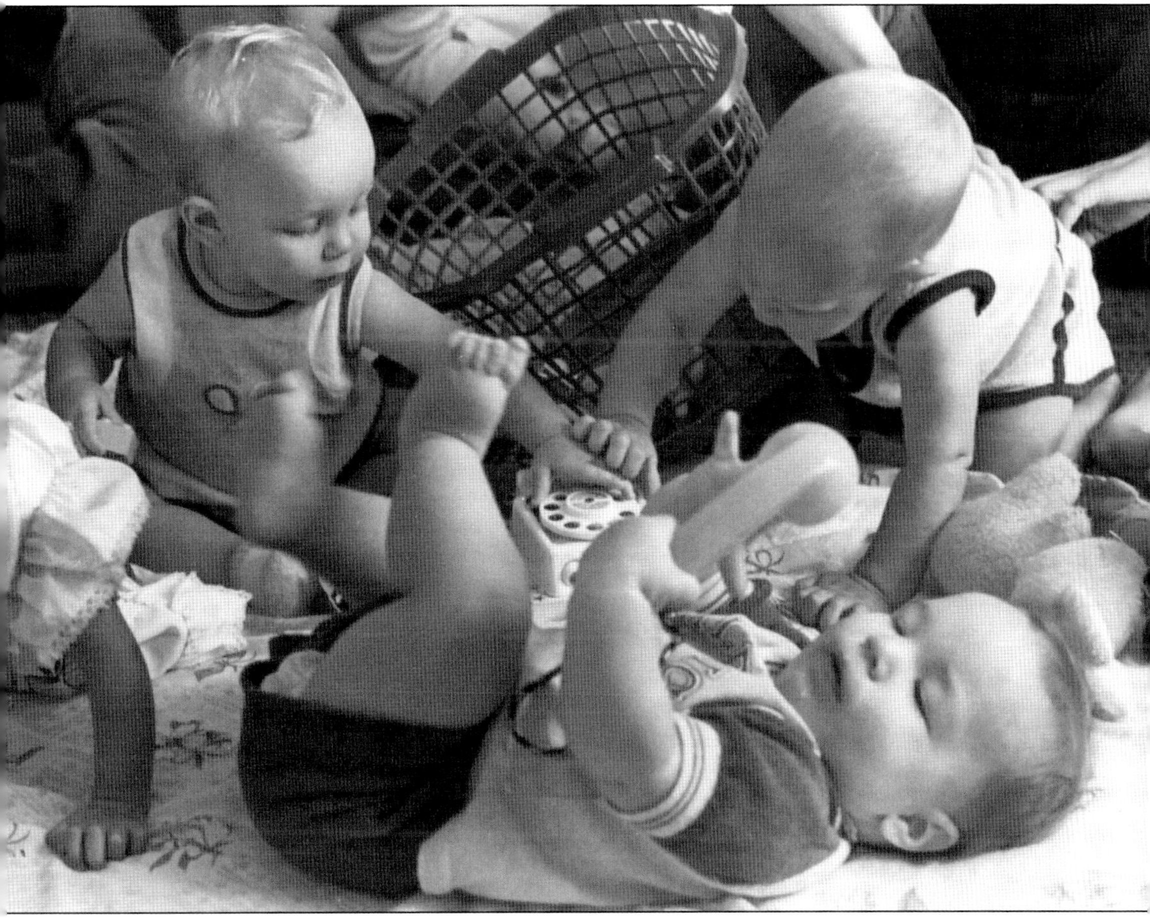

One aspect of Sonoma's community life was decidedly different from previous decades. The first wave of a generation soon identified as the baby boomers was ready for elementary school, and city leaders rushed to find solutions for the dearth of classrooms. (Courtesy SVHS.)

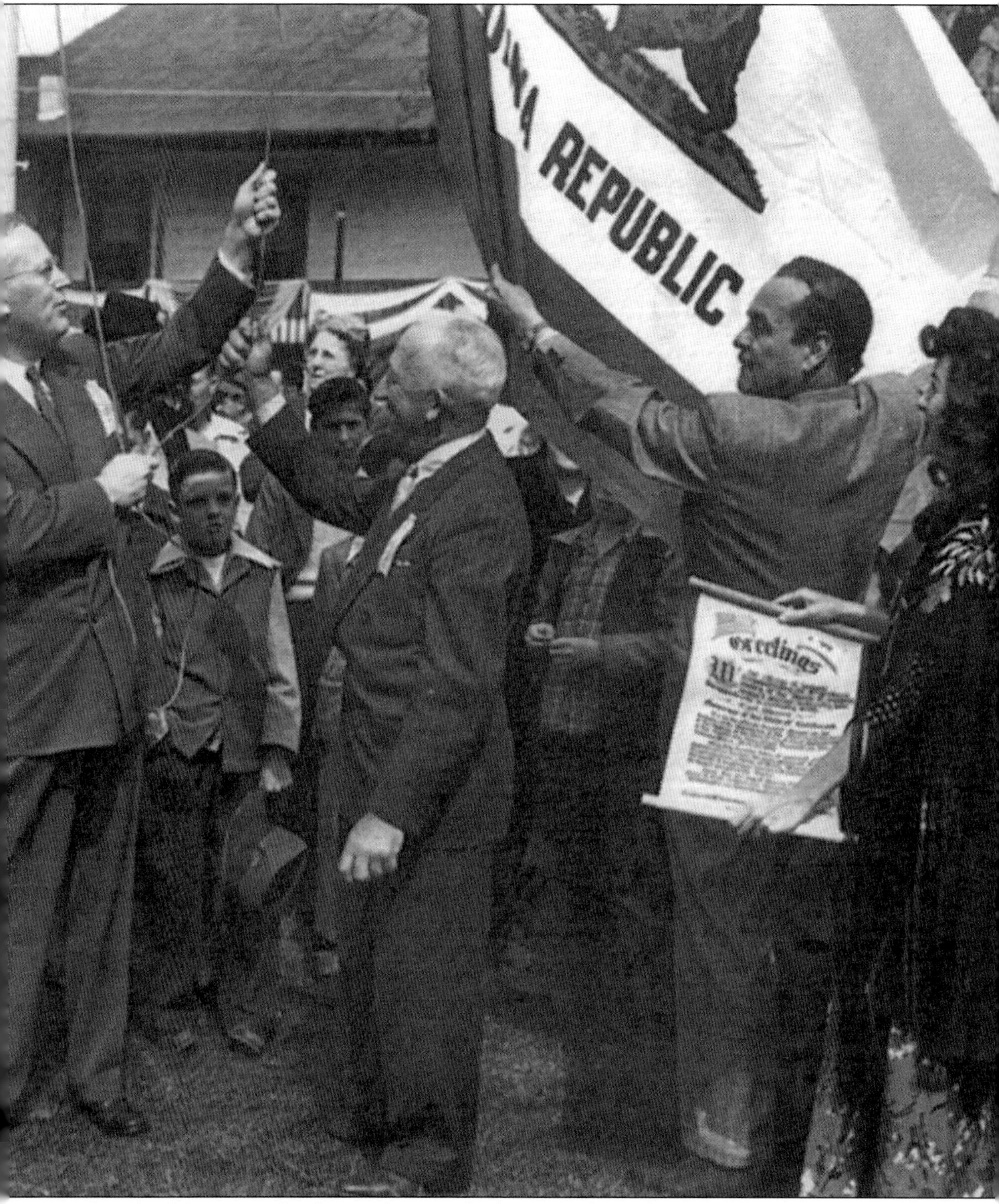

The school district was hard pressed to provide classrooms for students after the Sonoma Grammar School was condemned in 1948. Two weeks before the 1949–1950 school year commenced, trustee John Picetti announced, "only the whereabouts of the second and part of the third graders are in doubt." Picetti is shown above at center in 1946 with Gov. Earl Warren (left) and Leo Carrillo (right) during the Bear Flag celebration on the Sonoma Plaza. (Courtesy SVHS.)

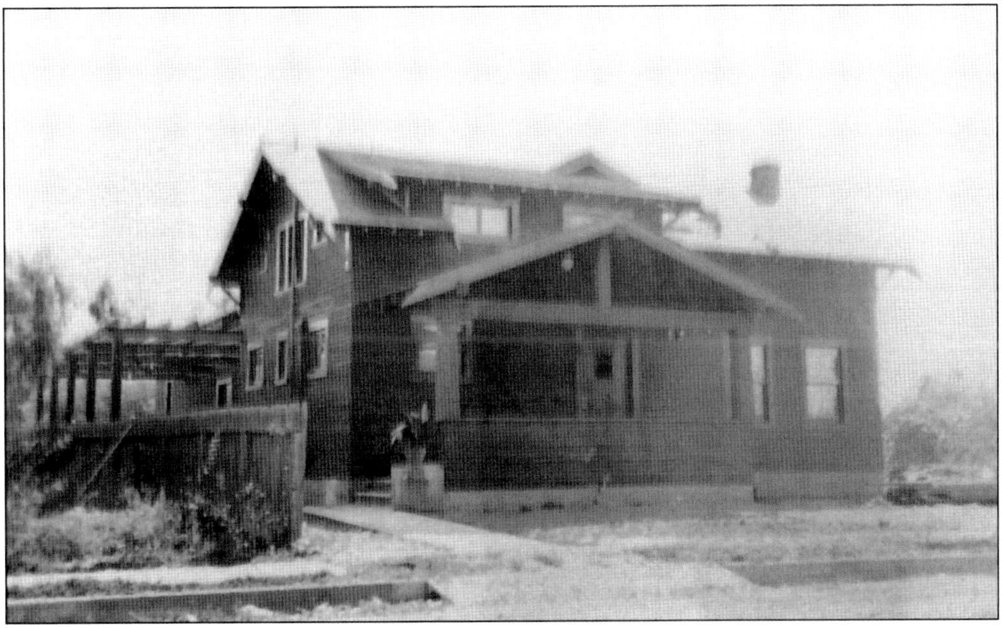

The Sonoma Valley Women's Clubhouse was a natural site for a temporary home for Frances Brocco's seventh graders. Only a block away from the old grammar school, the Woman's Club had been a civic force since it was founded in 1901. Clubwomen raised funds and acted as volunteer labor for the plaza beautification project, started and staffed the first public library, and helped preserve the crumbling Sonoma Mission. (Courtesy SVHS.)

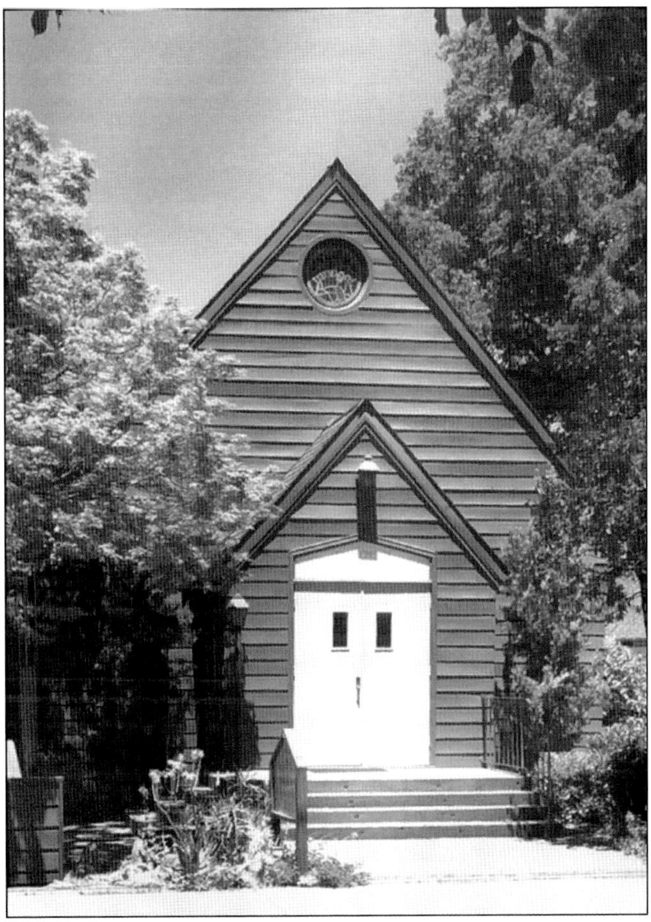

Sonoma Grammar School's entire first-grade class was housed at the Episcopal Parish Hall on the corner of Second Street East and East Napa Street—now home to the First Church of Christ, Scientist. The grammar school trustees requested that parents take their little ones to school on the first day, as there was much confusion about which grades reported to which building. (Courtesy of SVHS.)

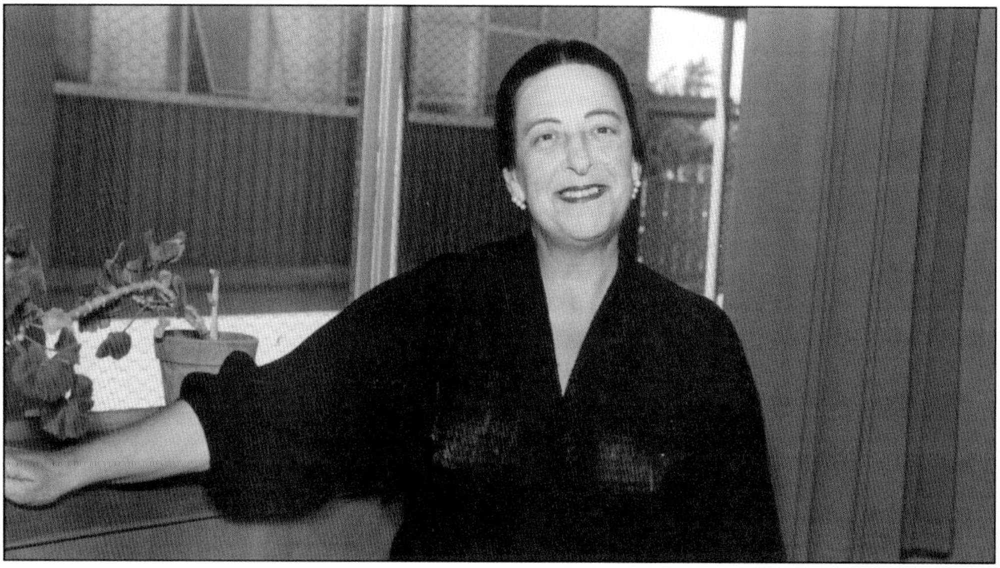

The Batto Building, on First Street West, was the classroom for Zolita Bates's second graders. A teacher since the early 1930s, Zolita was respected for dedicating her meager teaching salary to the restoration of the historic Patton-Nash Adobe on Fourth Street East. The old adobe had previously belonged to Zolita's grandmother Nancy Bones Patton—a survivor of the ill-fated Donner Party who had purchased it in 1848. (Courtesy of SVHS.)

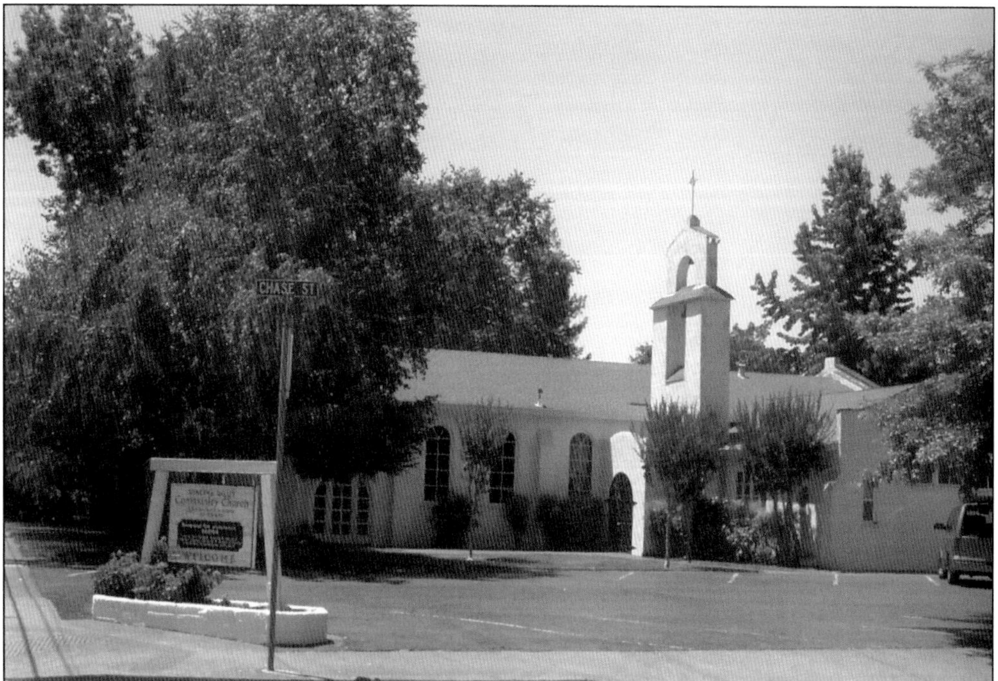

Third graders reported to Wanda Kearney at the Grace Reformed Church on Second Street East and Chase Street. This church is now the Sonoma Valley Community Church. Seventh and eighth graders attended class at the Youth Center Building—now the site of the Valley of the Moon Nursery School. (Courtesy of SVHS.)

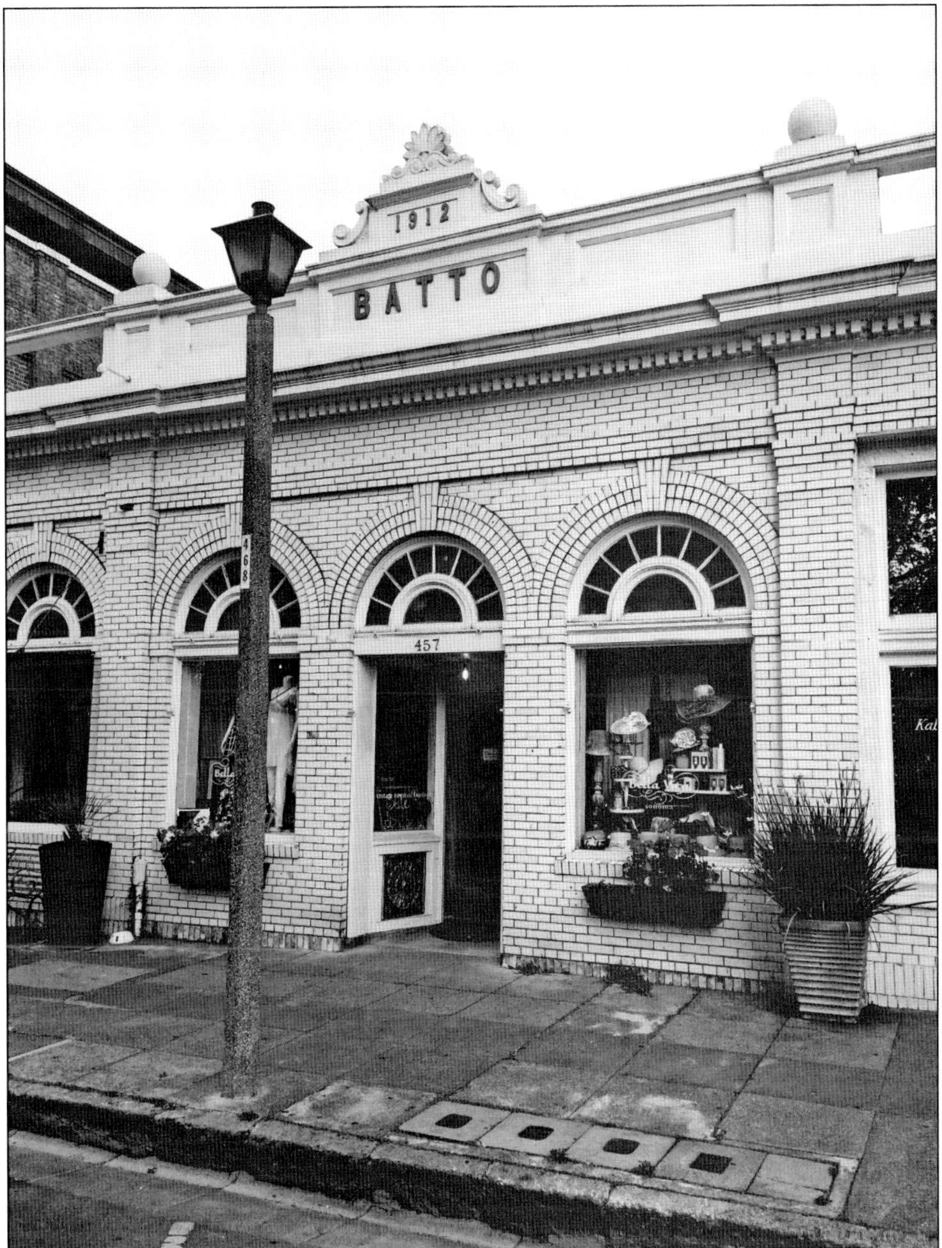

The school district was forced to run double school sessions in many community buildings (including the Batto Building, shown above). This confusion compounded by the stress of constructing a new elementary school quickly led to a clash between Principal Prestwood and the school district trustees. As reported by the *Sonoma Index-Tribune* at the beginning of the 1949–1950 school year, "the long smoldering feud between Principal J.F. Prestwood and two members of the Grammar School Board of Trustees burst into flames at the trustees meeting." The principal accused the board of "trying to get him out of the school." Prestwood finally decided to retire in 1950, and the Sonoma Grammar School District trustees honored his years of service by naming the new school Prestwood Elementary School. (Courtesy of David Goodison.)

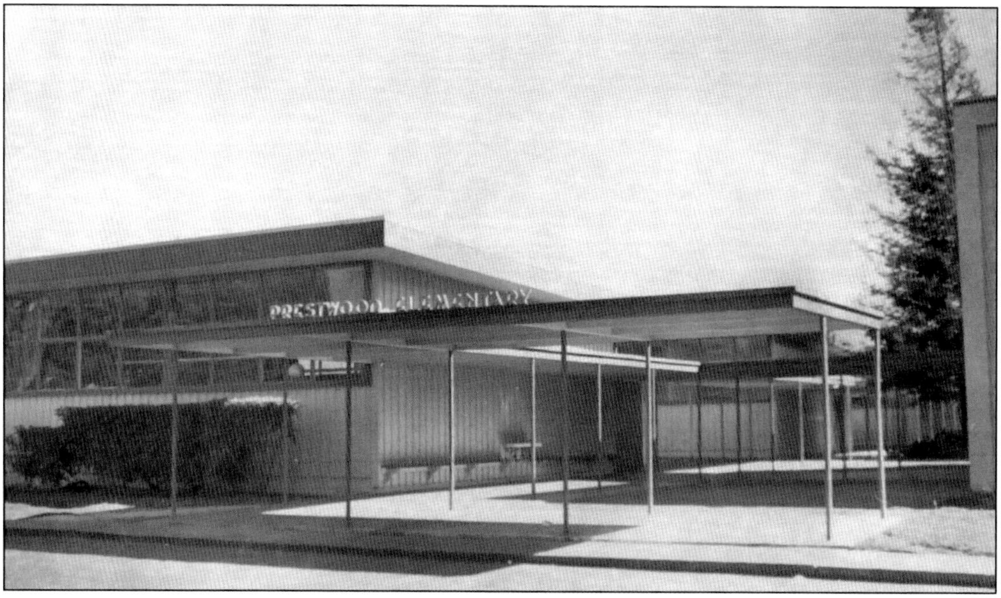

By January 1951, the new school already suffered from over-enrollment, was running double sessions for kindergartners, and was at capacity for all other grades. An investigative committee, led by Dr. Carroll Andrews, recommended that the old Sonoma Grammar School be resurrected to alleviate the situation, but the State of California ruled against it. Finally, in November 1951, voters approved a $100,000 bond to add three classrooms and a multipurpose room to the Prestwood School. (Courtesy of SVHS.)

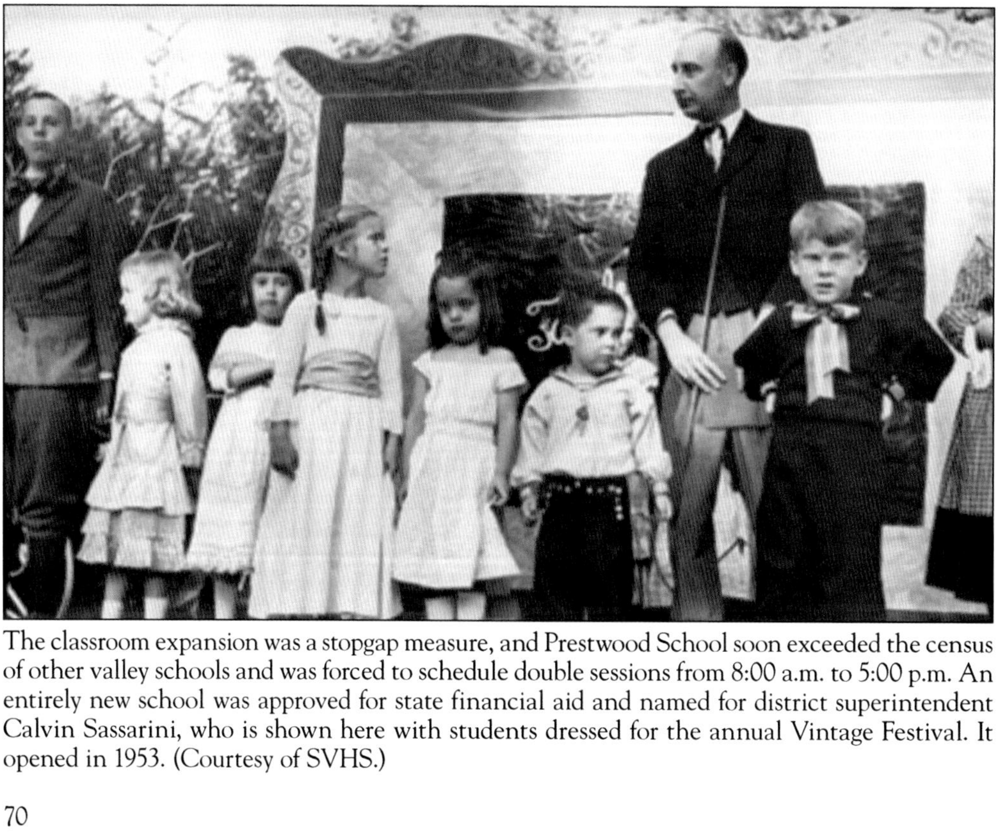

The classroom expansion was a stopgap measure, and Prestwood School soon exceeded the census of other valley schools and was forced to schedule double sessions from 8:00 a.m. to 5:00 p.m. An entirely new school was approved for state financial aid and named for district superintendent Calvin Sassarini, who is shown here with students dressed for the annual Vintage Festival. It opened in 1953. (Courtesy of SVHS.)

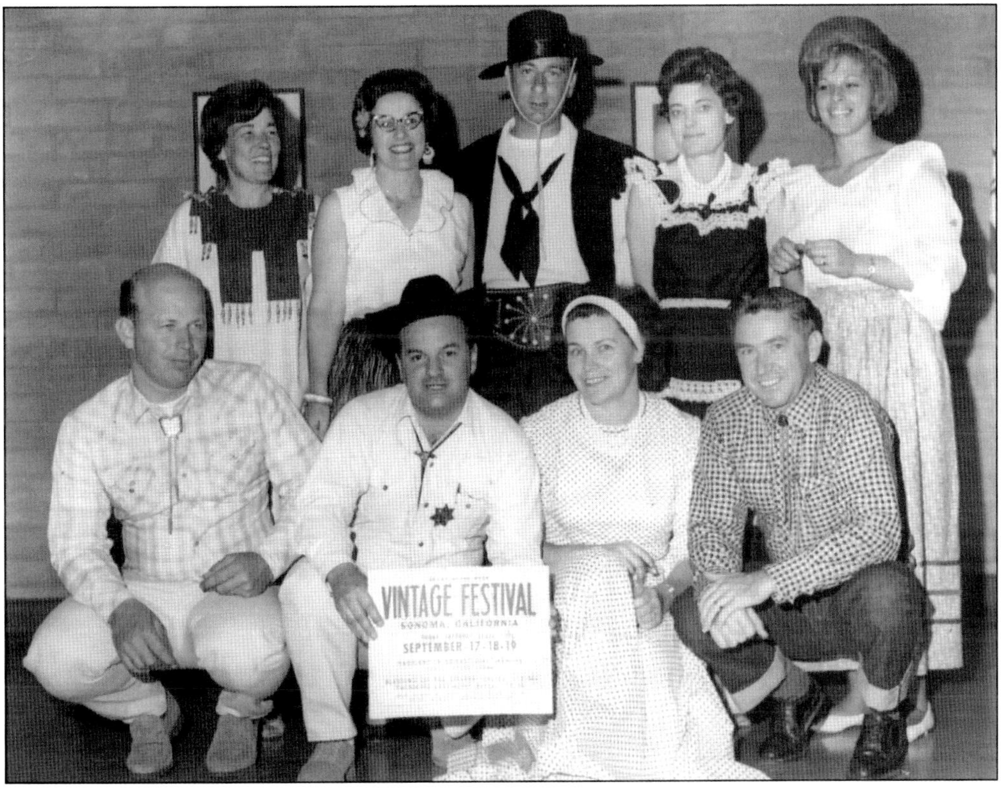

The grammar school's fate remained a challenge. After offering it for sale for $75,000 and receiving no offers, the board put it up for auction with an opening bid of $40,000. When no bidders came forward, the old building seemed destined for the wrecking ball until community leaders of the revered Vintage Festival Association proposed that the school be reimagined as a community center. (Courtesy of SVHS.)

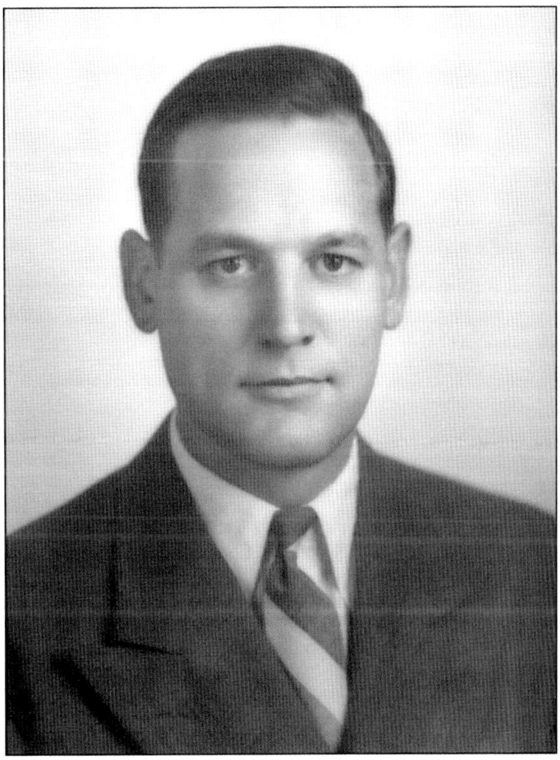

Dr. Carroll Andrews, a Nebraska-bred graduate of Stanford Medical School, adopted Sonoma as his home in 1933. He envisioned the school's new future and began a passionate campaign for its rebirth as a community center. On February 20, 1952, he and his wife, Katherine, purchased the building and four-acre lot at auction for $28,500 and turned it over to a new nonprofit board of directors. (Courtesy of SVHS.)

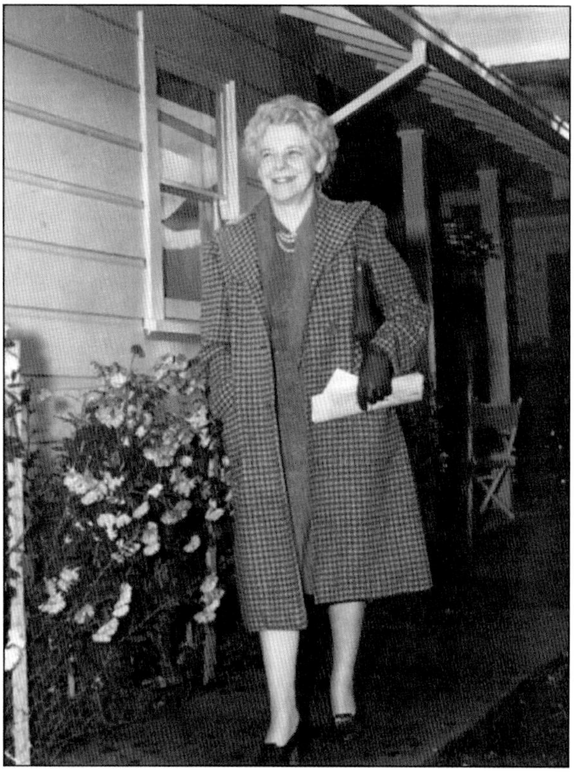

In a note to Dr. Andrews that accompanied her donation in support of the building's purchase, Eleanor Arnold—wife of the highly regarded Gen. Hap Arnold—wrote, "I have to tell you how much I appreciate the great effort you are making to obtain the old grammar school for the citizens of Sonoma. . . . We are most grateful for your initiative and hard work in serving our community." (Courtesy of SVHS.)

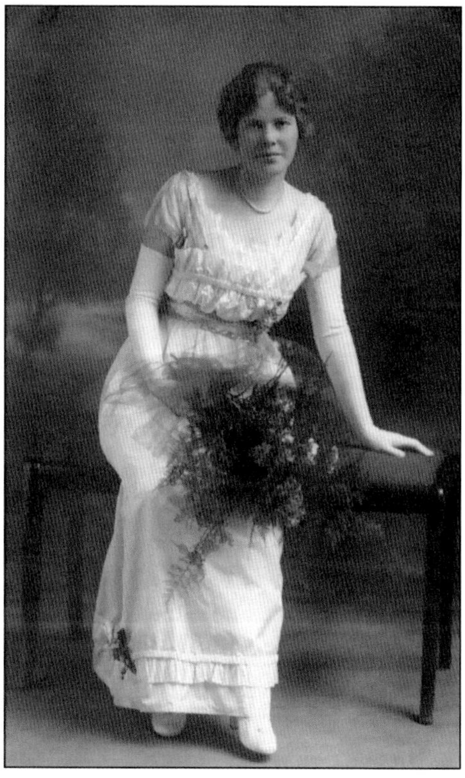

Dr. Andrews kept the issue before Sonoma's newspaper-reading public with letters and opinion pieces about the importance of a community center. Gladys Dodge, née Simmons, from one of the old families of the valley, was so stirred by his vision of cultural education that she wrote out a $1,000 check on the spot. She is shown here upon her graduation from Sonoma High in 1915. (Courtesy of SVHS.)

Winemaker August Sebastiani was keenly interested in obtaining the school. He was rumored to have an interest in turning it over to the Catholic diocese for a parochial elementary school. Some said that he wanted to expand his winery operations onto the property. A friendly but spirited rivalry between Sebastiani and Andrews resulted but was finally settled when Sylvia Sebastiani told her husband to let the doctor have it. (Courtesy of SVHS.)

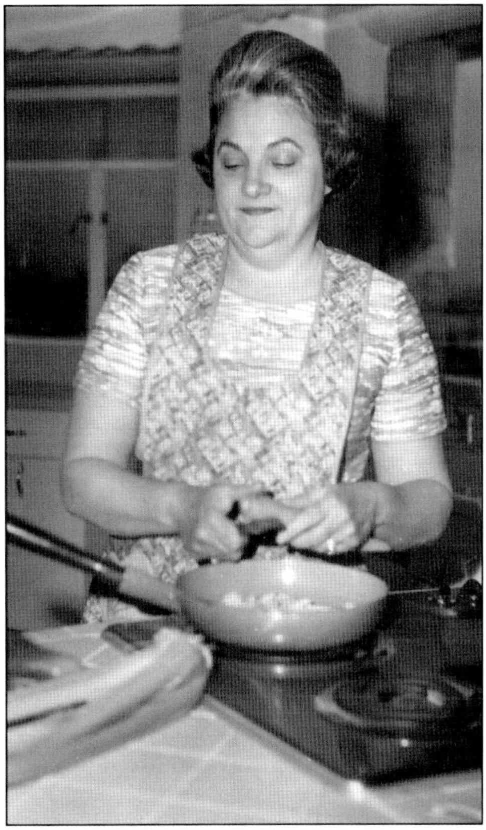

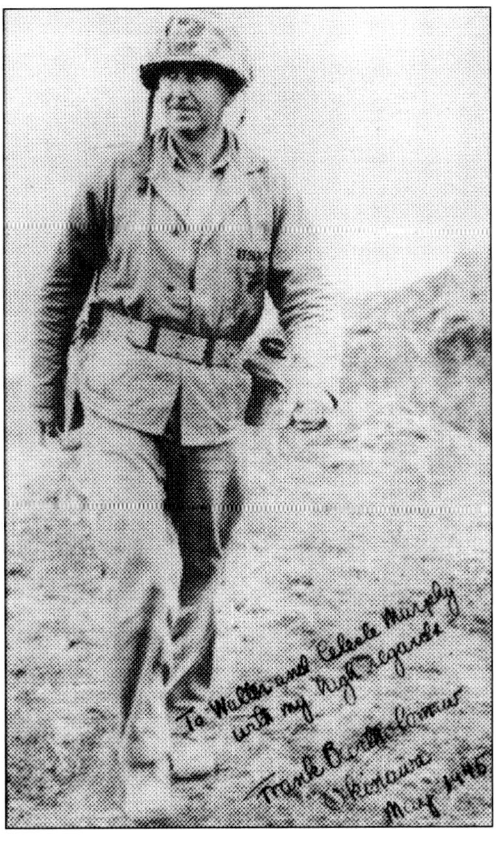

Community enthusiasm was palpable. The Andrewses were flooded with congratulations and letters of thanks. Frank Bartholomew, president of United Press International and owner of Sonoma's Buena Vista Winery, wrote, "Hearty congratulations upon emerging as successful bidder for the former Sonoma Grammar School. I know it will be put to the very best possible use and I am positive that the investment will pay dividends in many ways." (Courtesy of SVHS.)

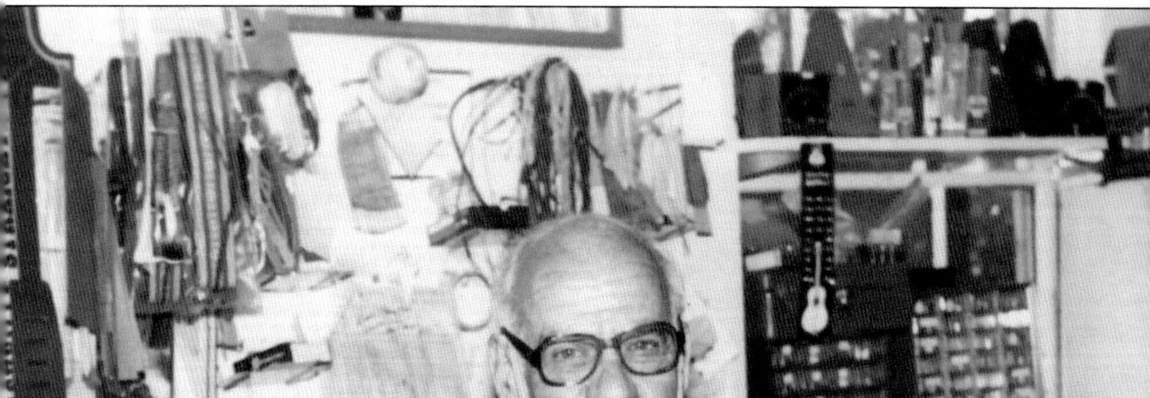

Dan Ruggles, whose first love was music, saw the acquisition of the old grammar school as an enormous step forward for the cultural life of Sonoma. He quickly became part of the nucleus of Sonoma Community Center organizers and ensured that music would be a dominant component of the new center. (Courtesy of SVHS.)

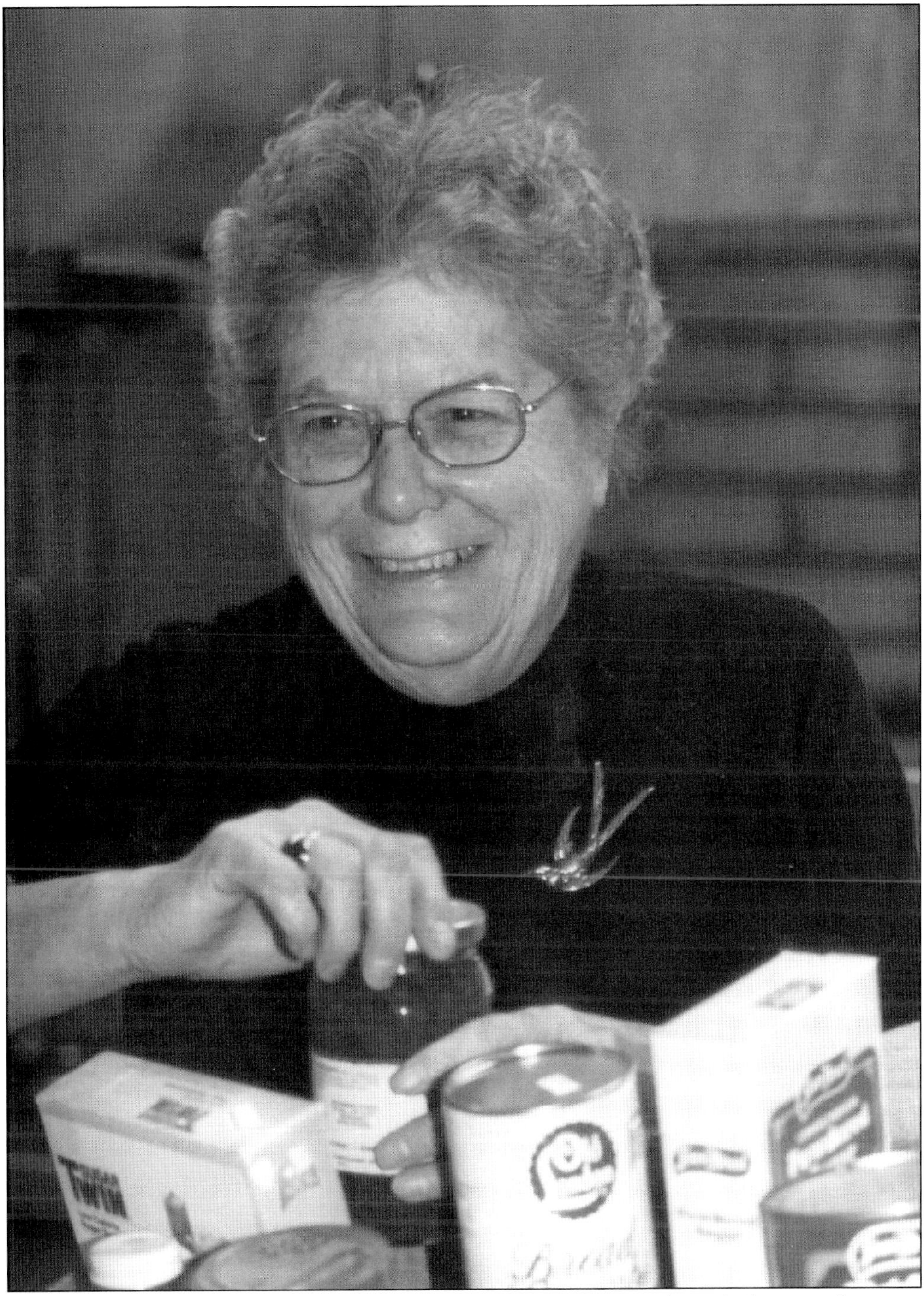

Balancing out Dan Ruggles's musical contribution, Jerry Casson brought her social service background and practical approach to the center. She was central to SCC's long history of altruism toward the community and used SCC as a launching site for a dozen other charitable ventures. She was instrumental in acquiring funding for the Vintage House Senior Center, and the building is named in her honor. (Courtesy of SVHS.)

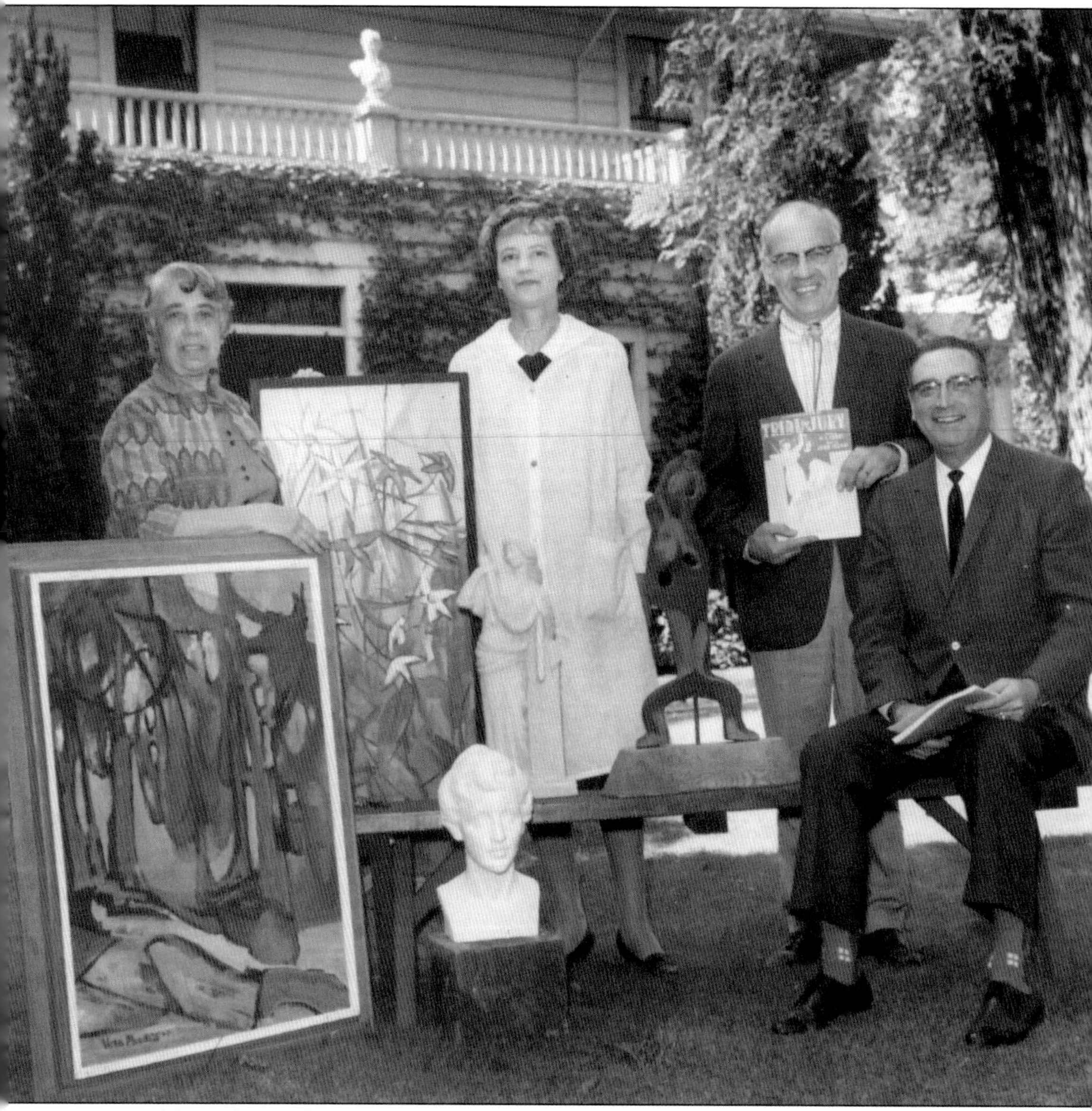

Pictured here, from left to right, are SCC organizers Jerry Casson, Marian Brackenridge, Dan Ruggles, and Dr. Andrews. A renowned sculptor, Brackenridge brought a cultural sophistication and intelligence to the start-up operation while also keeping an eye on the building from her home, La Brenta, which sat directly across the street from the center. (Courtesy of SVHS.)

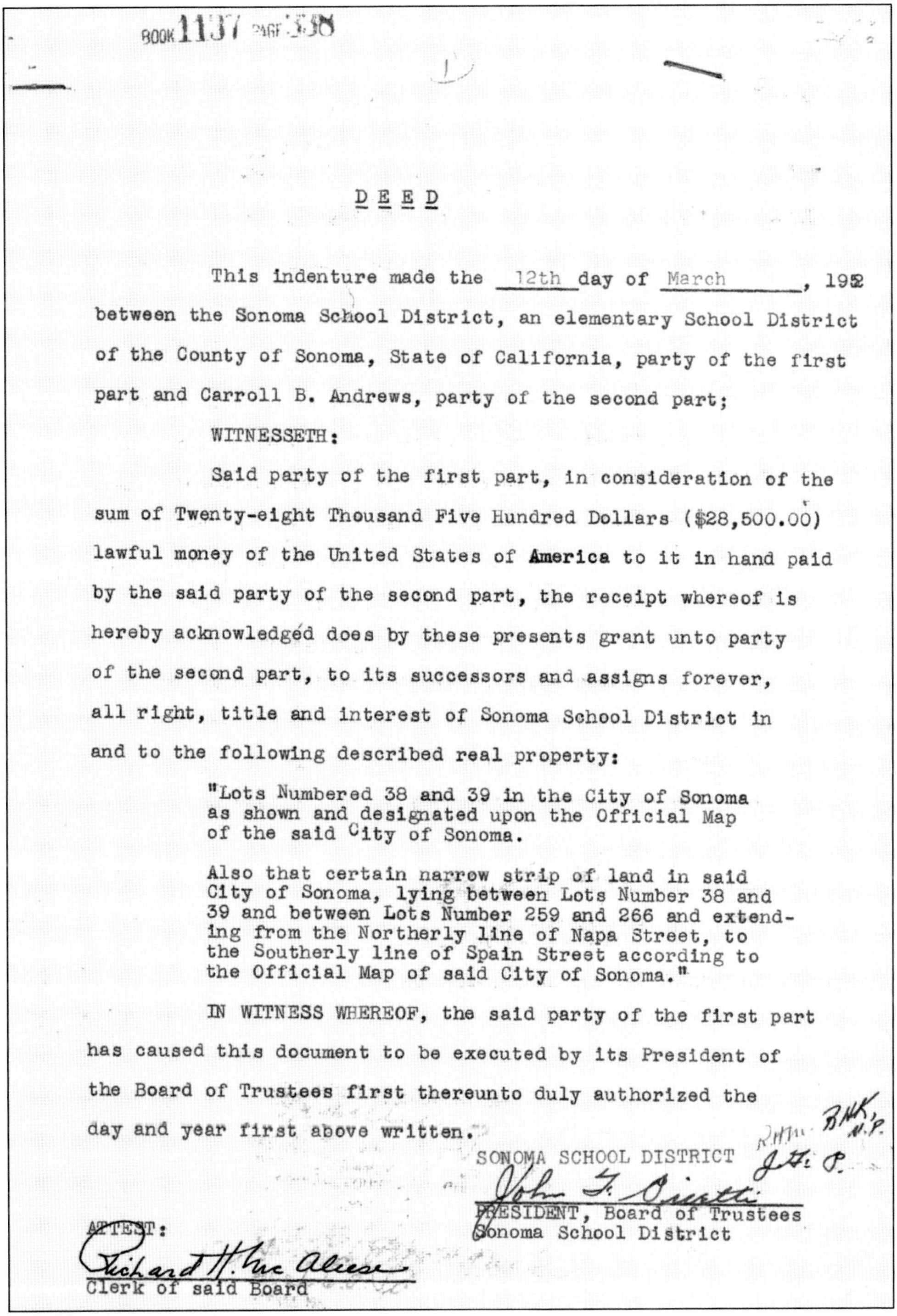
BOOK 1137 PAGE 338

D E E D

This indenture made the 12th day of March, 195

between the Sonoma School District, an elementary School District of the County of Sonoma, State of California, party of the first part and Carroll B. Andrews, party of the second part;

WITNESSETH:

Said party of the first part, in consideration of the sum of Twenty-eight Thousand Five Hundred Dollars ($28,500.00) lawful money of the United States of America to it in hand paid by the said party of the second part, the receipt whereof is hereby acknowledged does by these presents grant unto party of the second part, to its successors and assigns forever, all right, title and interest of Sonoma School District in and to the following described real property:

"Lots Numbered 38 and 39 in the City of Sonoma as shown and designated upon the Official Map of the said City of Sonoma.

Also that certain narrow strip of land in said City of Sonoma, lying between Lots Number 38 and 39 and between Lots Number 259 and 266 and extending from the Northerly line of Napa Street, to the Southerly line of Spain Street according to the Official Map of said City of Sonoma."

IN WITNESS WHEREOF, the said party of the first part has caused this document to be executed by its President of the Board of Trustees first thereunto duly authorized the day and year first above written.

SONOMA SCHOOL DISTRICT

John F. Oriatti

PRESIDENT, Board of Trustees
Sonoma School District

ATTEST:

Richard H. Mc Aliese

Clerk of said Board

On March 26, 1951, trustees of the Sonoma Elementary School District signed over the deed to Carroll and Katherine Andrews. In turn, Dr. Andrews bestowed its management upon a new board of directors. He became the board's first chairman and retained the position for a number of years. (Courtesy of SVHS.)

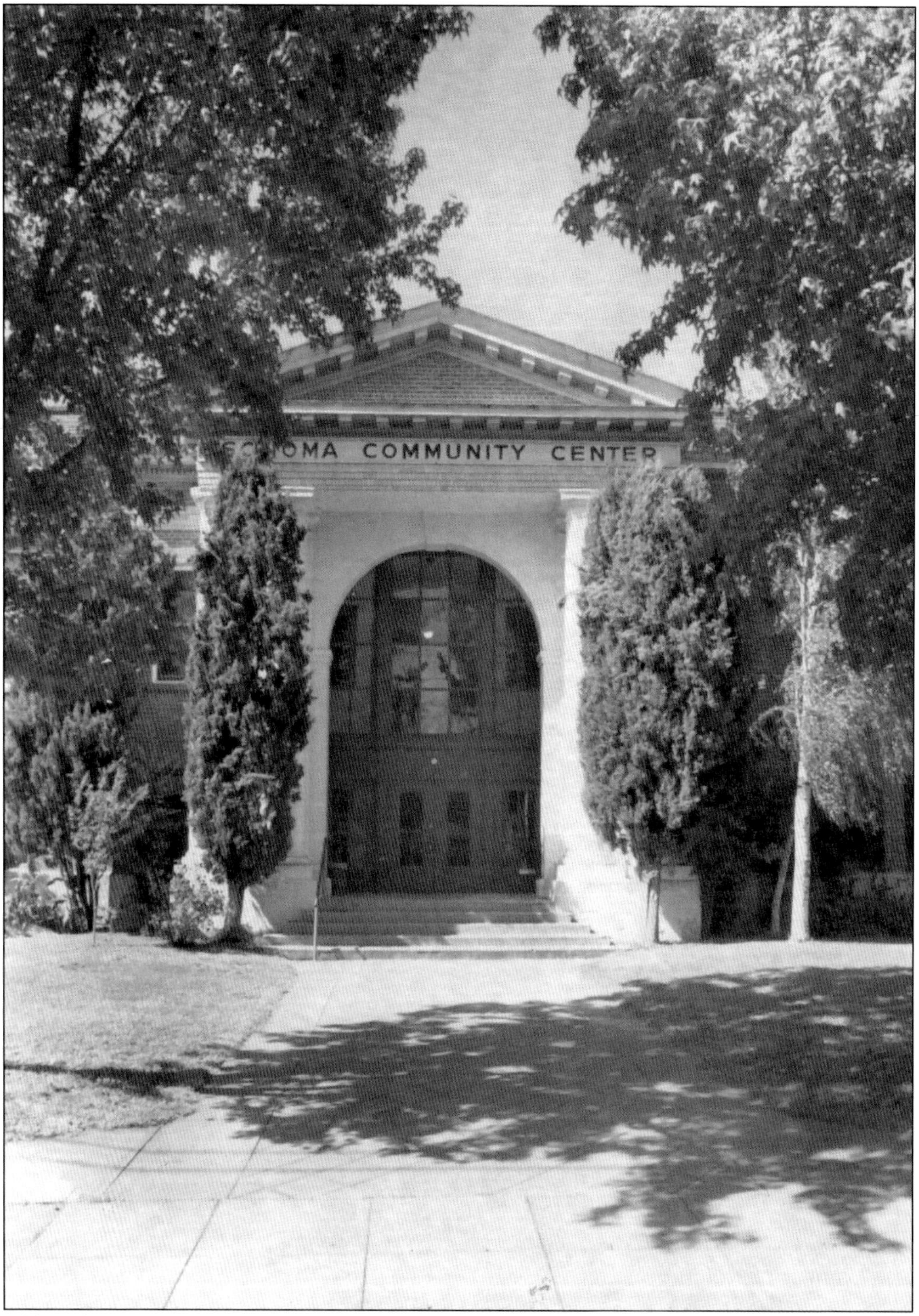

Although Sonoma Grammar School began its new career as a center of community and cultural life in a building that was already beginning to age, the organizers had great enthusiasm for its mission and little worry about how it would be supported. This lack of fiscal planning would be lamented many times in the future. (Courtesy of SVHS.)

Five

Community Takes Center Stage

Sonoma quickly embraced its new community center. Eight months after the school district sold the school to Dr. Andrews, the fledgling organization was awarded nonprofit 501c3 status by the IRS. The board of directors quickly hammered out a mission that was broad in scope and lofty in ideals. Board chairman Andrews spelled it out in a letter to the board: "The Sonoma Community Center's function is to provide a voluntary community organization with space for those who would not otherwise be able to develop activities and programs. The center will expand community-wide services to fill the gap between the tax supported school entities and the voluntary lay organizations."

With Dan Ruggles heading an ambitious music education program and Jerry Casson building a social service network for Sonomans in need, SCC became Sonoma's cultural nerve center. It incubated many of the crucial nonprofit organizations that still serve Sonoma today—churches, Scouting organizations, the Red Cross, arts clubs, the Vintage Festival Association, Pet Population Control, Adobe Grange, square dancing clubs, and the Valley of the Moon Garden Club all rented space there. Some start-ups were completely rent-subsidized by SCC, and the Boys Club (now the Boys and Girls Club) spent its first 10 years at the center rent-free.

SCC also developed programs and traditions that continue to define Sonoma's community identity. The Thanksgiving dinner, which boasts more volunteers than its hundreds of patrons; the annual Fourth of July parade that attracts thousands of visitors; and the annual *Thanksmas* (now renamed the *Fabulous Follies*), which celebrates community talent and the spirit of giving, were all started in these early days and continue even now.

Supporting these organizations, programs, and the associated building maintenance came at substantial cost, however. During its first years, SCC relied on a philanthropic community whose members raised money through memberships, developed a room rental program, and thought up a number of fundraising events.

In 1976, Carroll and Katherine Andrews forgave the $14,000 principal owed to them by SCC's board of directors, but the generous gesture did not alleviate the financial pall that hung over the building. From SCC's inception, the board struggled to support the operation and pay for maintenance on the 27,000-square-foot building. By the early 1980s, building safety was a major concern. Deferred maintenance projects could no longer be postponed. Something had to be done.

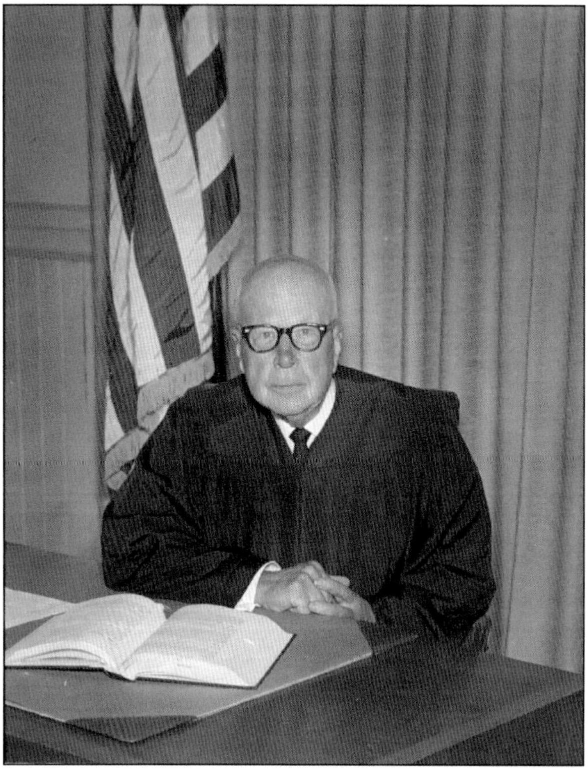

Local attorney Allan Grinstead stepped forward to guide the unseasoned Sonoma Community Center on its legal path to 501c3 status—formally bestowed in November 1952. The attorney also joined the center's new finance committee, comprised of Harriet Jones, Leslie Pace Armstrong, William Houston, and Dr. Andrews. That same year, he was named justice of the peace of the Sonoma Township. (Courtesy of SVHS.)

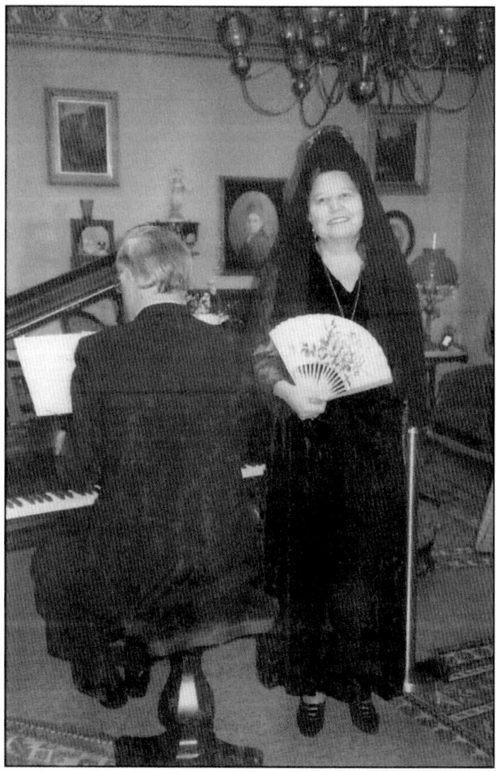

Among the strategies suggested by the finance committee to raise funds was a series of musicals that were developed by Dan Ruggles and scheduled throughout the year. Pictured is Evelyn Gregory, a linchpin of SCC's choral group, whose voice was described by the local paper as "a brilliant and rich soprano." At this particular Depot Park Museum Bear Flag celebration, Owen Thomas accompanied her on the piano. (Courtesy of SVHS.)

Fundraisers attempted to help raise money for the operating budget through monthly Sunday brunches, antique fairs, flea markets, bake sales, and a hundred other well-intentioned grassroots activities that were great social events but not too helpful to SCC's bottom line. (Courtesy of SVHS.)

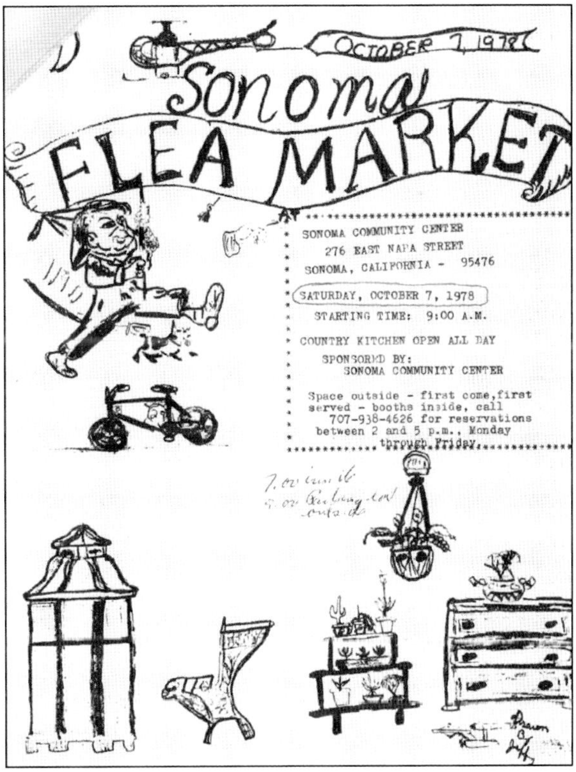

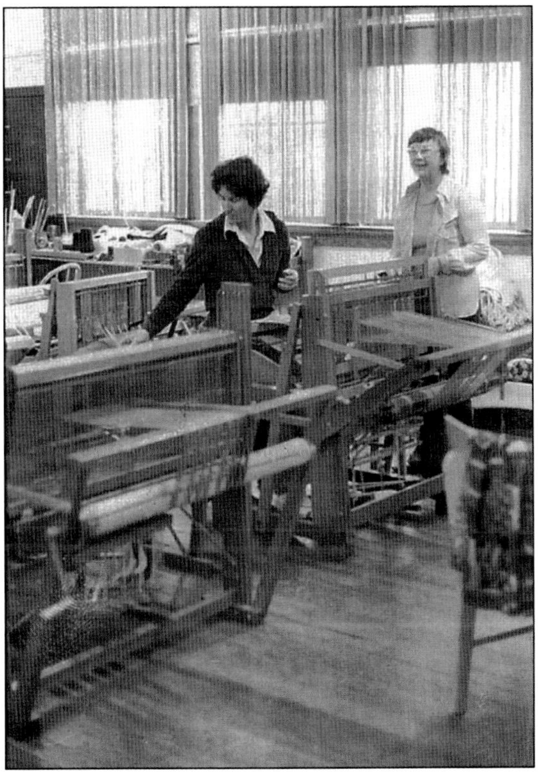

For 30 years, the board relied heavily on volunteers to accomplish most SCC work, and renters who used the center as their base of operation helped out as much as possible. Lois Purdom, an expert weaver, filled an upstairs classroom with various kinds of looms and taught generations of interested Sonoma residents the art of weaving. She also cleaned and maintained her own room. (Courtesy of SVHS.)

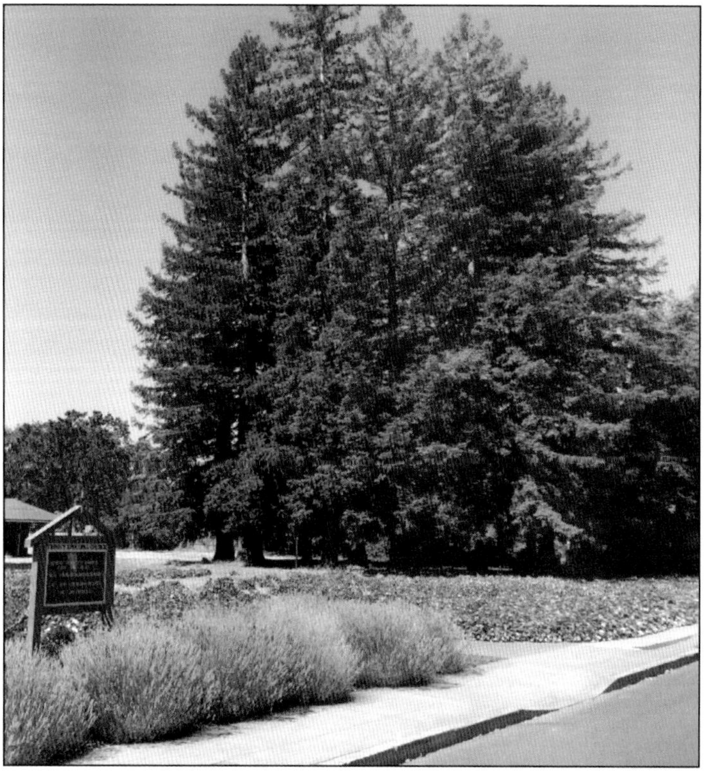

From the beginning, SCC intended to play an important role in Sonoma life. In 1953, it joined the Valley of the Moon Garden Club to plant a redwood grove in honor of the Sonoma men who had died serving in the armed forces. The grove is now located on the north edge of the Trinity Episcopal Church property and affords citizens a place of contemplation. (Courtesy of SVHS.)

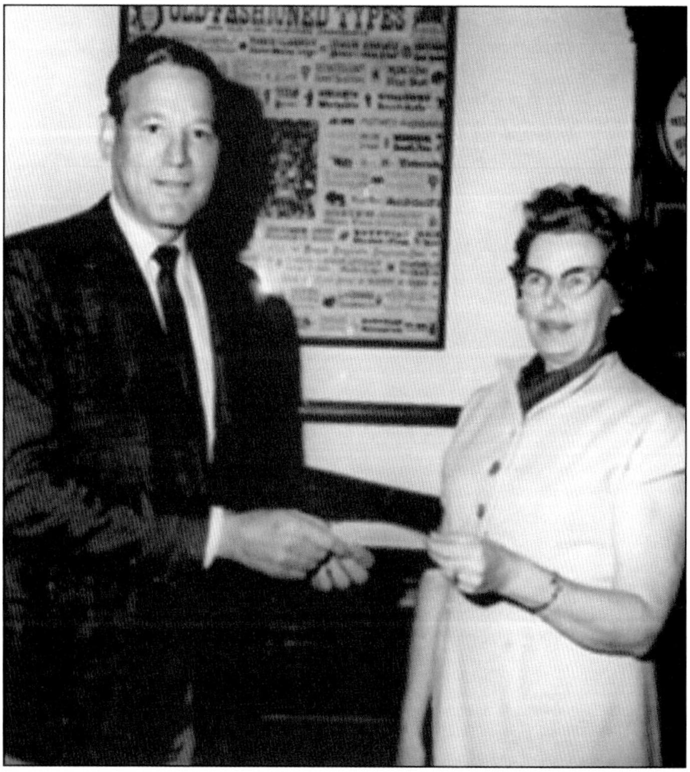

SCC initiated and developed Valley of the Moon Boys Club in 1964, set up as an independent organization and as a unit of the Boys' Clubs of America. SCC donated the downstairs to the club rent-free. Dr. Andrews was a tireless fundraiser for the organization and is shown here accepting a donation from Helen Clary. The club stayed at SCC for 10 years before acquiring its own larger building. (Courtesy of SVHS.)

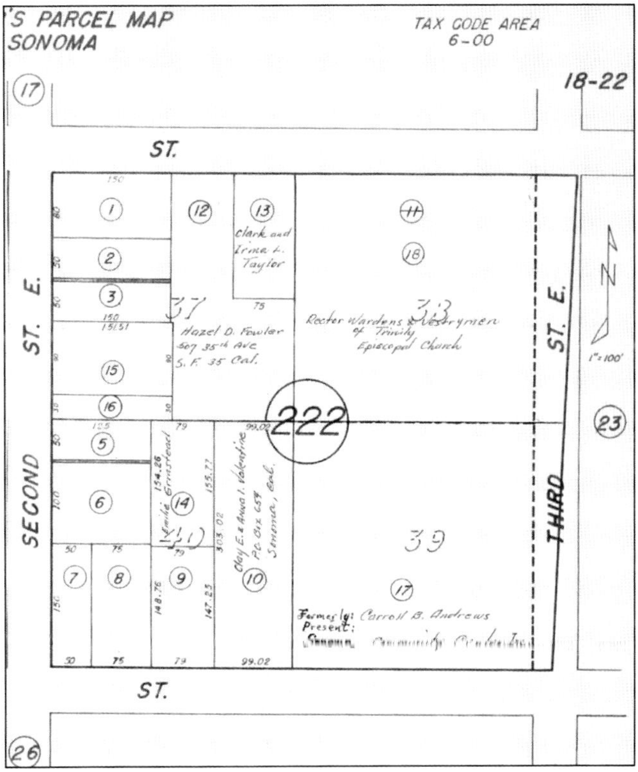

Dr. Andrews still held the title to the Sonoma Community Center and the four acres on which it was situated. In 1964, he recouped some of the original purchase price by subdividing the property and selling two acres to the Trinity Episcopal Church for $20,000. The swelling congregation had outgrown its home at Parrish Hall on East Napa Street, which is now the Christian Science church. (Courtesy of SVHS.)

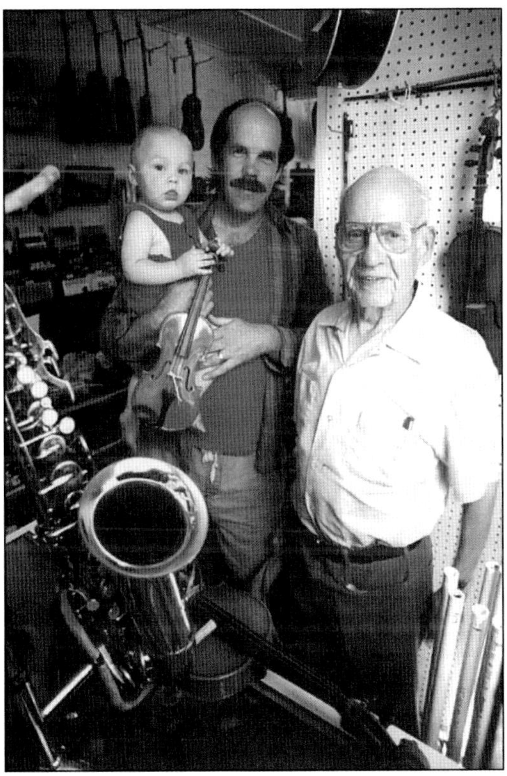

Dan Ruggles's musical expertise and enthusiasm were essential to a thriving music program during the early years. He was well versed in attracting crowds and twisting arms for funding. His well-loved store, Ruggles Music, was adjacent to the plaza and was often headquarters for planning the next Sonoma Community Center musical event. He is shown here with his son and grandchild. (Courtesy of SCC.)

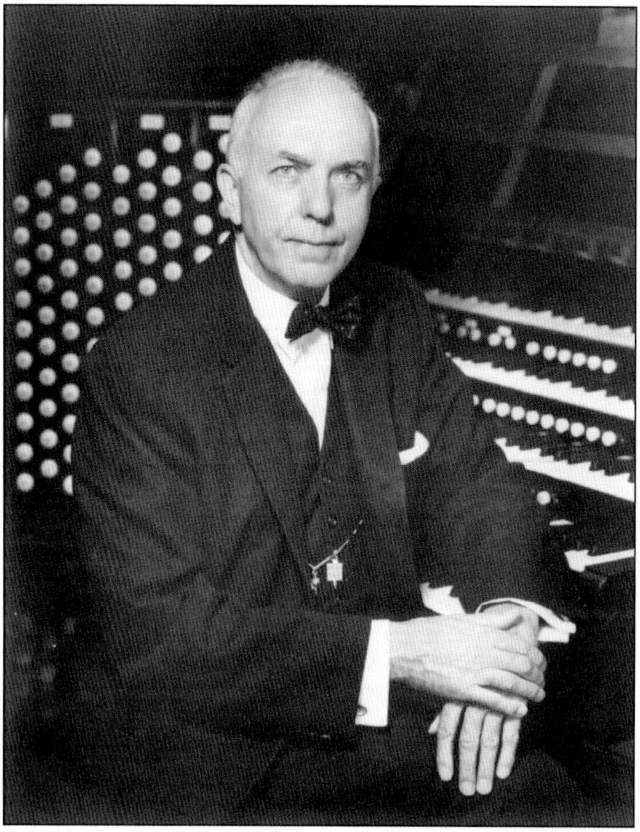

In the late 1960s, Dan Ruggles was successful in acquiring the donation of a Kimball pipe organ and, with donated and paid labor, rebuilt it to an excellent instrument that was key to a variety of performances over the years. In 1969, the organ was dedicated during a performance by Dr. Alexander Schreiner, an internationally famous organist at the Mormon Tabernacle in Salt Lake City. (Courtesy of SVHS.)

Director Ruggles's music collection was housed at the center. He also collected other sheet music to be loaned to interested parties. At one time, the music library contained thousands of titles. Helen Clary was one of the many volunteers who worked to keep it current. (Courtesy of SVHS.)

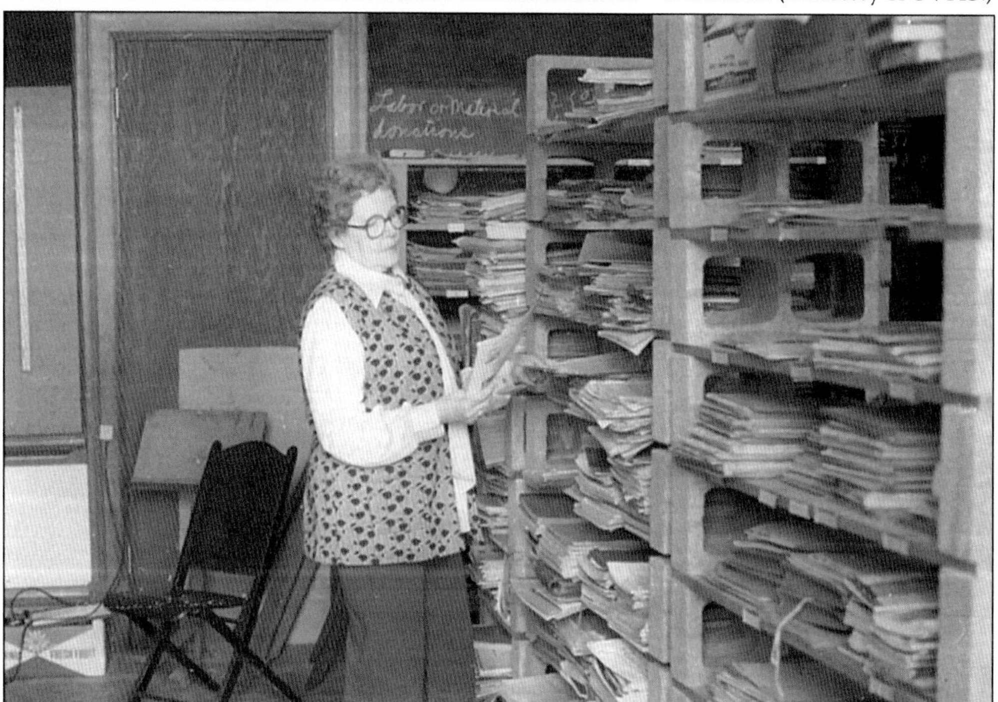

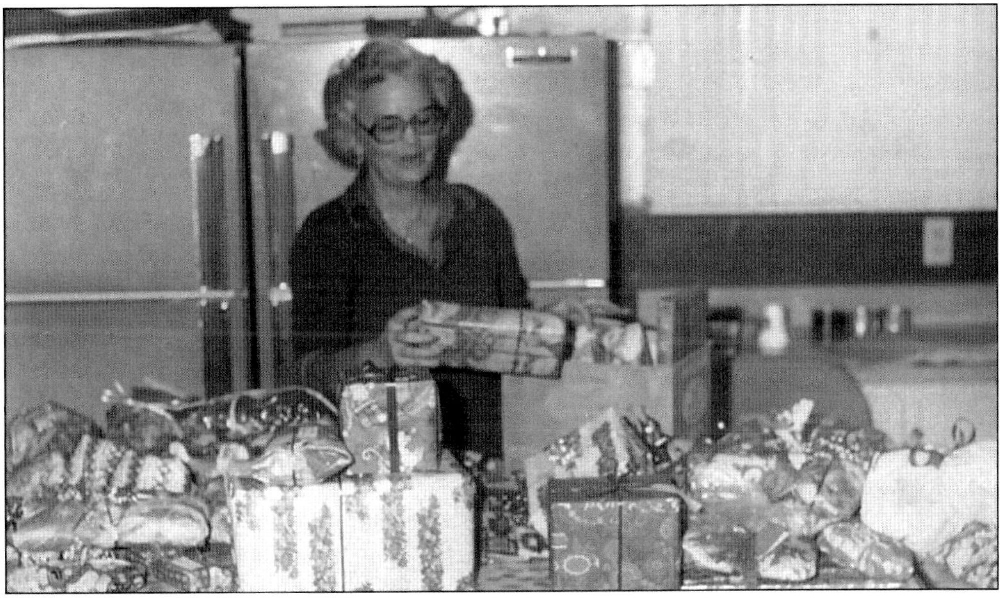

Jerry Casson put together a group that she called her "kitchen cabinet" and went to work on making sure no one went hungry or homeless. Her grassroots, no-nonsense approach to these issues was the right one for Sonoma at the time. The pictured Christmas basket project, a forerunner of the FISH (Friends in Sonoma Helping) program later established by local churches, made sure that no one would go hungry or be without gifts at Christmas. Volunteers wrapped hundreds of presents for the children on their lists. (Courtesy of SVHS.)

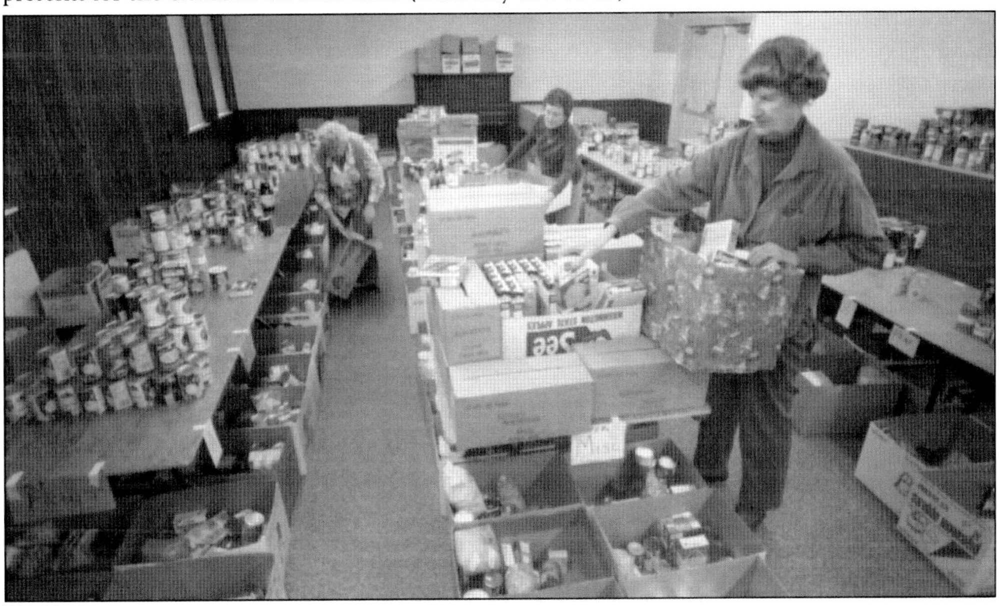

From Thanksgiving through Christmas, rooms were dedicated to charitable activities. Margo Hendricksen and others devoted their holiday hours to make sure Christmas baskets were organized and ready to go. In 1988, Jerry Casson recalled, "It started with 15 baskets and grew until we are now at 400." Adele Harrison, a member of Jerry's team who became the director of FISH, said, "Jerry used to check every basket herself." FISH took over the program and continues to feed hundreds of families every year. (Courtesy of SCC.)

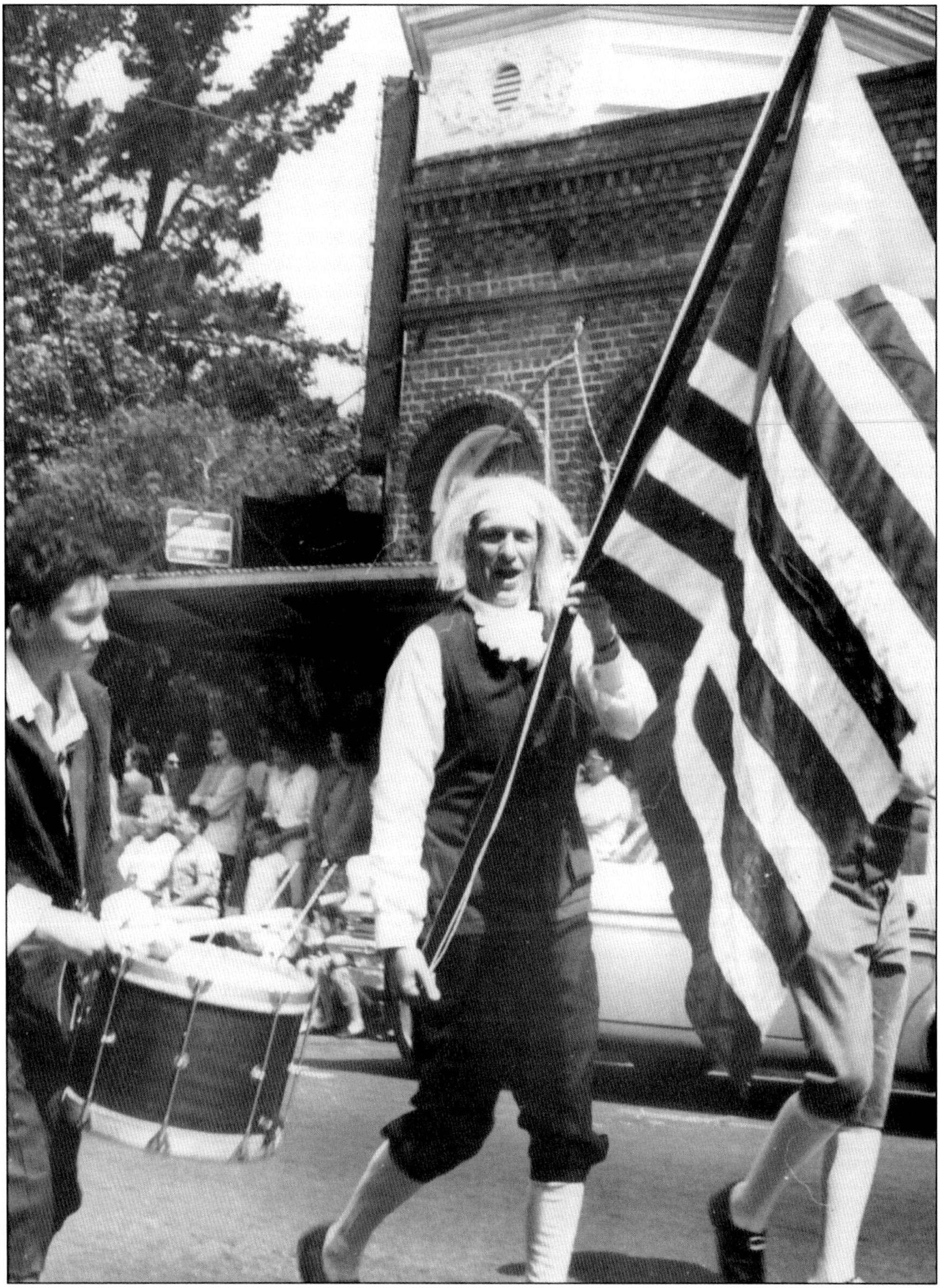

Sonoma Community Center reinvigorated civic pride by building strong community traditions like the Fourth of July parade—started in 1963. School district superintendent John Glaese created the Spirit of '76 entry and reprised it again over the years. In those days, the parade started and ended at the community center. Jerry Casson convinced city officials to have the parade circle the plaza, where it has provided Sonoma with a strong summer focal point ever since. (Courtesy of SVHS.)

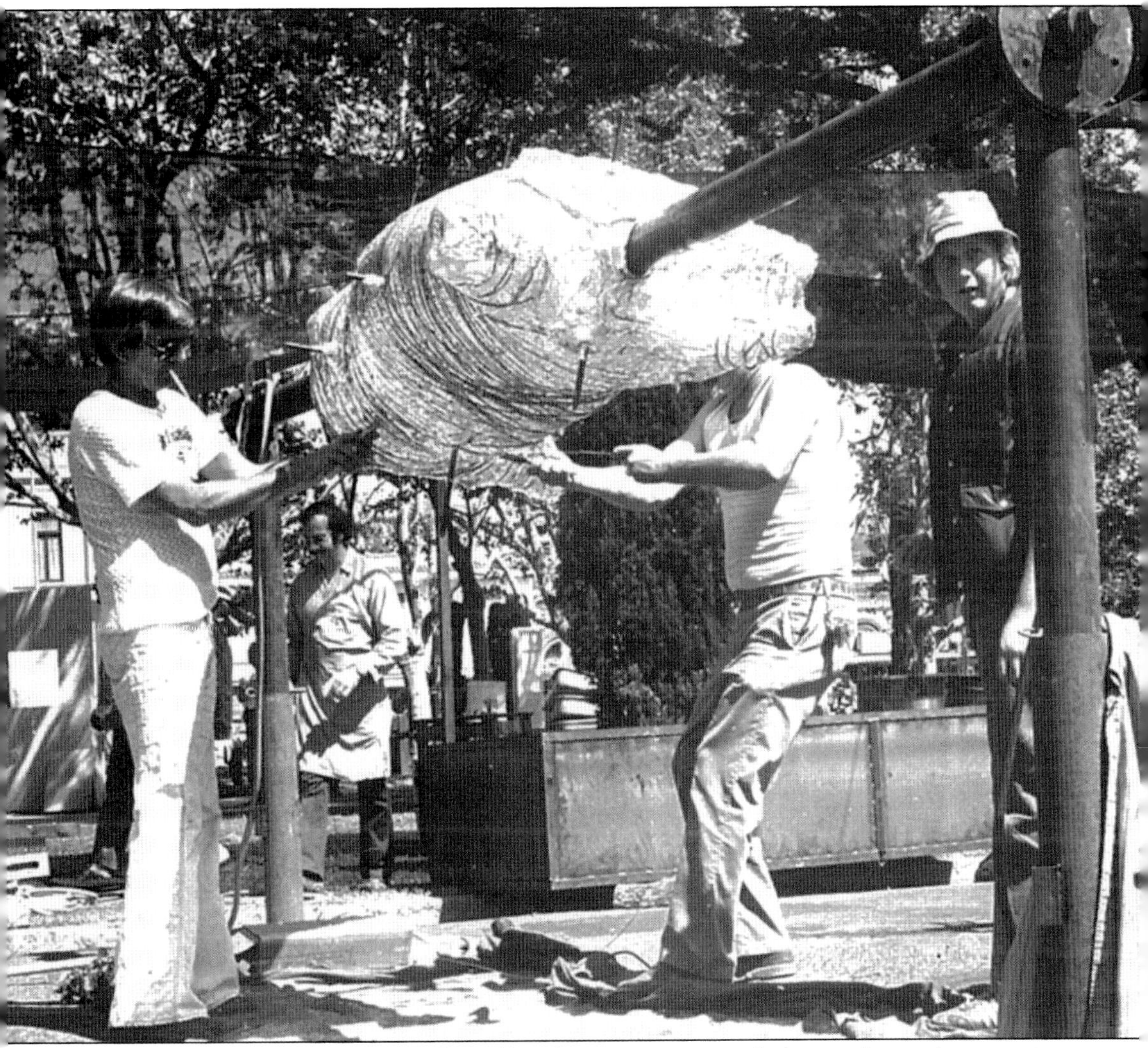

Volunteers for the Ox Roast stayed up all night spit roasting a whole cow for revelers to enjoy the next day. Originally created in 1963 under the leadership of Bob Cannard and the Sonoma Chamber of Commerce, SCC soon assumed control of the event. Generations of Sonomans volunteered, celebrated, and were entertained at this favorite local event until event organizer Howie Ehret died 2012. SCC retired the event in 2013. (Courtesy of SVHS.)

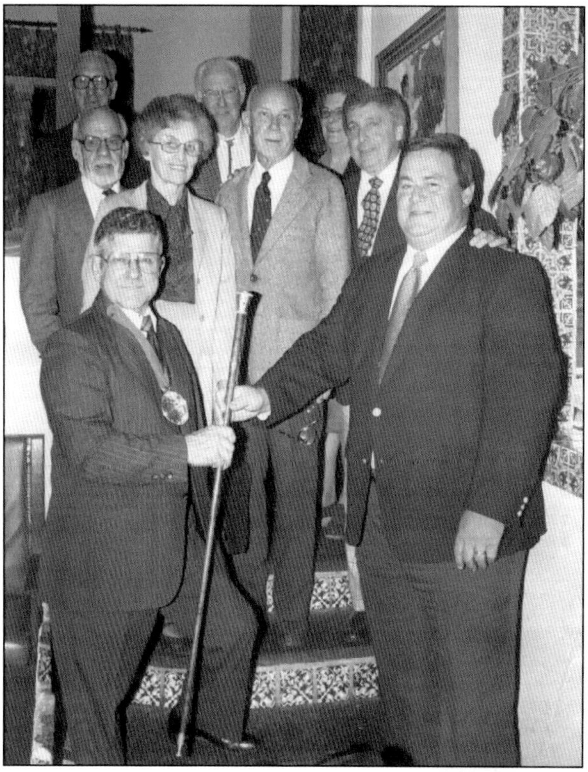

In 1975, Sonoma created a process to name an annual honorary alcalde to recognize community members who made unselfish contributions to the welfare of Sonoma. In this alcalde photograph from 1983, everyone pictured was critical to the success and mission of SCC. From left to right are (first row) Chet Sharek and Gail Fehrensen; (second row) Adele Harrison; (third row) Dan Ruggles, Paul Harrison, and Bob Lynch; (third row) August Pinelli, Henri Maysonnave, and Jerry Casson. (Courtesy of SVHS.)

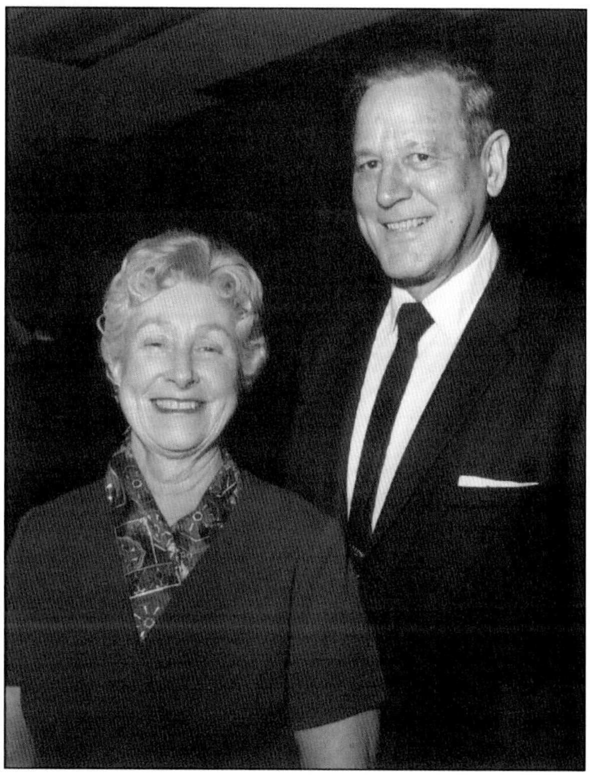

In 1976, Dr. and Mrs. Andrews were celebrated at a ceremonial dinner and SCC's auditorium was named in their honor. A bronze plaque was placed in the newly minted Andrews Hall in honor of the couple who revived the old grammar school, turned it into a much needed and used community center, and ensured that the building and land "fully belonged to its board of directors." (Courtesy of Jurine Biers.)

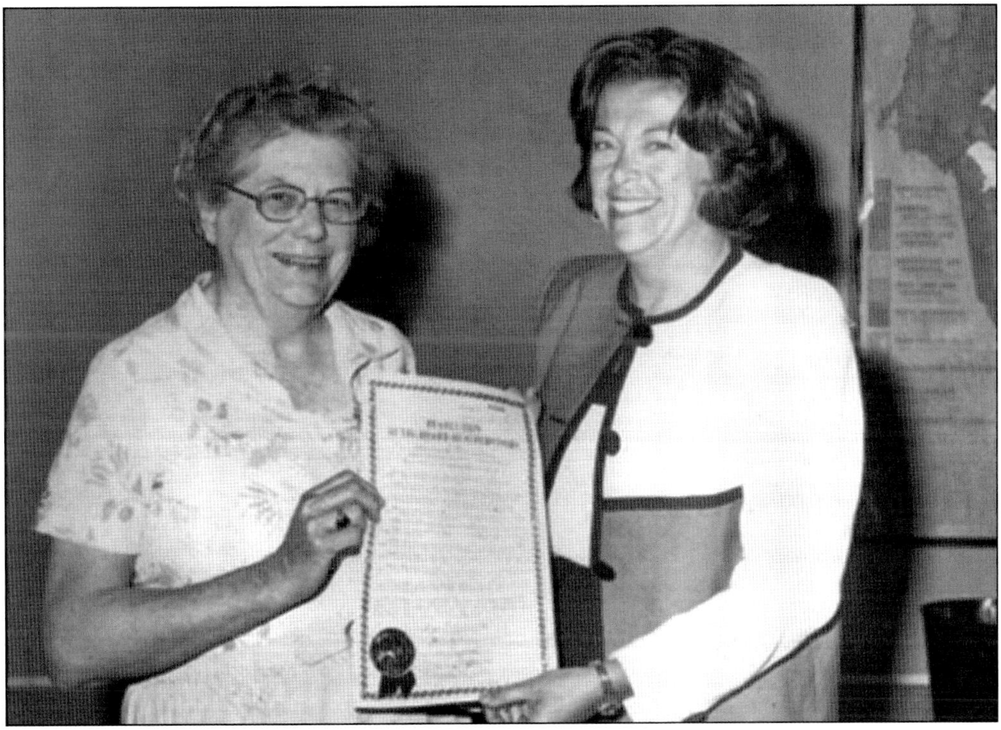

The old guard of SCC's early, critical decades was nearing retirement age, but they continued to give. While they were recognized for all they had done, SCC's wellbeing was becoming another generation's responsibility. Jerry Casson was honored by the Sonoma County Board of Supervisors for her many contributions to the city and county of Sonoma. In 1983, First District supervisor Janet Nicholas presented her with a proclamation honoring her years of service. (Courtesy of SVHS.)

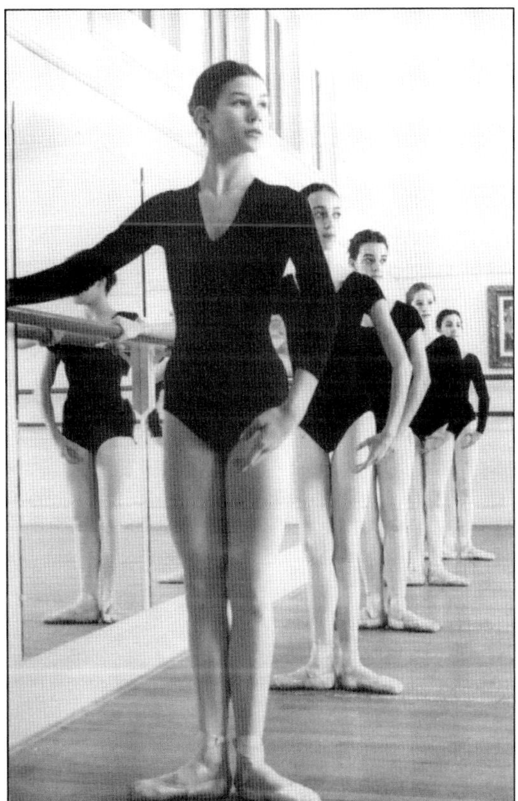

SCC continued to serve the community by renting dedicated classrooms to long-term tenants. Beth-Marie Deenihan's Sonoma Ballet was an institutional tradition for many young Sonoma girls. Other lease holders who contributed to the center's stability during these days included Samantha Maynard's Sonoma Dance Academy, Lois Purdom's weaving room, and Alcoholics Anonymous. (Courtesy of SVHS.)

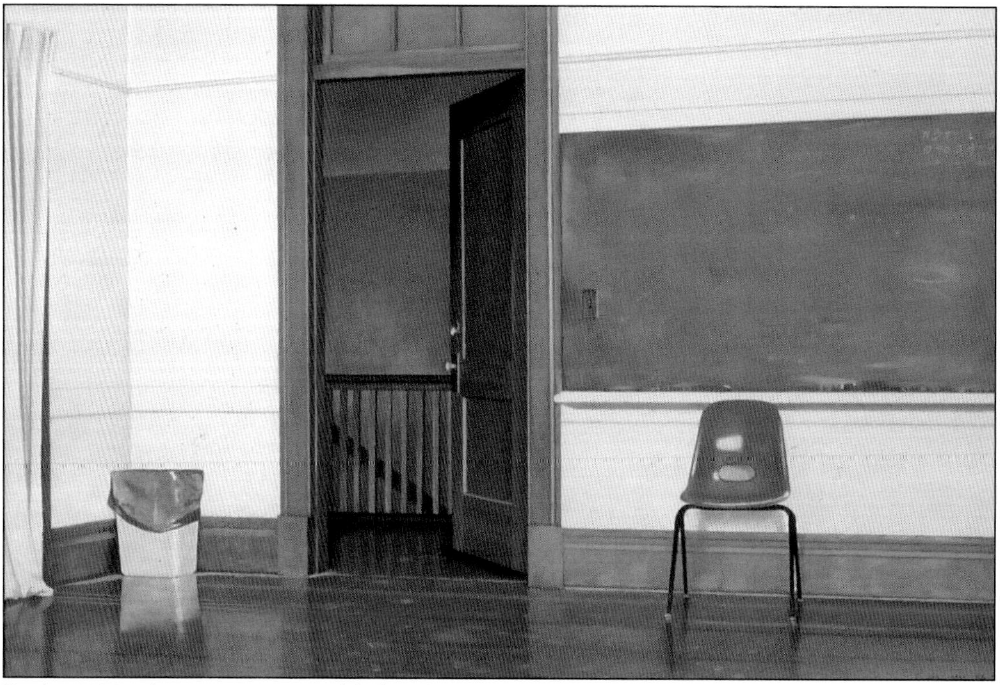

By the 1980s, the consequences of deferred maintenance loomed. SCC needed a sound building to attract a public that had other choices for town meetings and entertainments. While the shabby classrooms stayed empty, local artist Don Williams painted the empty rooms over a period of years. The beauty he found in the historic spaces is compelling, but it did not attract a population with its eye on the future. (Courtesy of Don Williams.)

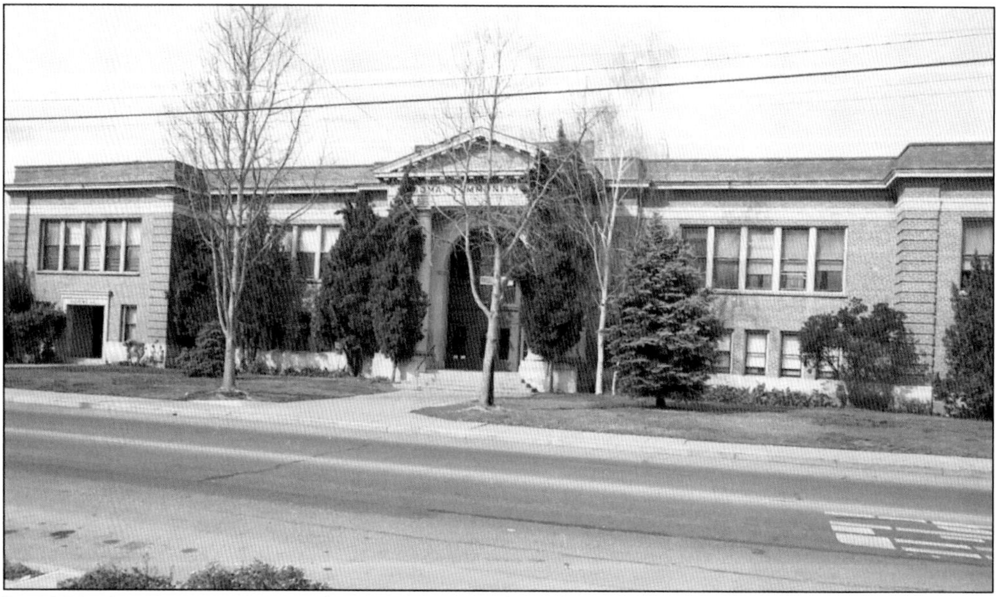

In 1980, the center was at its lowest point. Its board of directors worked valiantly to attract community attention to the sorry state of the building, but to no avail. Finally, a wake-up call came from an unexpected source and dramatically changed Sonoma Community Center's future. (Courtesy of SCC.)

Six

Reconstruction

The Sonoma Community Center's board of directors faced a serious dilemma. Restoring the building to its former grandeur required the attention and financial support of its community, but the building's depressing physical state kept away those it was trying to attract.

Even as the board of directors pondered its next move, Sonoma's new city manager Brock Arner proposed a potential solution to the building's failing health: tear down the existing brick building, sell the land for residential development, and use those funds to build a brand new center in another central city location.

The proposal caused consternation among a board of directors who valued the building's importance to local history more than any benefits a modern but impersonal facility could provide. Led by board president Kathleen Hill, it applied for the building's designation as a National Historic Landmark, receiving confirmation in less than six weeks. This ensured that the building could not be demolished nor the exterior changed from its original and also made it eligible for a federal preservation grant to help finance structural, fire, and safety improvements.

Additional construction soon followed when the City of Sonoma embraced the project and found funding for a fire sprinkler system, electrical improvements, and renovations to both Andrews Hall and the restrooms. Local businesses contributed free labor and materials, while community members gave cash donations to the project. The center's first paved parking lot was installed through in-kind donations from local paving contractor John Serres and others.

The renovation program proved to be the key to the center's revival. A flood of new renters increased the building's occupancy rate to 70 percent. Membership sharply increased, and the center soon received the first of some substantial financial gifts.

By the mid-to-late 1990s, a new board successfully implemented a strong cultural arts program that included pottery, fine arts, theater, writing, and culinary departments headed by professionals of each discipline. Successful annual fundraisers, such as the well-received Art Auction and an ongoing and profitable rummage sale dubbed Chez Rummage, helped the budget's bottom line.

A critical question remained, however: how could the necessary building upgrades and maintenance be sustained over time?

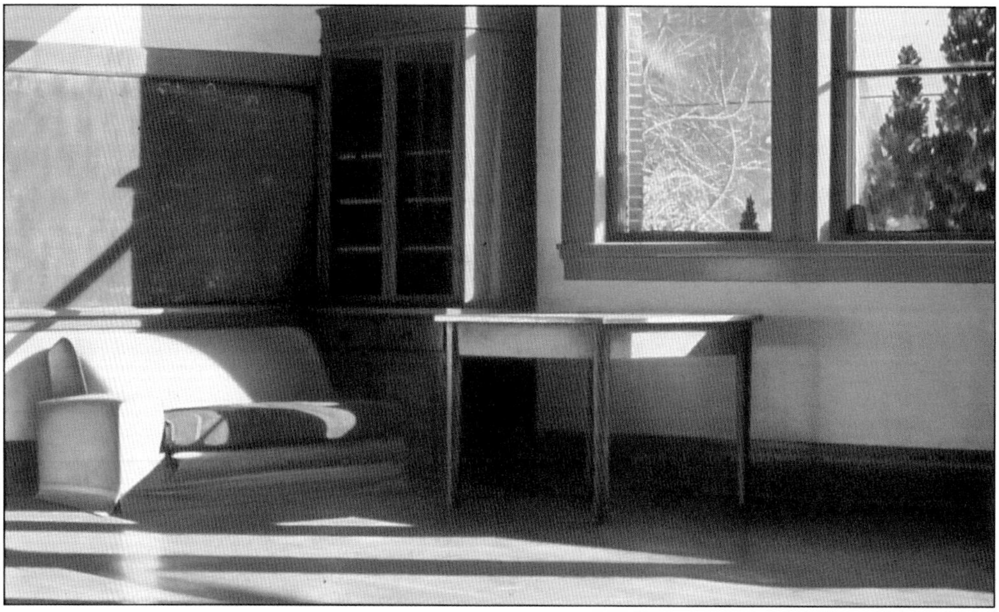

As Sonoma artist Don Williams's haunting pastel images show, the majority of the old classrooms remained empty and evocative of better times. In 1980, when seeking permission to paint the interiors, the artist was given ready access, as most of the rooms were only used for storage. (Courtesy of Don Williams.)

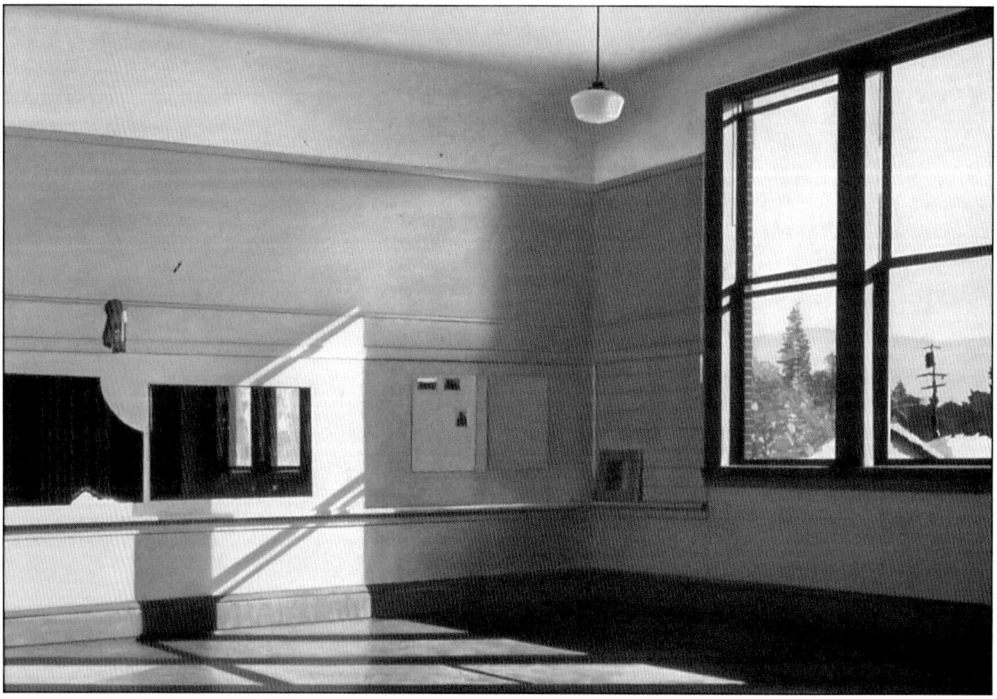

Williams says he painted the rooms because he "was struck by the wonderful light and spaciousness of these old classrooms and hallways. They brought back vivid memories of the schools I went to years ago with their blackboards, creaky wood floors, and large double-hung windows." Williams estimates he has created 20 pastels of the building's interiors over the years. (Courtesy of Don Williams.)

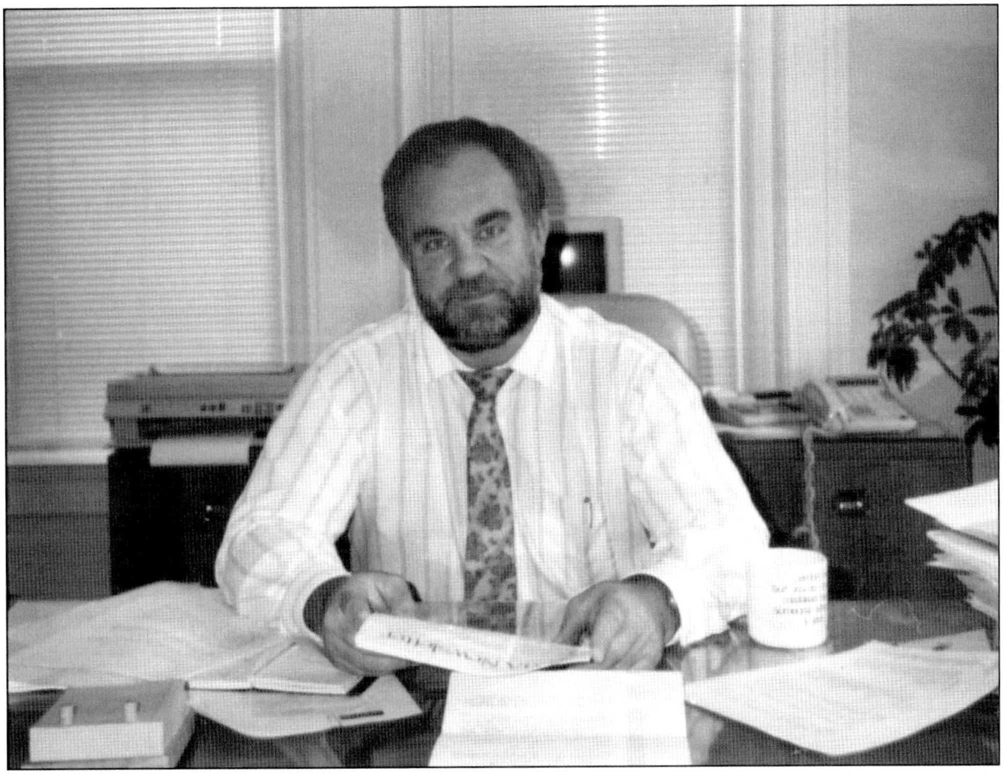

City manager Brock Arner was freshly arrived from Southern California's Orange County when he approached the Sonoma Community Center board about selling the ailing community center building and using the proceeds of the sale to erect a new, modern building across town. The board's reaction was not positive. (Courtesy of David Goodison.)

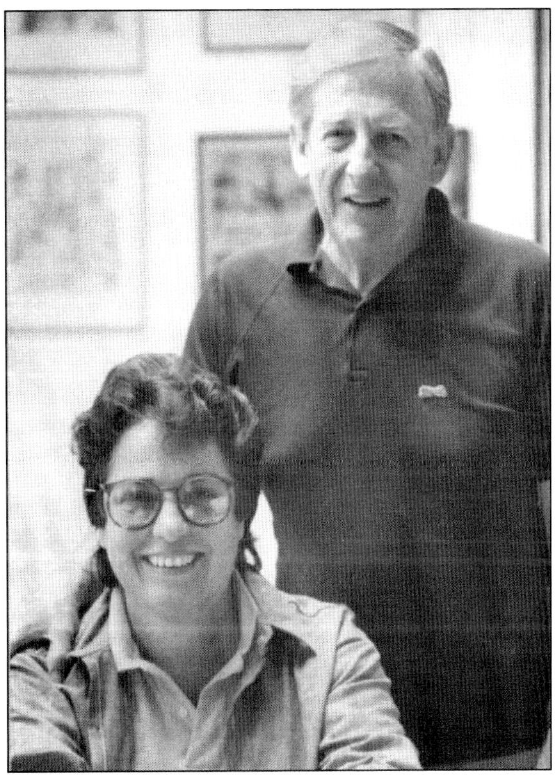

Board president Kathleen Hill led the board of directors to seek National Historic Register status for the building. Galled by the suggestion that SCC held no real value, the board acted quickly to acquire certification and—on November 28, 1980, only six weeks after its application was filed—SCC was granted historic status. Kathleen and her husband, Gerald, are pictured here. (Courtesy of SVHS.)

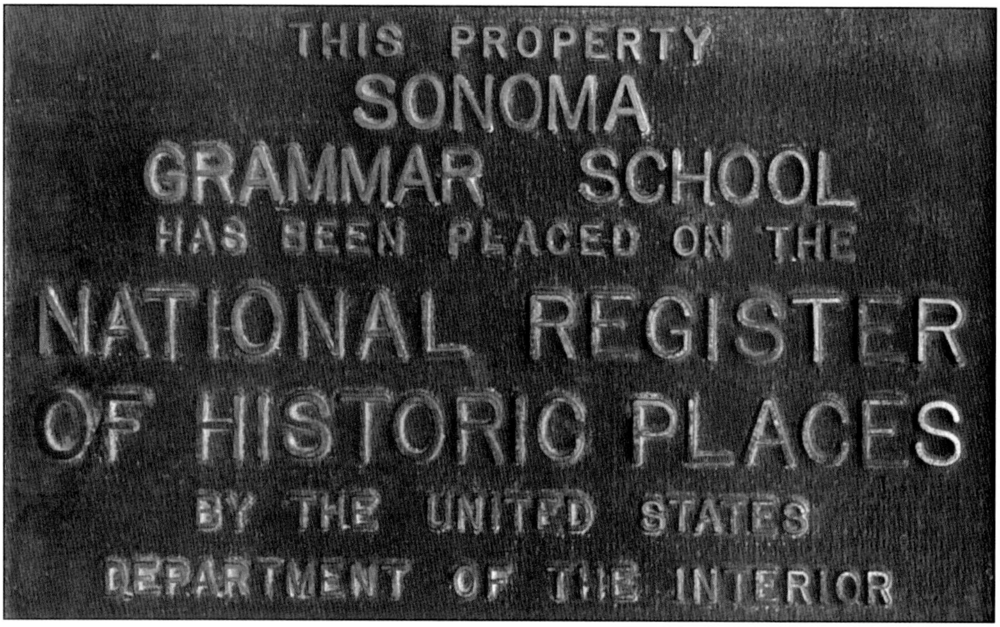

The bronze plaque acknowledging the Sonoma Grammar School's historic status was placed at the main entry of SCC. Sonoma Grammar School graduates were invited to a picnic to celebrate the old school's inclusion on the National Register of Historic Places. The board of directors expected 50 people, but over 200 former students turned out to honor the old building. (Courtesy of SCC.)

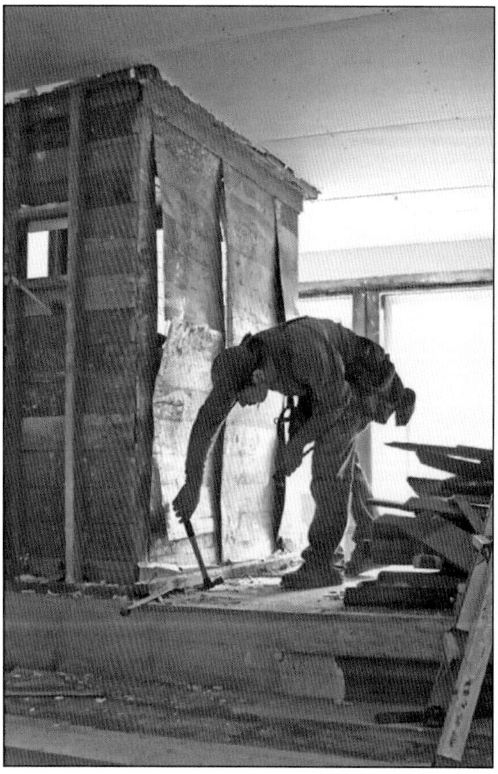

Once the city council understood that the community still revered the old building, it moved forward to help. The city was instrumental in obtaining a number of government grants, and additional funding was received from private foundations and individuals. The ambitious restoration improved structural, fire, life, and seismic safety components of the building. (Courtesy of Owen Orser.)

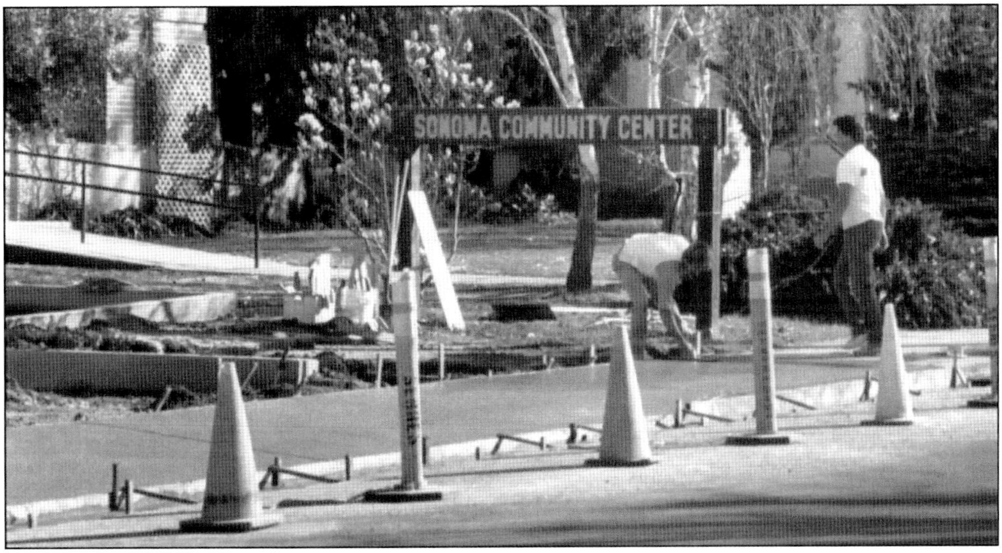

There was much to be done that was not visible to the public eye, but everyone was happy when the ground-floor restrooms were remodeled and the floor and theater were improved in Andrews Hall. Due to the generosity of local contractors, SCC also got its first paved parking lot. Led by John Serres, contractors donated in-kind labor and materials to the cause, including E.K. Excavating, Ron Church, Jim Price, Yaeger & Kirk, Shamrock Materials, and Charles Webster. (Courtesy of SVHS.)

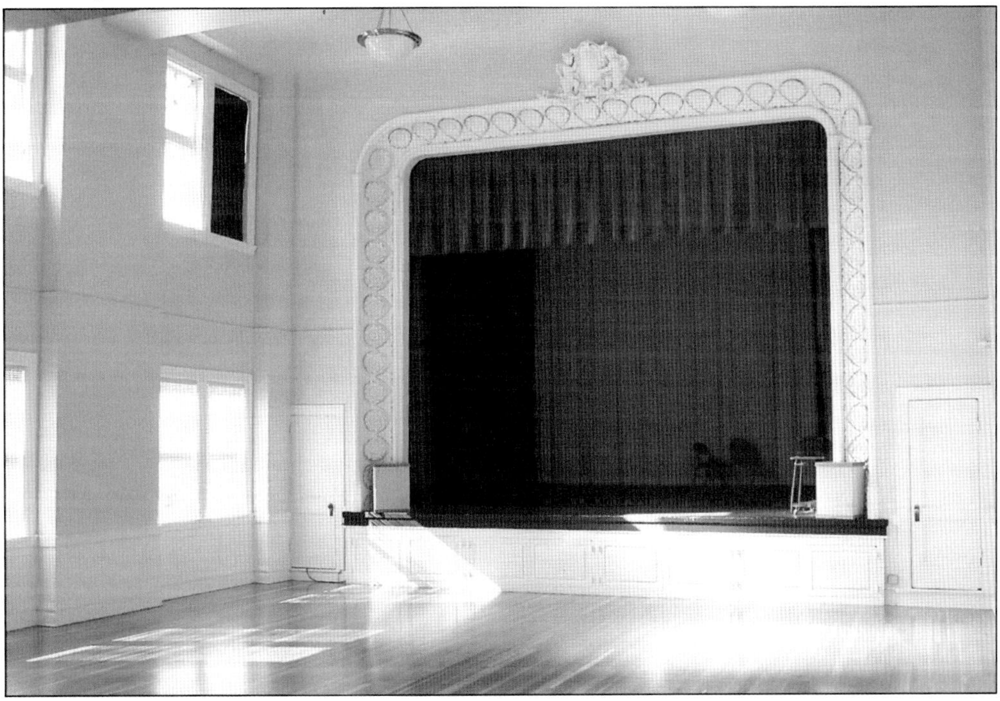

On February 20, 1988—exactly 36 years since Dr. Andrews purchased the building at auction—a gala was held to celebrate the end of the five years of construction and restoration. The hall named in Andrews's honor gleamed like a jewel box, and SCC once again became a center for community life. (Courtesy of SCC.)

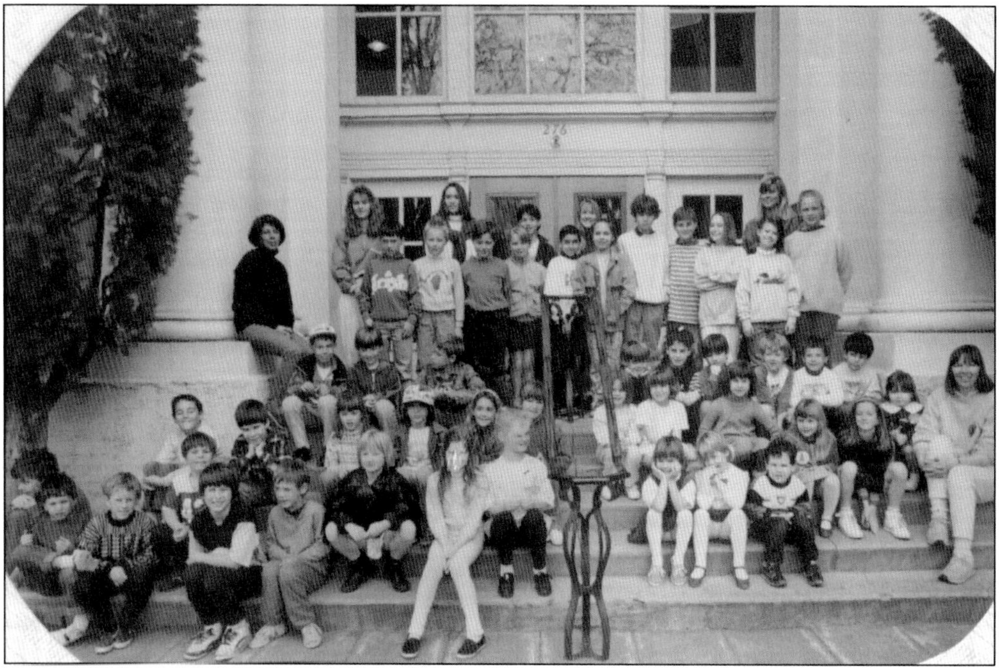

The promise of a safe and upgraded SCC attracted tenants who returned it to its roots. In 1986, a private elementary school, Vintage Country Day School, approached SCC to rent several rooms for a new school. Karin Neihoff, one of the school's original teachers, assumed ownership of the school in 1994 and renamed it Crescent Montessori School. It now includes a middle school curriculum and has thrived at SCC. (Courtesy of Crescent Montessori School.)

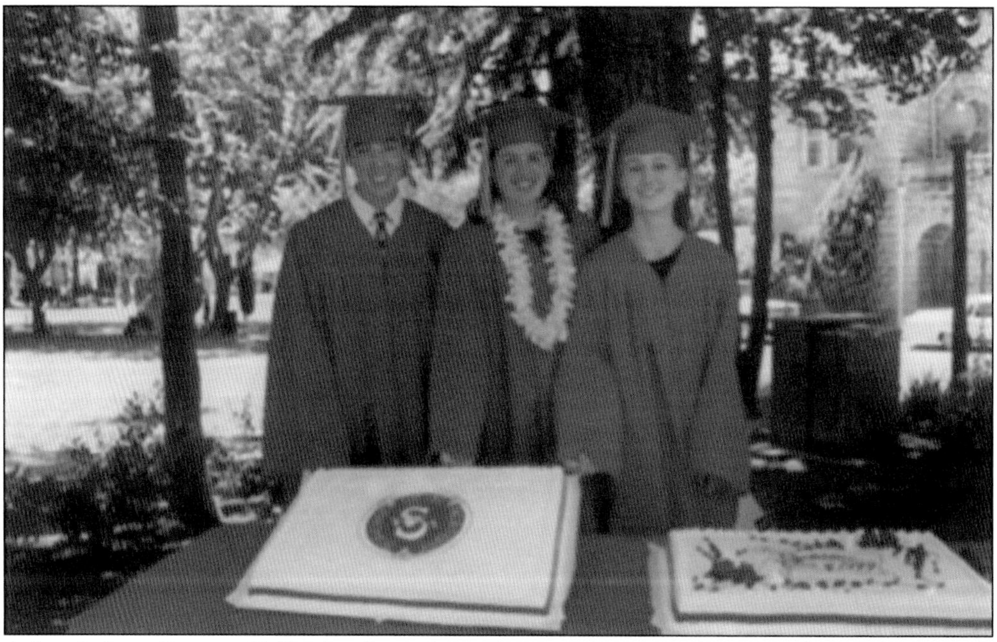

A decade later, Sonoma Valley Academy also took up residence at SCC. It was founded to provide an alternative high school and its mission was "to make education personal." The school will celebrate its 20th anniversary in 2015. (Courtesy of Sonoma Valley Academy.)

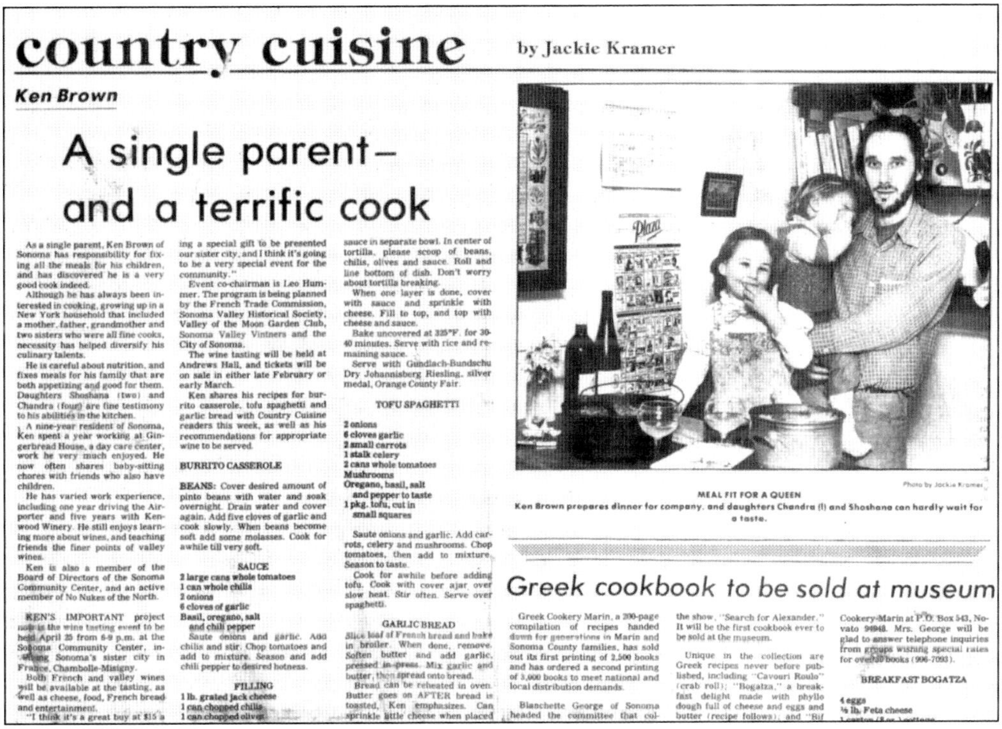

country cuisine

by Jackie Kramer

Ken Brown

A single parent– and a terrific cook

As a single parent, Ken Brown of Sonoma has responsibility for fixing all the meals for his children, and has discovered he is a very good cook indeed.

Although he has always been interested in cooking, growing up in a New York household that included a mother, father, grandmother and two sisters who were all fine cooks, necessity has helped diversify his culinary talents.

He is careful about nutrition, and fixes meals for his family that are both appetizing and good for them. Daughters Shoshana (two) and Chandra (four) are fine testimony to his abilities in the kitchen.

A nine-year resident of Sonoma, Ken spent a year working at Gingerbread House, a day care center, work he very much enjoyed. He now often shares baby-sitting chores with friends who also have children.

He has varied work experience, including one year driving the Airporter and five years with Kenwood Winery. He still enjoys learning more about wines, and teaching friends the finer points of valley wines.

Ken is also a member of the Board of Directors of the Sonoma Community Center, and an active member of No Nukes of the North.

KEN'S IMPORTANT project now is the wine tasting event to be held April 25 from 6-9 p.m. at the Sonoma Community Center, involving Sonoma's sister city in France, Chambolle-Misigny.

Both French and valley wines will be available at the tasting, as well as cheese, food, French bread and entertainment.

"I think it's a great buy at $15 a ing a special gift to be presented our sister city, and I think it's going to be a very special event for the community."

Event co-chairman is Leo Hummer. The program is being planned by the French Trade Commission, Sonoma Valley Historical Society, Valley of the Moon Garden Club, Sonoma Valley Vintners and the City of Sonoma.

The wine tasting will be held at Andrews Hall, and tickets will be on sale in either late February or early March.

Ken shares his recipes for burrito casserole, tofu spaghetti and garlic bread with Country Cuisine readers this week, as well as his recommendations for appropriate wine to be served.

BURRITO CASSEROLE

BEANS: Cover desired amount of pinto beans with water and soak overnight. Drain water and cover again. Add five cloves of garlic and cook slowly. When beans become soft add some molasses. Cook for awhile till very soft.

SAUCE

2 large cans whole tomatoes
1 can whole chilis
2 onions
6 cloves of garlic
Basil, oregano, salt and chili pepper

Saute onions and garlic. Add chilis and stir. Chop tomatoes and add to mixture. Season and add chili pepper to desired hotness.

FILLING

1 lb. grated jack cheese
1 can chopped chilis
1 can chopped olives

sauce in separate bowl. In center of tortilla, please scoop of beans, chilis, olives and sauce. Roll and line bottom of dish. Don't worry about tortilla breaking.

When one layer is done, cover with sauce and sprinkle with cheese. Fill to top, and top with cheese and sauce.

Bake uncovered at 325°F. for 30-40 minutes. Serve with rice and remaining sauce.

Serve with Gundlach-Bundschu Dry Johannisberg Riesling, silver medal, Orange County Fair.

TOFU SPAGHETTI

2 onions
6 cloves garlic
2 small carrots
1 stalk celery
2 cans whole tomatoes
Mushrooms
Oregano, basil, salt and pepper to taste
1 pkg. tofu, cut in small squares

Saute onions and garlic. Add carrots, celery and mushrooms. Chop tomatoes, then add to mixture. Season to taste.

Cook for awhile before adding tofu. Cook with cover ajar over slow heat. Stir often. Serve over spaghetti.

GARLIC BREAD

Slice loaf of French bread and bake in broiler. When done, remove. Soften butter and add garlic, pressed in press. Mix garlic and butter, then spread onto bread.

Bread can be reheated in oven. Butter goes on AFTER bread is toasted, Ken emphasizes. Can sprinkle little cheese when placed

Photo by Jackie Kramer

MEAL FIT FOR A QUEEN

Ken Brown prepares dinner for company, and daughters Chandra (l) and Shoshana can hardly wait for a taste.

Greek cookbook to be sold at museum

Greek Cookery Marin, a 200-page compilation of recipes handed down for generations in Marin and Sonoma County families, has sold out its first printing of 2,500 books and has ordered a second printing of 3,000 books to meet national and local distribution demands.

Blanchette George of Sonoma headed the committee that col- the show, "Search for Alexander." It will be the first cookbook ever to be sold at the museum.

Unique in the collection are Greek recipes never before published, including "Cavouri Roulo" (crab roll); "Bogatza," a breakfast delight made with phyllo dough full of cheese and eggs and butter (recipe follows); and "Bif

Cookery-Marin at P.O. Box 543, Novato 94948. Mrs. George will be glad to answer telephone inquiries from groups wishing special rates for over 30 books (906-7093).

BREAKFAST BOGATZA

4 eggs
½ lb. Feta cheese

The newly remodeled Andrews Hall attracted weddings, presentations, dances, and hundreds of other community uses, and the need for a responsible live-in caretaker became increasingly important. Ken Brown, who had both volunteered for SCC events and been president of its board, moved into the caretaker's quarters with his two young daughters. The *Sonoma Index-Tribune* wrote the above story about his parenting and expanded role at SCC. (Courtesy of SVHS.)

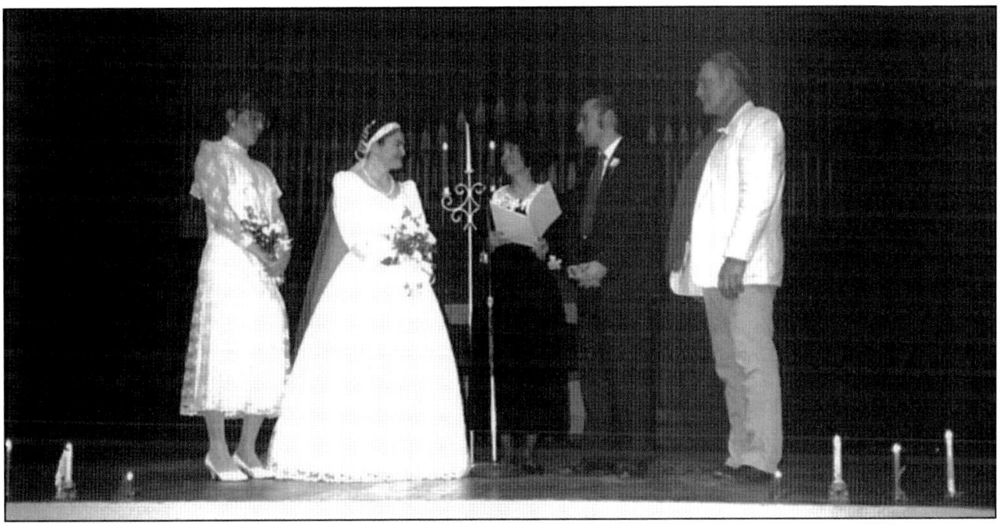

Ken Brown's long association with SCC helped hold it together during this time of change. He recalls enthusiastically nodding his head when Jerry Casson first told him to volunteer in the late 1970s. He served as a member of the board, a caretaker, an event worker, and the center's general manager. He married Jewel Matthiessen on the Andrews Hall stage and brought their first child, Moses, home to SCC. (Courtesy of Ken Brown.)

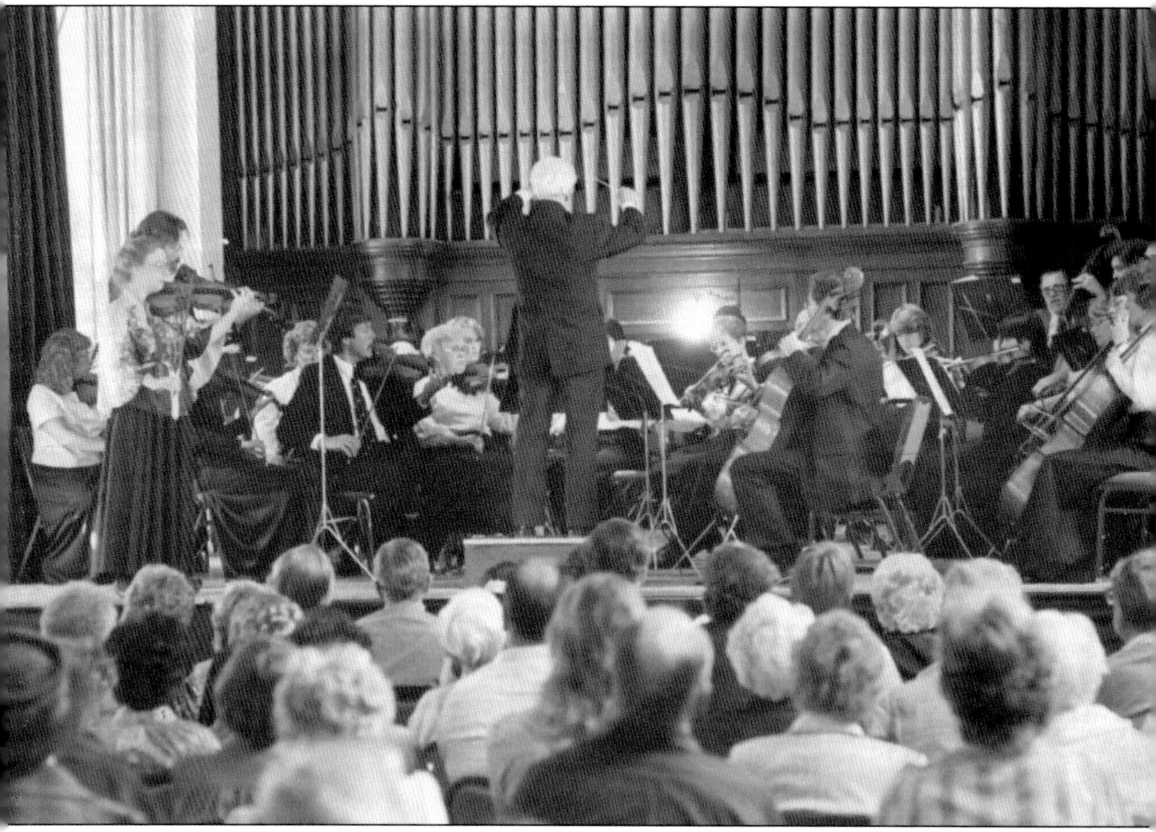

The board of directors and staff stepped up their programming to reestablish ongoing music and arts education classes. Baroque Sinfonia partnered with SCC to offer a popular series of classical music performances for Sonoma. Note the pictured pipes, which were part of the Kimball organ. (Courtesy of SVHS.)

SCC began to partner with other valley nonprofits to broaden its scope of events. Andrews Hall became the site for a lecture series entitled "Conversations on Food and Wine," which was presented in partnership with the Sonoma Valley Vintners Association. The inaugural speaker was M.F.K. Fisher. As reported on the front page of the *Sonoma Index-Tribune*, the "sometimes rambling but always entertaining" conversation captivated its sold-out audience. (Courtesy of SVHS.)

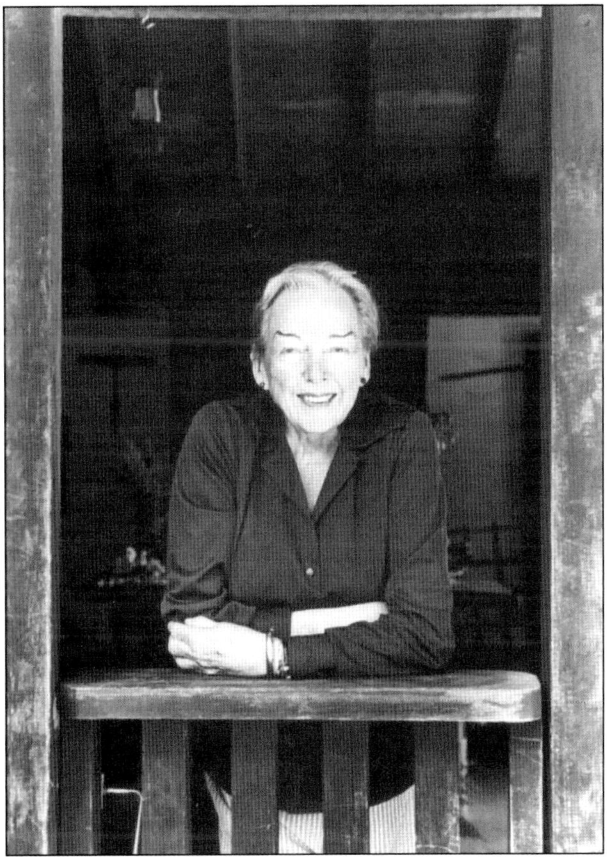

By the late 1990s, SCC's board of directors and staff were on a mission to create focused, art-centered programming. Music, theater, writing, pottery, and fine art departments had been developed and were overseen by talented directors of each discipline. Board president Charlotte Lamb is widely credited with developing this successfully implemented program structure. (Courtesy of SCC.)

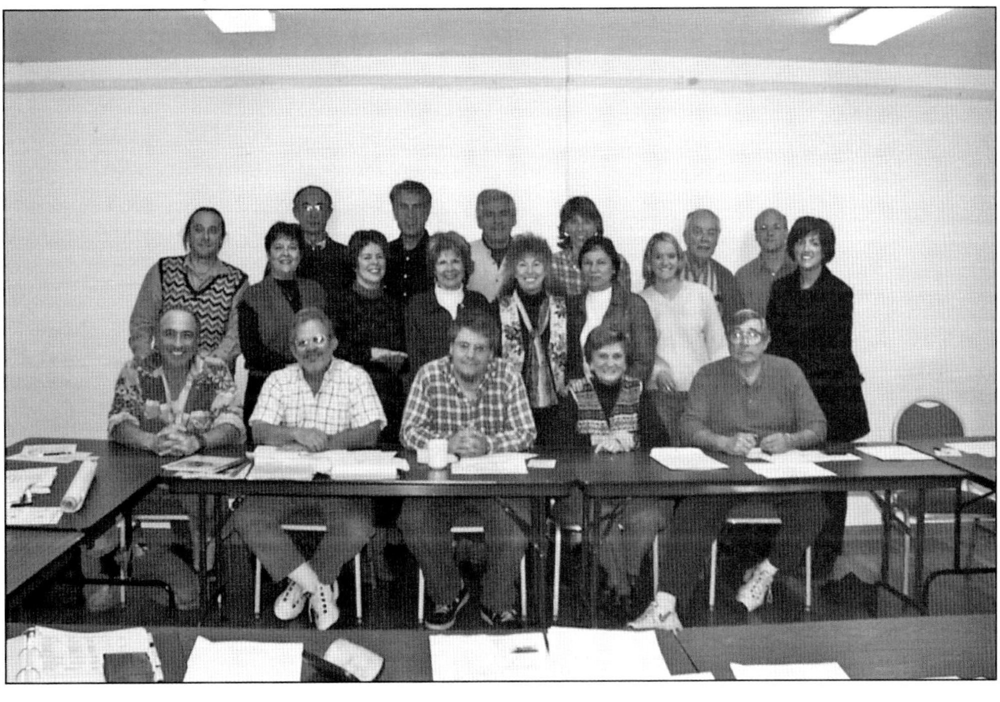

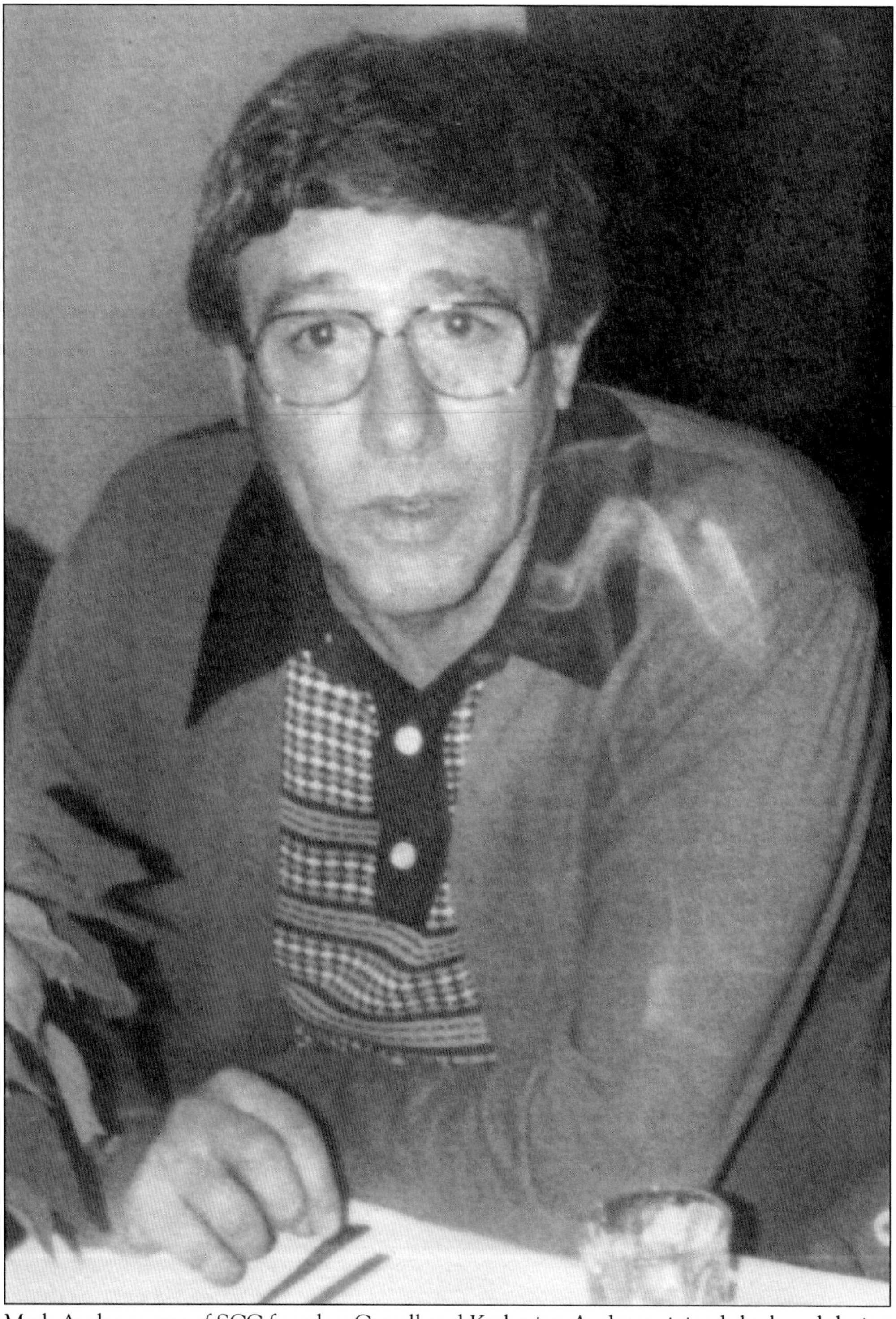

Mark Andrews, son of SCC founders Carroll and Katherine Andrews, joined the board during this period of organizational growth. He served as board president and announced the Fourth of July parade for a number of years. (Courtesy of Mark Andrews.)

The talented and larger-than-life potter Tom Collins (left) was hired as the director of the ceramics department. He worked with the board to create a pottery studio and to install a number of kilns. Here, he and board member Jim Lamb (right) prepare the floor. The program continues to thrive to this day. (Courtesy of SCC.)

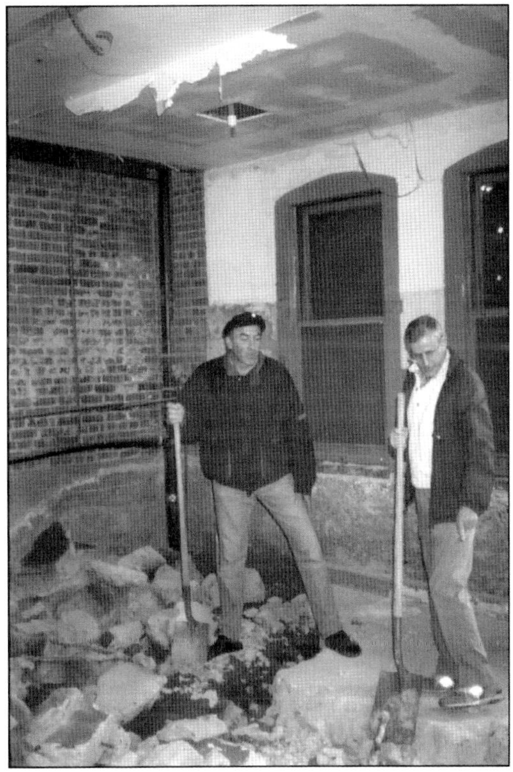

Fine arts and sculpture thrived under the leadership of Lia Transue (left) and later under Alex Parman Cole (right). Lia and the board created a sculpture park on the front lawn of SCC for a series of installations. She and Alex are seen here welcoming a work by well-known sculptor Linda Flemming. (Courtesy of Lia Transue.)

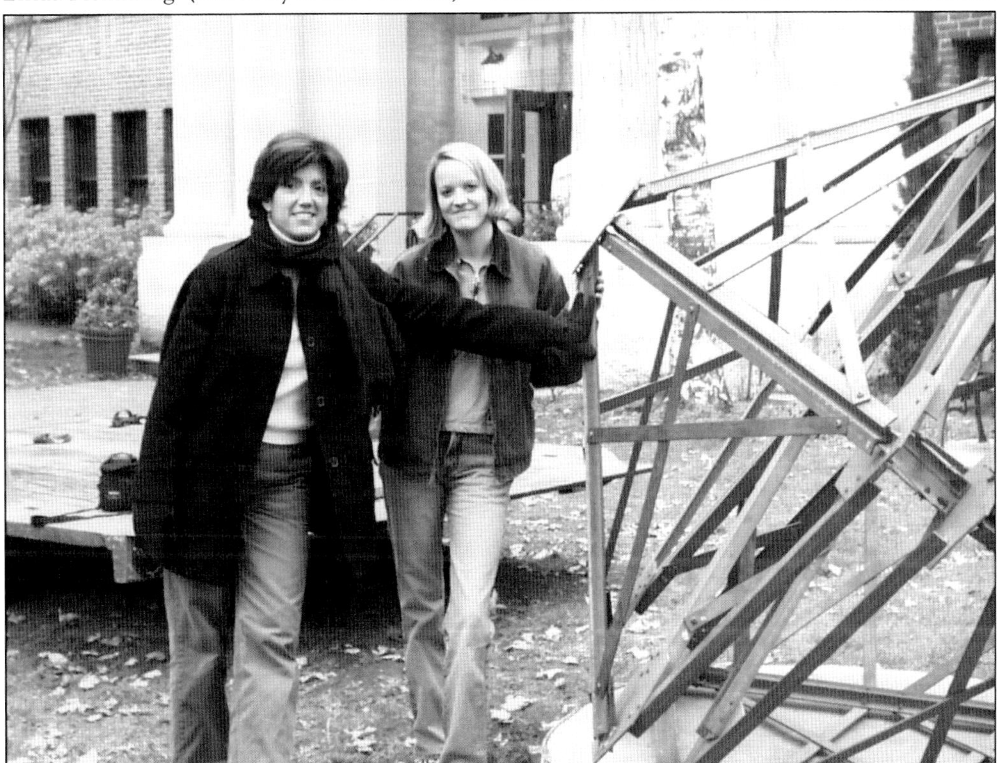

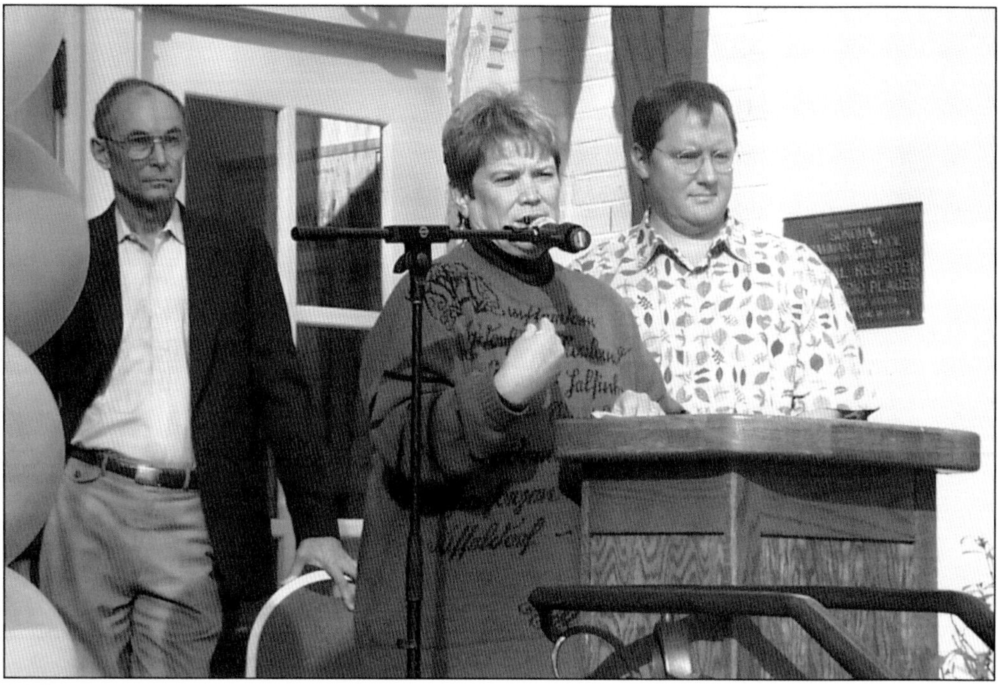

SCC was creating exciting new programs, and the board wanted to make sure the community knew it. When the sculpture garden was complete, Mayor Phyllis Carter (center) dedicated the garden, with Pixar producer John Lasseter (right) acting as master of ceremonies. Board member Peter Hohorst is visible at left. (Courtesy of Lia Transue.)

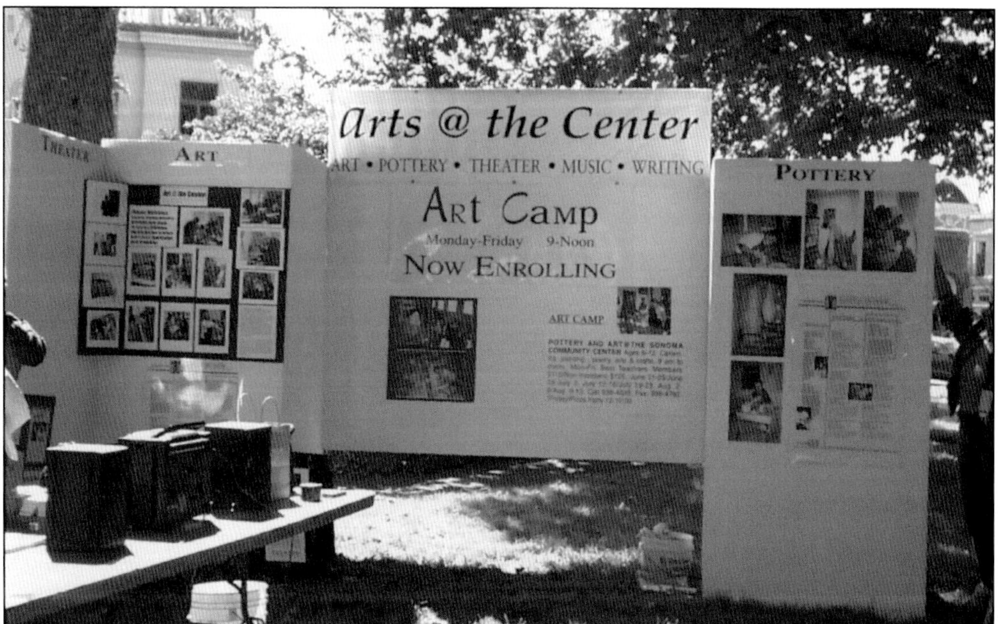

The Ox Roast and the Fourth of July, held annually in the Sonoma Plaza, continued to be beloved by the community. They were natural venues to promote classes and activities for all of the SCC departments. (Courtesy of Lia Transue.)

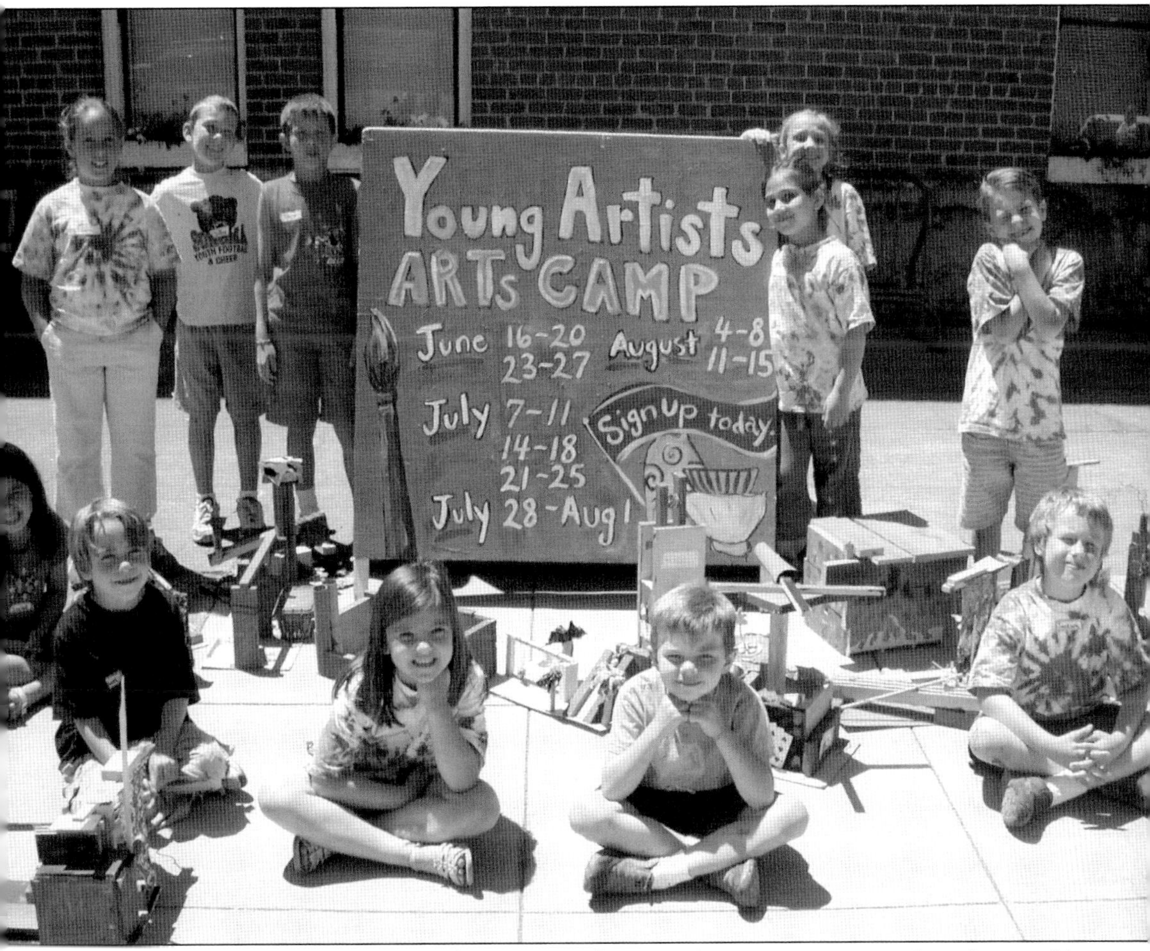

Another successful innovation was the creation of a series of summer art camps. A student could sign up for a week or spend the entire summer learning pottery and the fine arts while having a wonderful time. The camps quickly sold out. (Courtesy of SCC.)

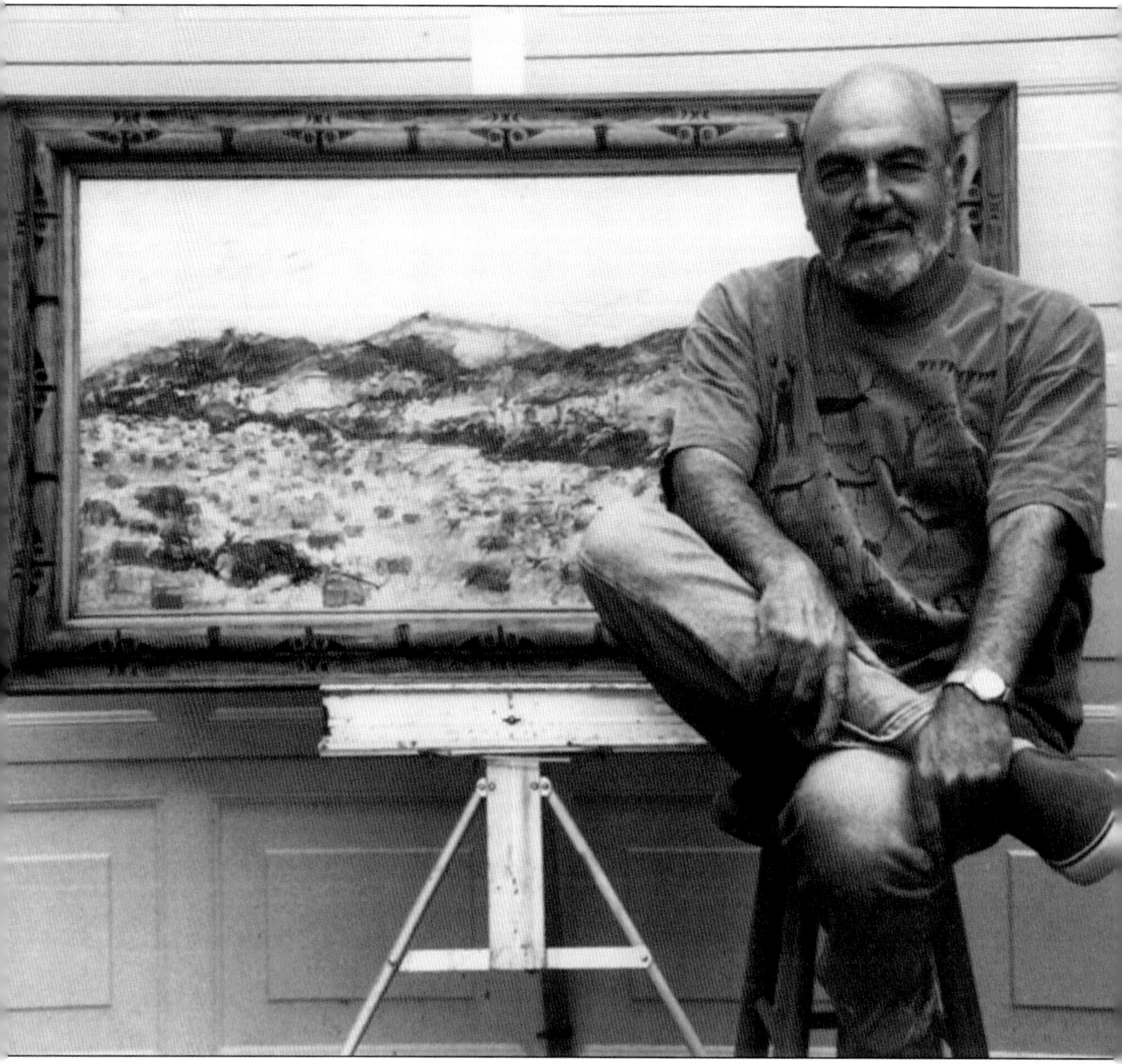

The community flocked to the Guest Artist Series, which featured such well-known artists as Dennis Ziemienski, Chester Arnold, and Neil Watson. In addition to the formal lecture, a two-day workshop with each artist was offered. The painter Karl Rawicz (pictured) was a well-received speaker. (Courtesy of Lia Transue.)

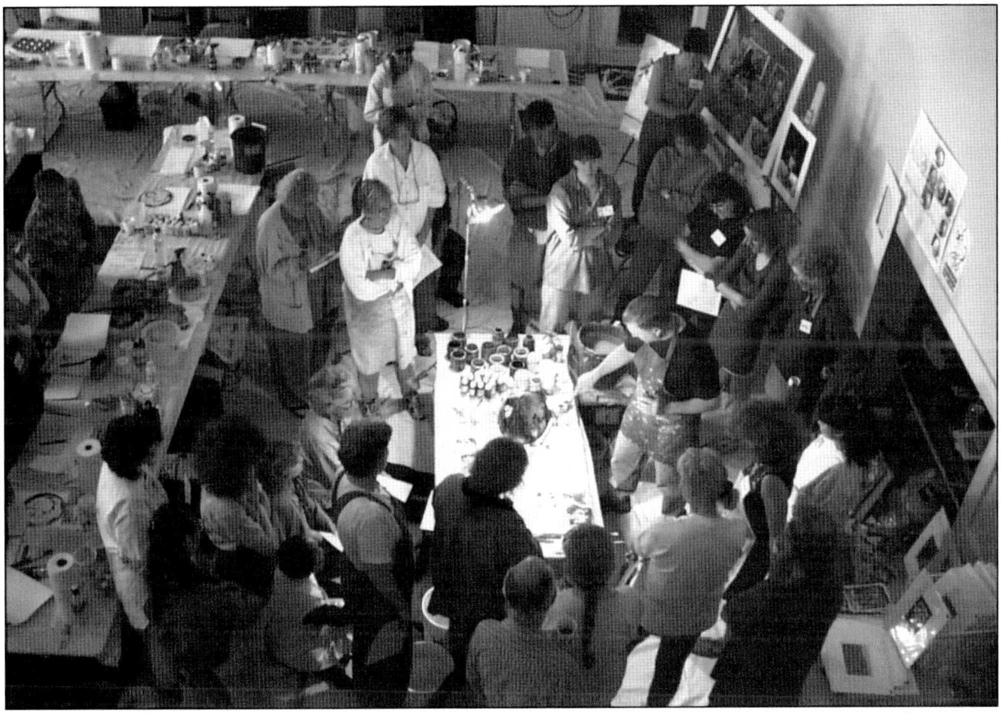

Artist Bob Burridge was a perennial favorite at SCC, and his workshops always sold out. He encouraged his students to be unafraid of the creative process, and his workshops became so large that they had to be held in Andrews Hall. (Courtesy of SCC.)

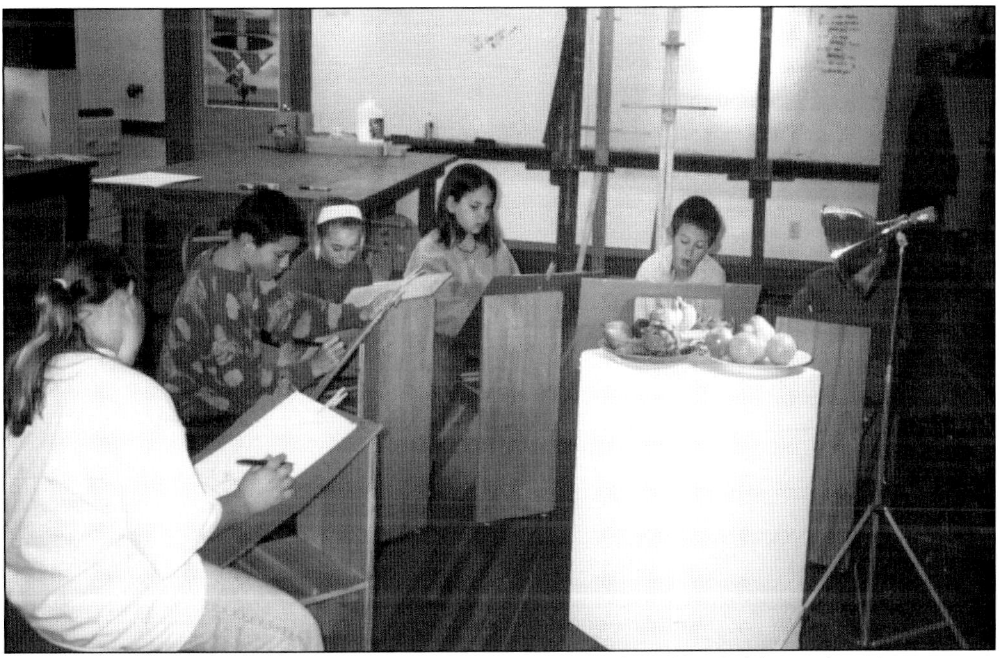

The Fine Arts Department developed a special curriculum for children after the summer camps proved so popular. Classes in painting, drawing, and pottery were available. (Courtesy of Lia Transue.)

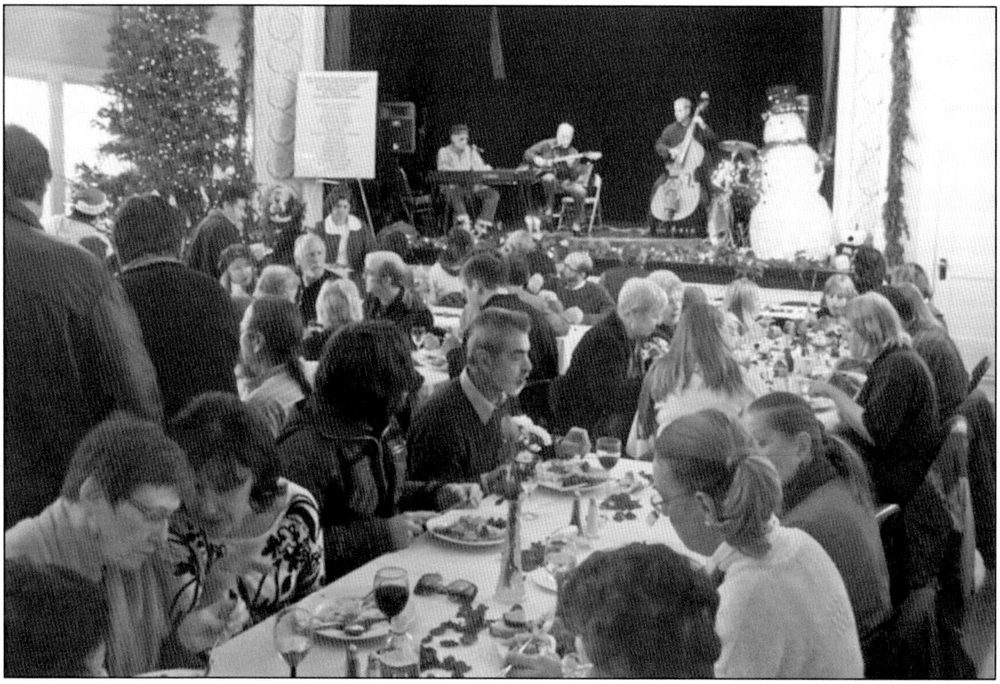

SCC's traditional events, such as the holiday dinners, grew during this period, and the annual communal meals soon exceeded capacity. Somehow, the volunteer chefs always managed to find a way to feed the overflowing crowd. (Courtesy of SCC.)

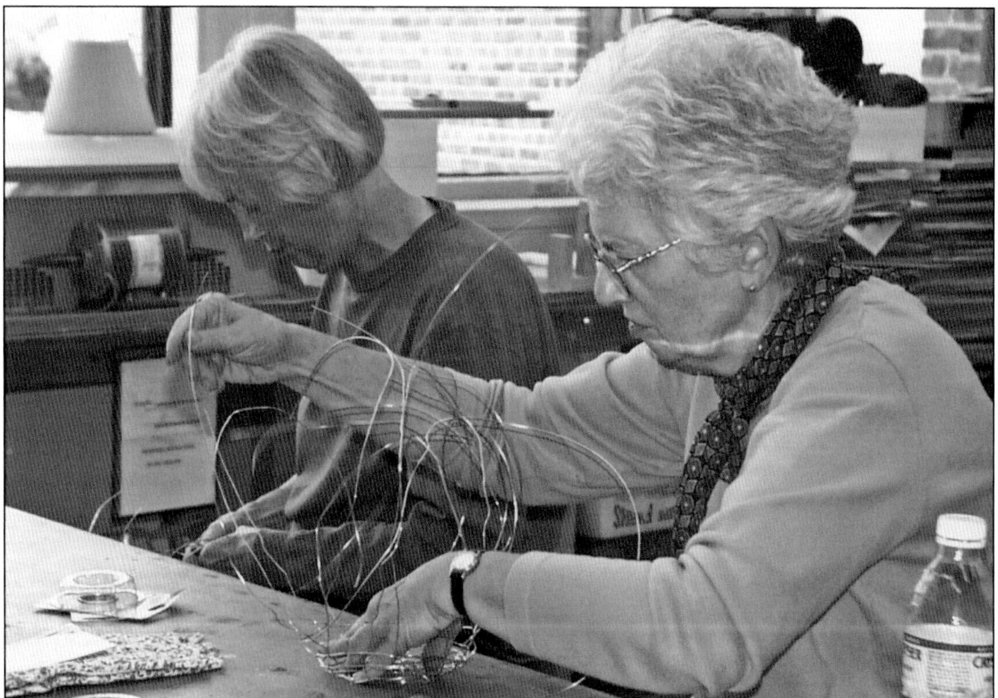

In addition to fine arts instruction, the staff scheduled a number of interesting and sometimes quirky classes that caught the imagination of many students. (Courtesy of Alex Cole.)

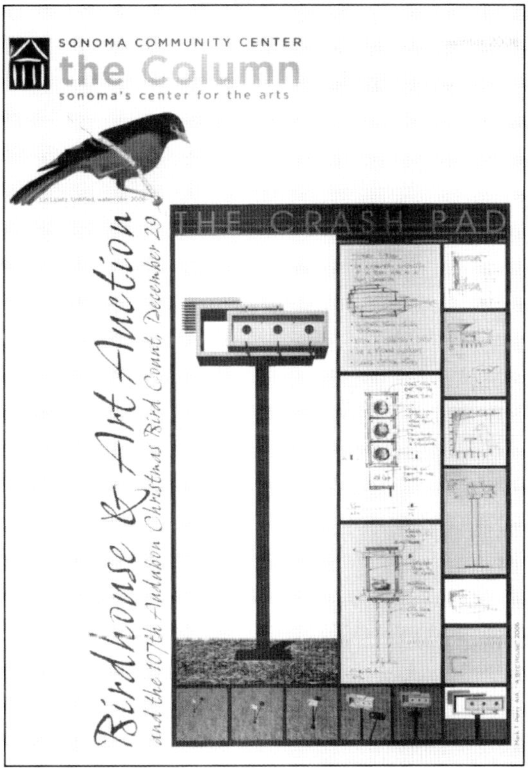

As SCC's education and entertainment offerings grew, the monthly newsletter evolved into a publication called the *Column*. With its magazine format and schedule of classes and events, the periodical became so popular that it remained in this format until becoming a digital publication. (Courtesy of Alex Cole.)

SCC's first annual art auction was a gala affair, with board members in formal dress and an enthusiastic audience competing against each other for paintings and sculpture. Staff members Lia Transue and Tom Collins worked with board members and volunteer staff to create a lovely and lucrative evening. The board was becoming more sophisticated in its event fundraising, and the community noticed. (Courtesy of Lia Transue.)

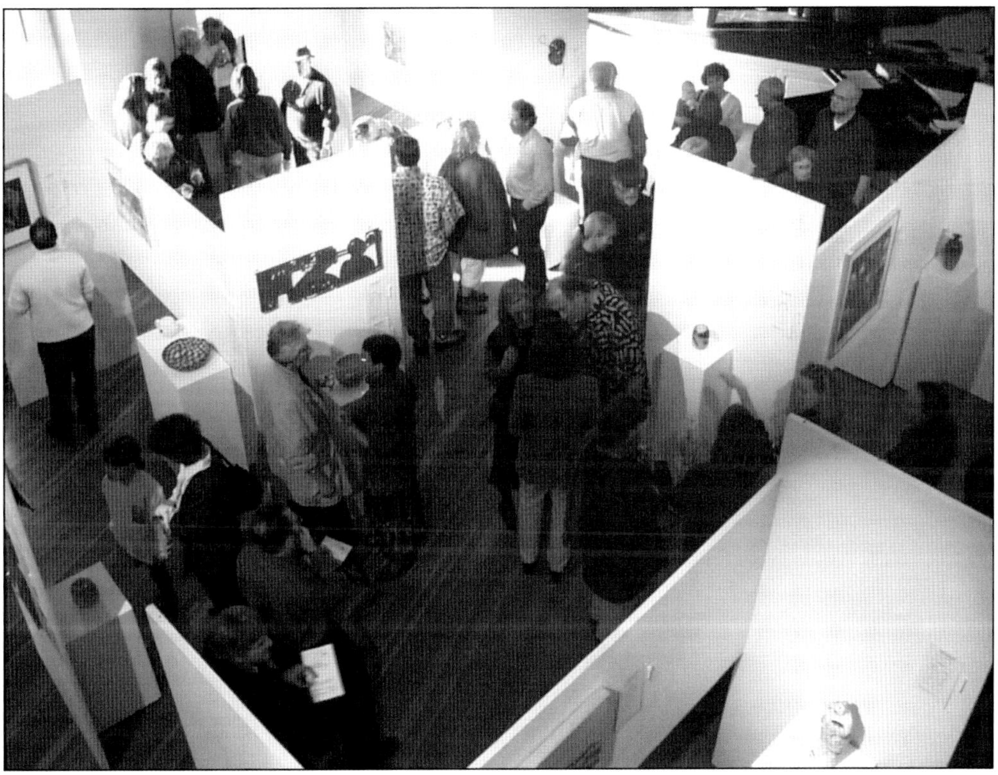

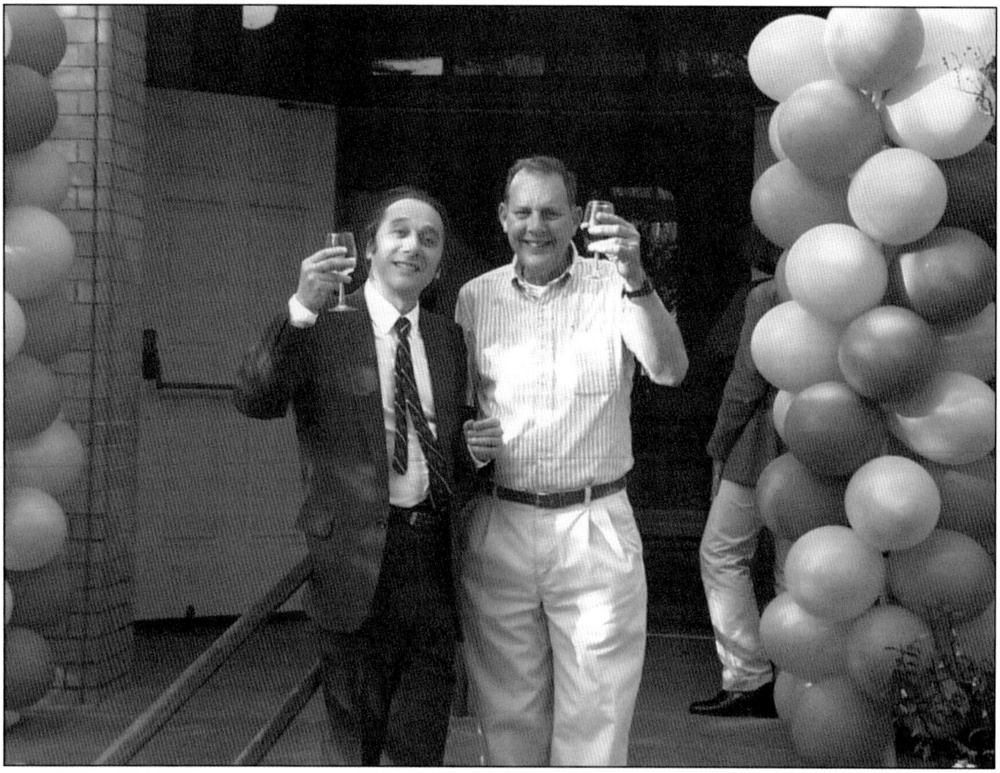

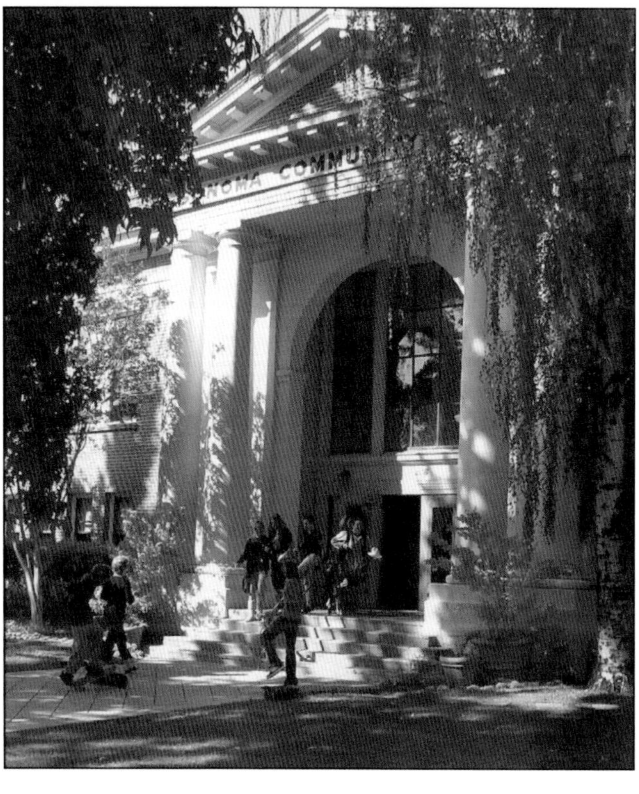

Many people, like Ken Brown (left) and Howie Ehret (right), dedicated their efforts to grassroots fundraisers, but major funding was needed to substantially remodel the building. SCC needed HVAC systems, a new kitchen, plumbing and electric systems, and a new roof. The seismic safety upgrades had to be finished as well. No matter how much art was sold at auction, it was not going to pay the construction bills. (Courtesy of Lia Transue.)

The building was bursting with activity, and the graceful exterior was beautiful. But the board needed to fund construction if SCC was to have a future. (Courtesy of SCC.)

Seven
Living History

During SCC's decades-long history as an independent community center, the core challenge extended to every set of board members was this: How do we keep pace with the cost of caring for an aging building while honoring our mission to provide low-cost programs?

By 2004, with another bout of deferred maintenance projects looming, the board settled in to plan long-range solutions that addressed its capital improvement program and generated new earned income. The board commissioned an assessment from an architect and structural engineer on the building's physical fitness and, in 2009, began a lengthy discussion with city council about potential funding to comprehensively renovate and restore the historic building.

In the meantime, Sonoma Community Center programming had entered into a true renaissance—expanding into new ventures and generating new income. By partnering with a number of organizations interested in ecological sustainability, an invigorated board of directors led the community in better water management by removing the center's lawn and installing a water-wise garden. This space was designed and overseen by Sonoma County Master Gardeners and maintained by Garden Club volunteers.

The board also cemented important funding and service relationships with local community groups such as Rotary of Sonoma Valley, who funded the center's remodeled kitchen. It generated new income by developing a partnership with the Sonoma Theater Alliance, which presented a full season of theater in Andrews Hall.

A talented and passionate staff initiated artist residency programs with the valley's middle schools, increased arts education classes, and began public art installations throughout the city and Sonoma Valley. Audiences flocked to the center's new programs, including the Trashion Fashion Show, a new dedicated gallery space, the artist in resident program, and new performances in Andrews Hall.

In 2012, after three years of discussion, the city council—led by councilman Steve Barbose and city manager Linda Kelly—agreed to fund the most ambitious capital improvement project in the center's history.

As the construction dust settled on the $2.5-million restoration in 2013, the board and staff look forward and began to prepare future generations to act as good stewards of SCC's mission. And the old building, newly strengthened and emboldened, goes on, as do the memories and dreams of this community's living history.

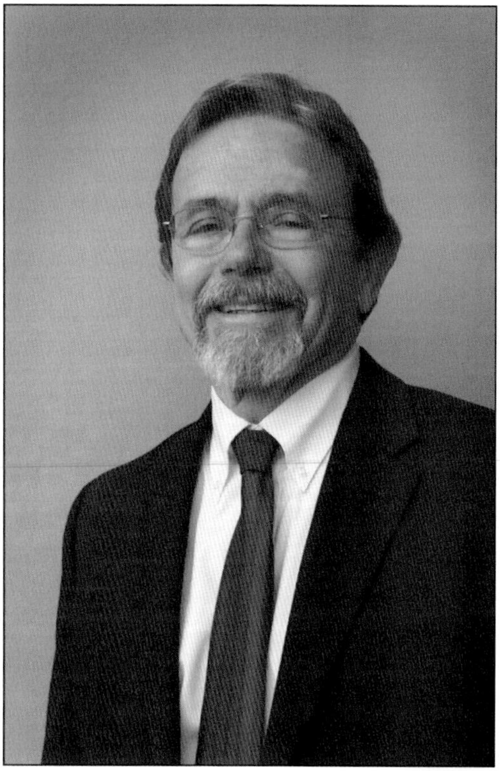

In 2004, the board of directors commissioned a comprehensive report on the structural needs of SCC. Faced with a daunting price tag of over $3 million, the board began a series of conversations with city councilman Steve Barbose (pictured) and city manager Linda Kelly in 2009 looking to find a way to restore the building and keep it serving for the next 100 years. (Courtesy of David Goodison.)

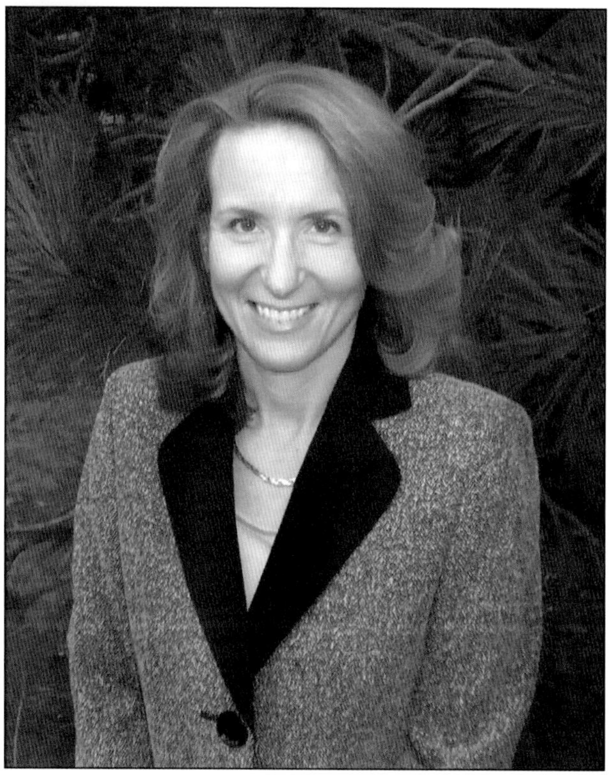

In the meantime, the staff and board began developing a series of strategic alliances that dealt with new community challenges and developed a higher profile for its programs. At the suggestion of Linda Kelly (pictured), SCC removed its grass lawn and replaced it with what was dubbed "The Water-Wise Garden." (Courtesy of David Goodison.)

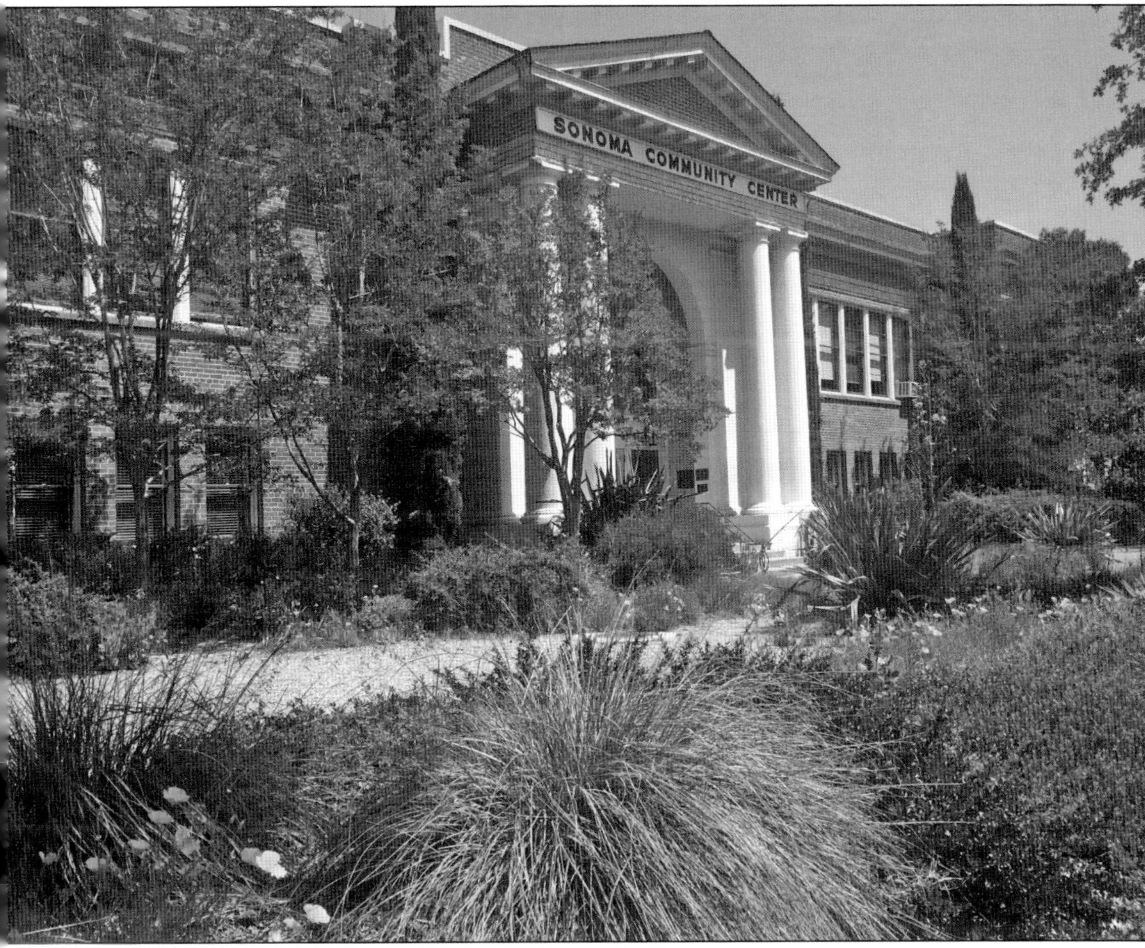

SCC partnered with Sonoma County Master Gardeners, who designed SCC's building exterior to demonstrate various ways gardens could be beautiful and use little water. After the board approved the design that maintained the existing sculpture garden, the Valley of the Moon Garden Club and many other volunteers helped install and maintain it. It was named in honor and memory of SCC board member Susan Maloney and her family, who died in a tragic automobile accident. (Courtesy of David Goodison.)

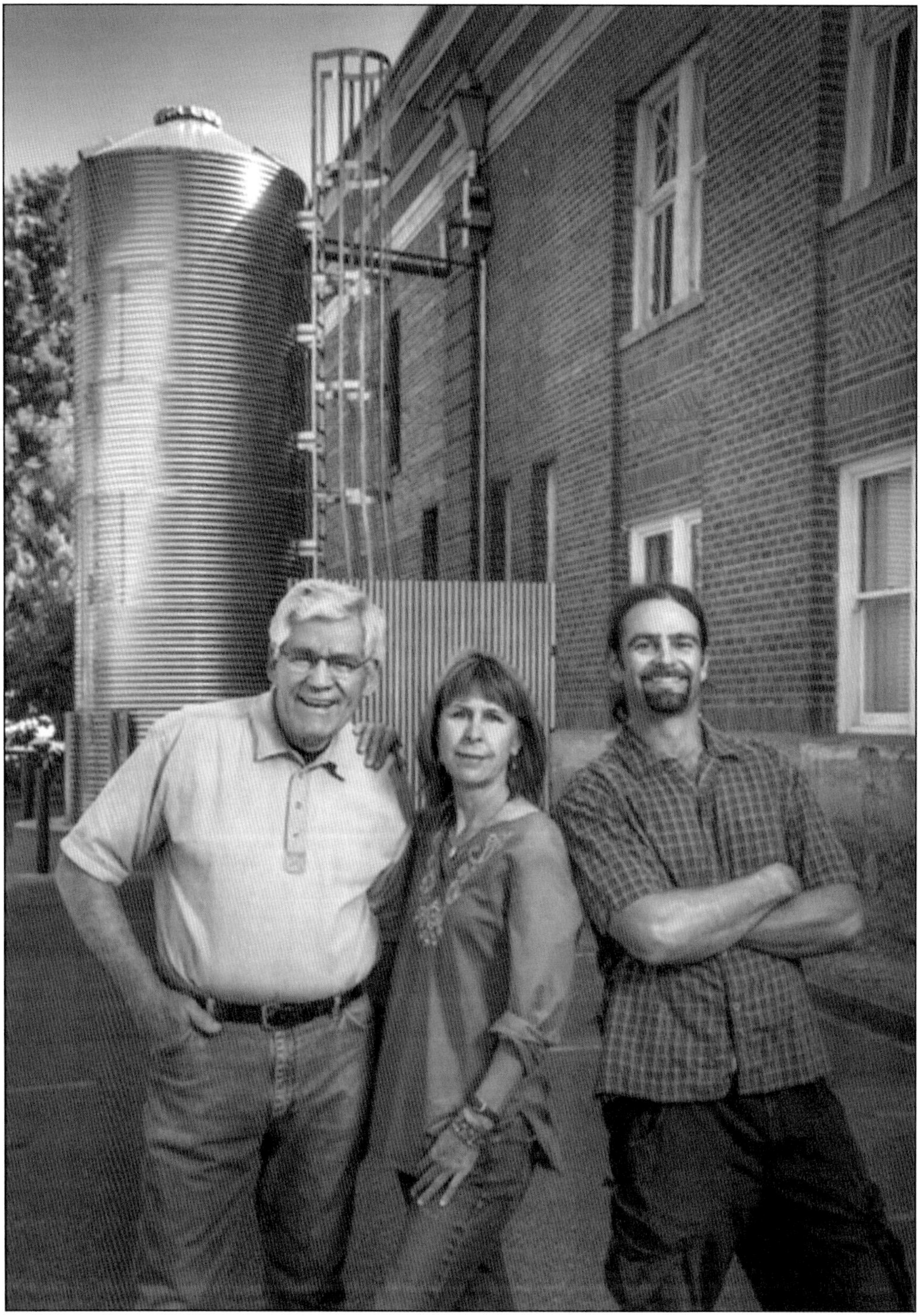

Thanks to the determination of local community activist Melinda Kelley and funding from the City of Sonoma, the North Bay Watershed Association, and the County of Sonoma, SCC was able to install a rain-harvesting tank that would be used to irrigate the property. (Courtesy of SCC.)

Gary Edwards served as a head chef at SCC's holiday dinners for many years, and he knew how limited the old kitchen was. As a leading member of the Sonoma Valley Rotary, he convinced his club to help replace the kitchen. The group's $50,000 "splash" grant made it happen. Gary is pictured at left, with SCC operations manager Marty Brinley (center) and city councilman Ken Brown (right), at a recent Ox Roast. (Courtesy of SCC.)

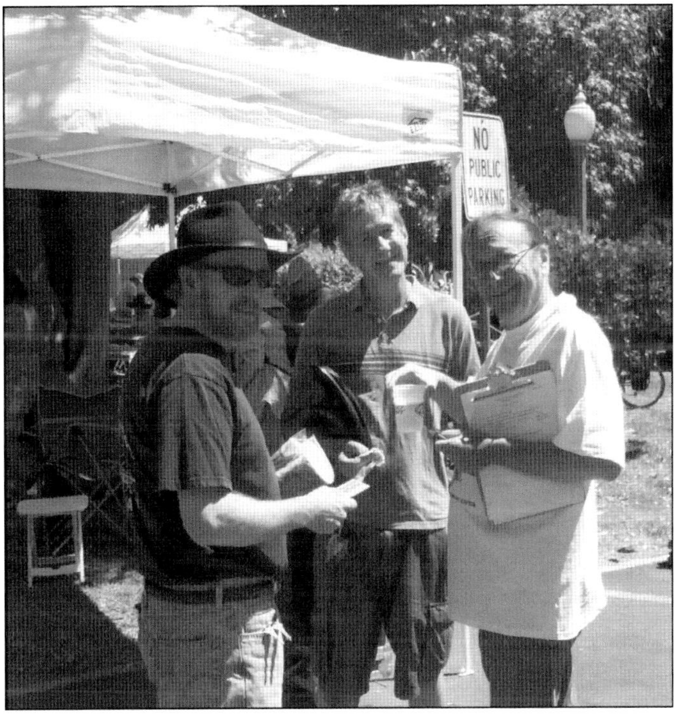

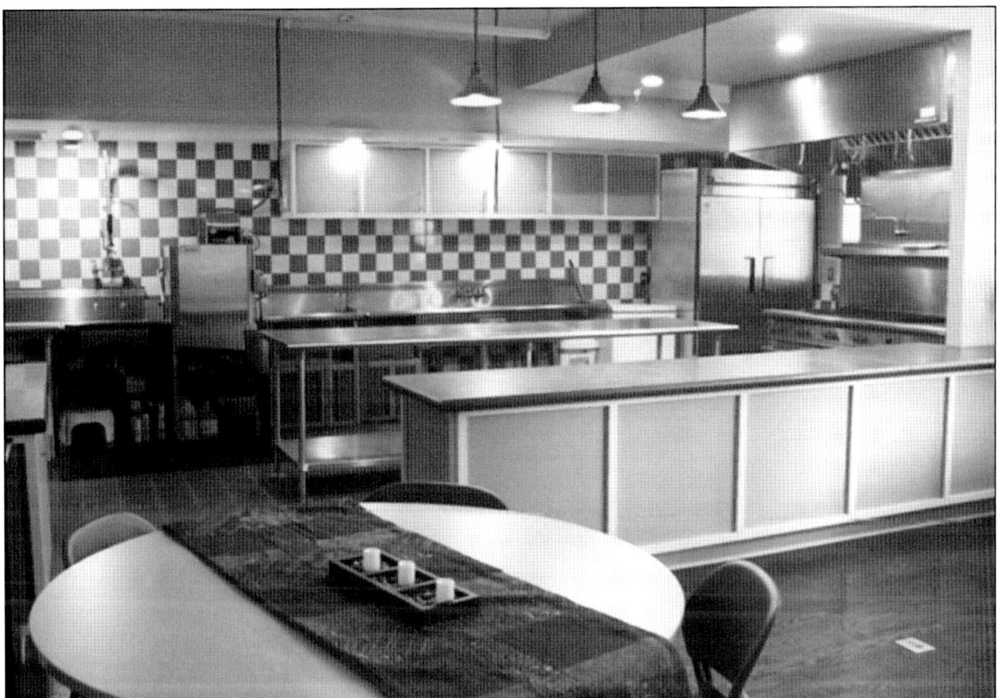

The beautiful new kitchen is named the Rotary Community Kitchen in honor of the club that was instrumental in realizing SCC's goal. Architect Mark Perry, who had worked on other SCC remodels, designed a space that also serves as a concession area for Andrews Hall events. (Courtesy of SCC.)

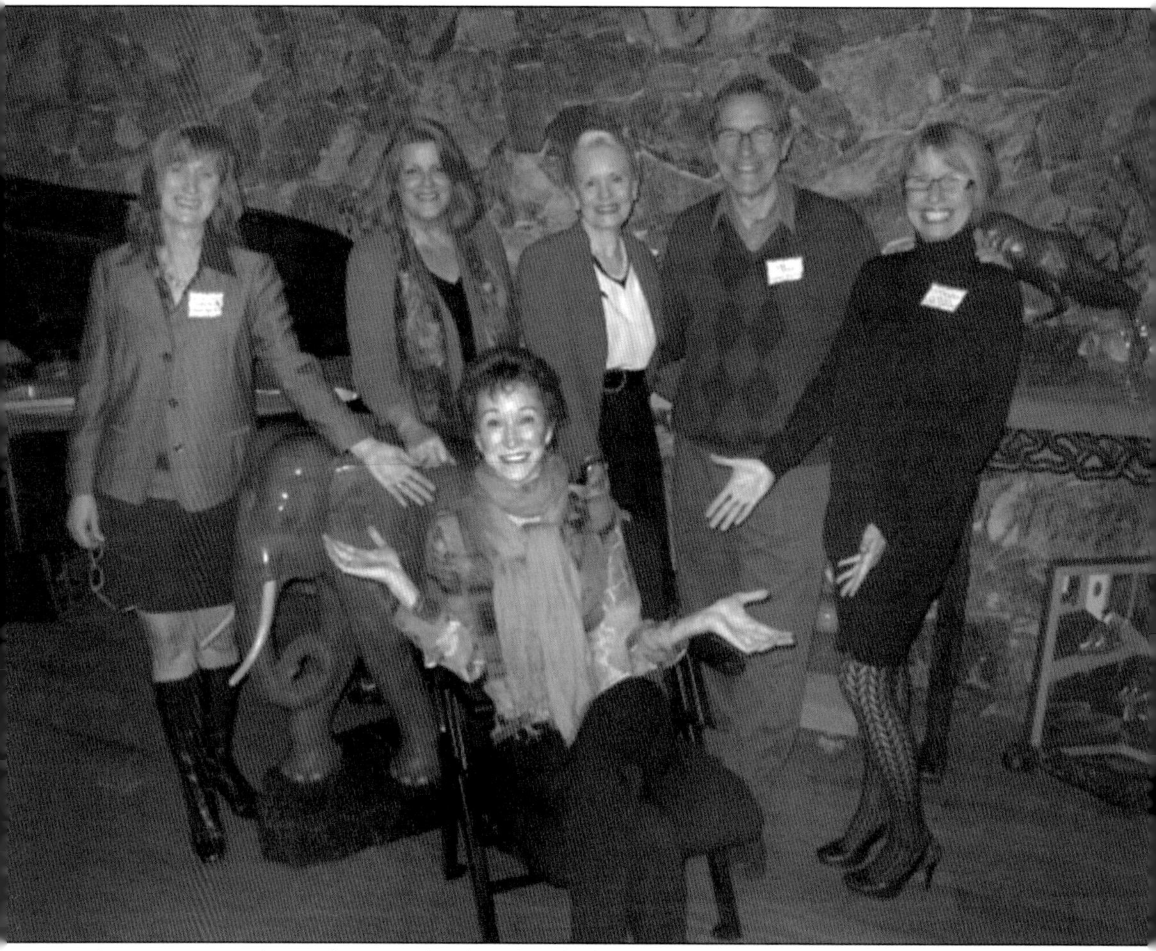

An important relationship was developed with the Sonoma Theater Alliance, a consortium of community theater groups that was looking for a dedicated space to create a true theater season. The partnership developed during a three-month summer theater festival, and the current season runs from April to November. Here, the founding members promote their "buy a seat" fundraising campaign, which provided Andrews Hall with comfortable, semi-permanent seating for the first time. (Courtesy of Sonoma Theater Alliance.)

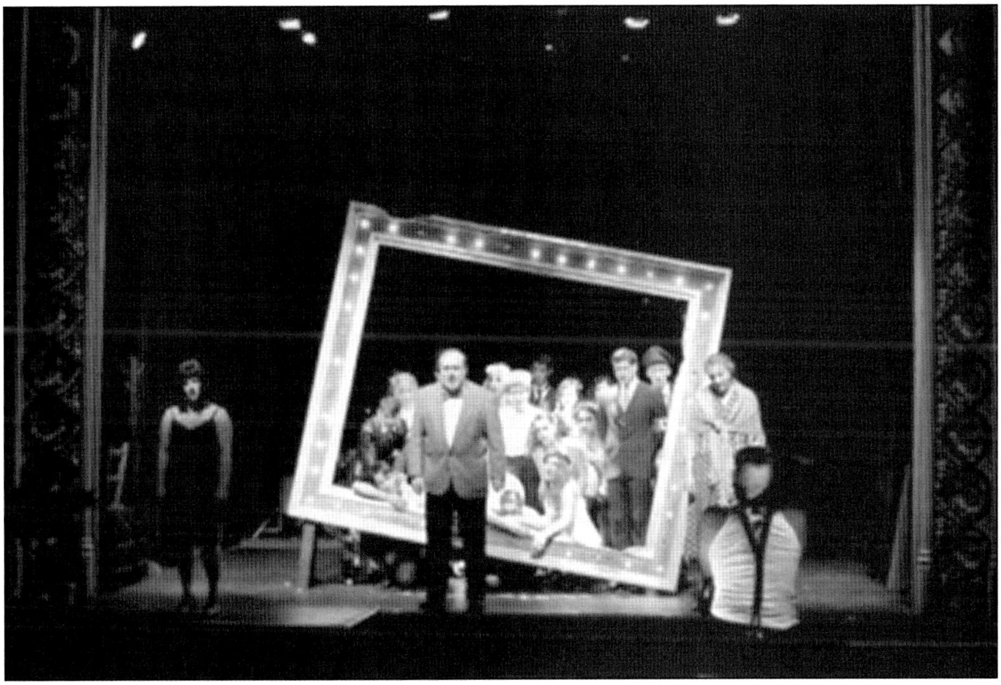

As the Sonoma Theater Alliance grows, a wider spectrum of theatrical experiences is offered each year. Cat Austin's ETC production of *Cabaret* was widely acclaimed for its excellent production values and acting. (Courtesy of SIT.)

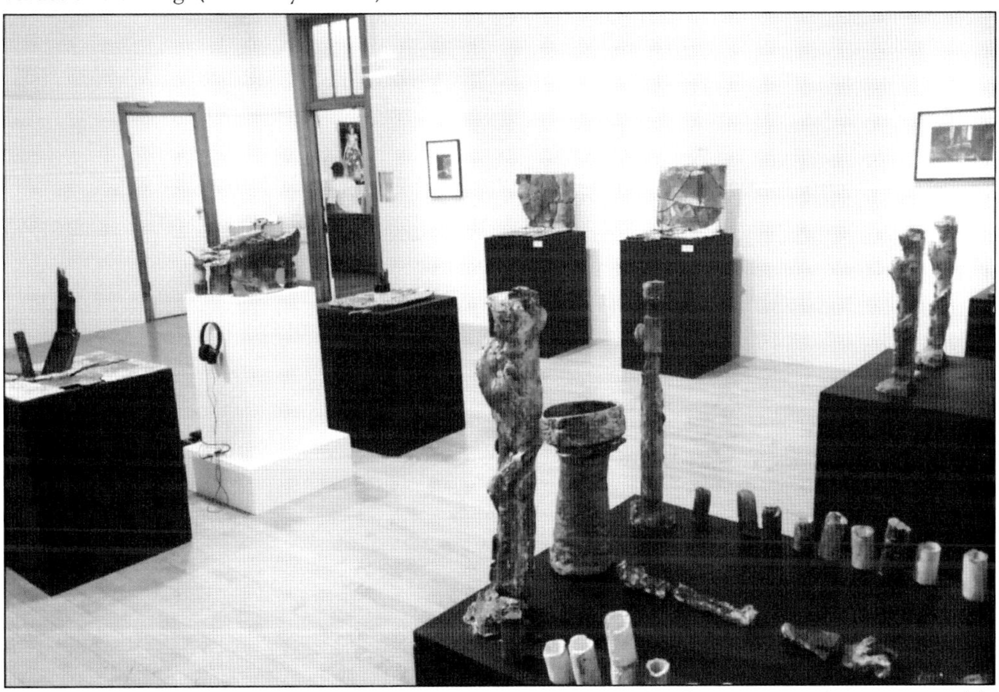

In 2007, SCC converted one of its classrooms into a dedicated gallery space. It features monthly exhibits by resident artists, as well as many local and regional artists. The photograph above shows the gallery's exit exhibit of resident artist Miles Votek. (Courtesy of SCC.)

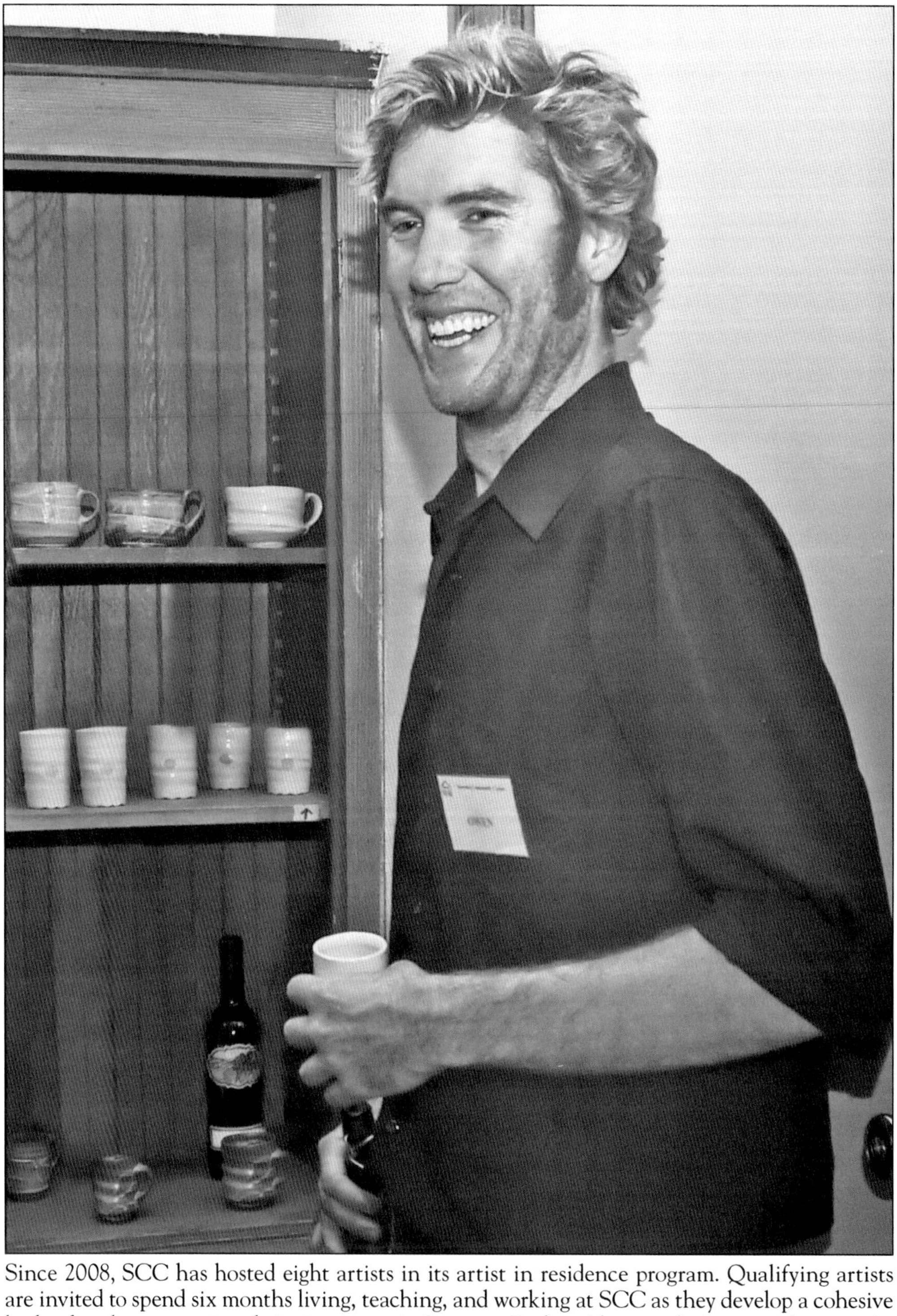

Since 2008, SCC has hosted eight artists in its artist in residence program. Qualifying artists are invited to spend six months living, teaching, and working at SCC as they develop a cohesive body of work representing their time spent in Sonoma. Each residence culminates with a month-long exhibit in SCC's Gallery 212. Pictured above is Owen Nelson, SCC's first resident artist. (Courtesy of SCC.)

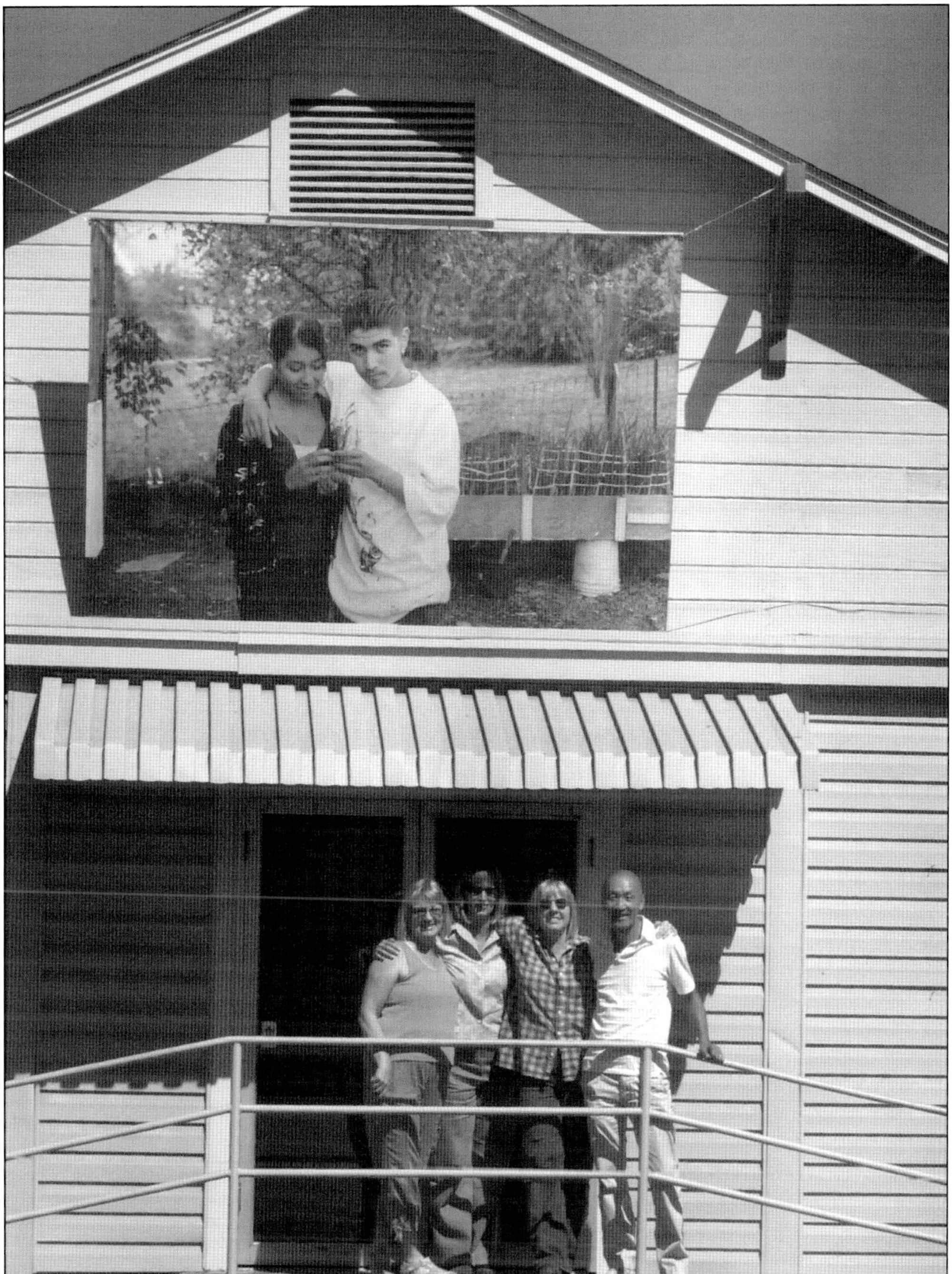

SCC also provides artist residencies in the community. Nationally noted photographer Wing Young Huie lived in the area of Boyes and Fetter Hot Springs for a month while he photographed community members' everyday lives. The residency culminated in an exhibition of enormous photographs displayed on both sides of Highway 12 where it runs through the area. Seen here with one of his images are, from left to right, volunteer Lucy Hamlin, SCC staff members Margaret Hatcher and Shelly Willis, and artist Wing Young Huie. (Courtesy of SCC.)

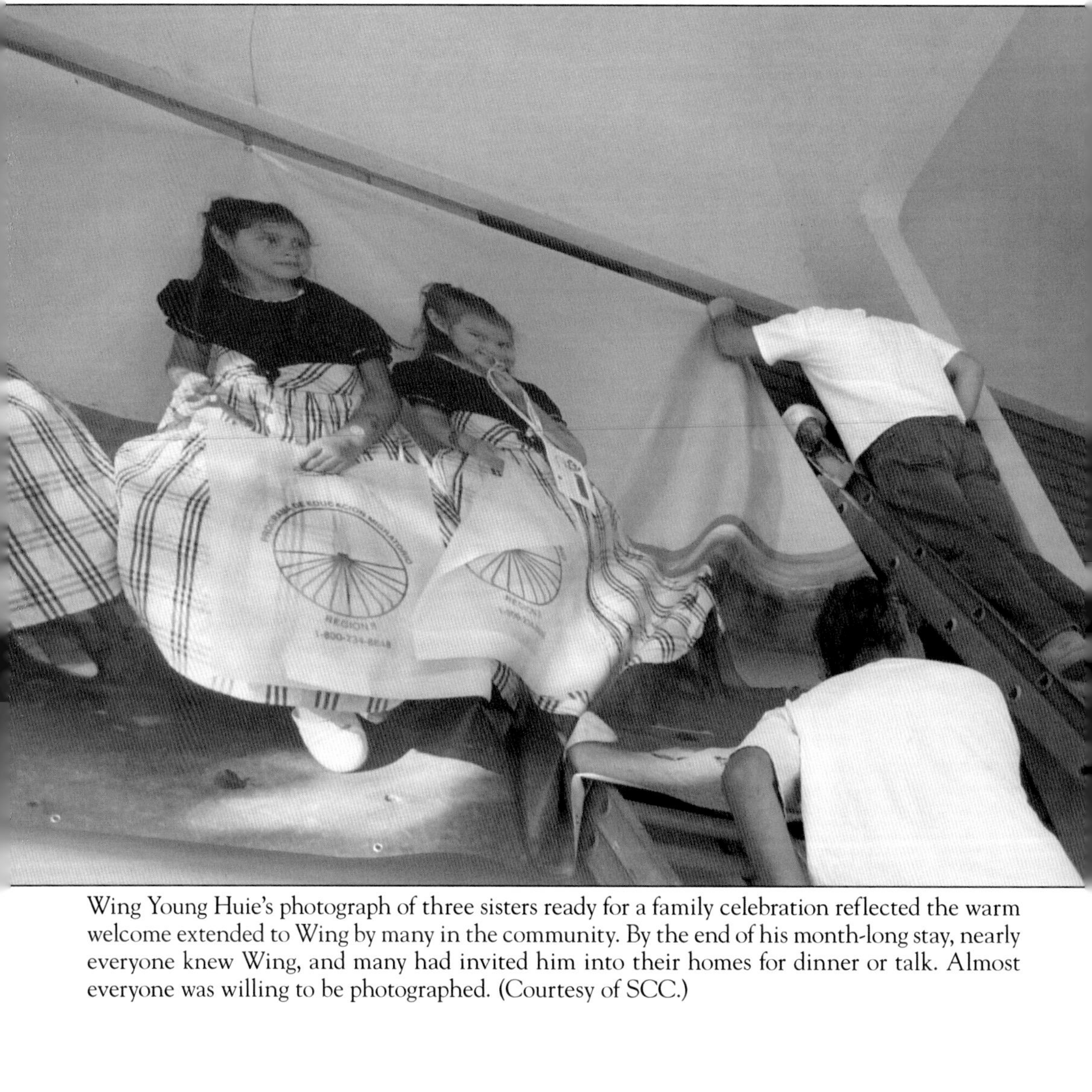

Wing Young Huie's photograph of three sisters ready for a family celebration reflected the warm welcome extended to Wing by many in the community. By the end of his month-long stay, nearly everyone knew Wing, and many had invited him into their homes for dinner or talk. Almost everyone was willing to be photographed. (Courtesy of SCC.)

In 2006, SCC began a signature fundraising event entitled the Sonoma Valley Muse. It raises substantial money through an auction but also celebrates the lives of individuals who have made a significant contribution to the cultural history of the valley, sharing a bit of the honoree's life and how he or she experienced the valley. One of the first Muse celebrations honored the life of Jack London. (Courtesy of SCC.)

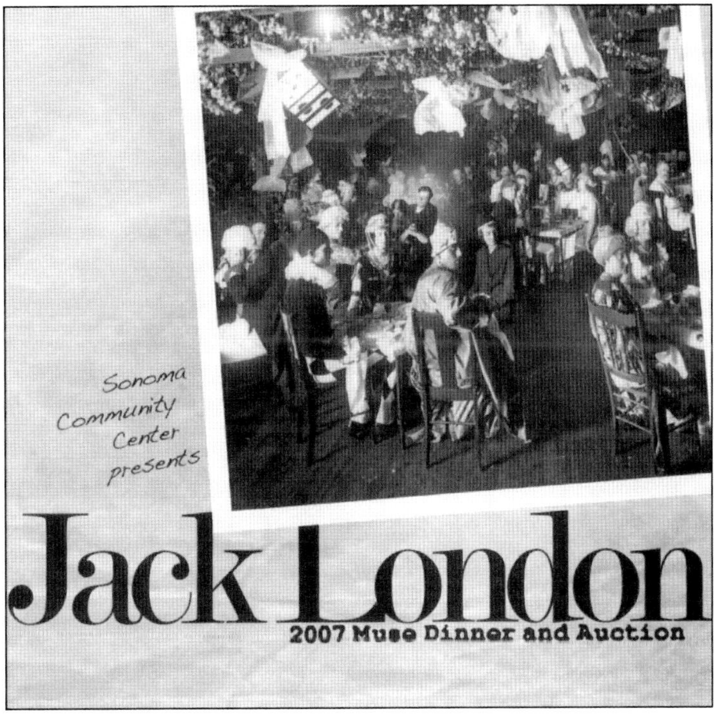

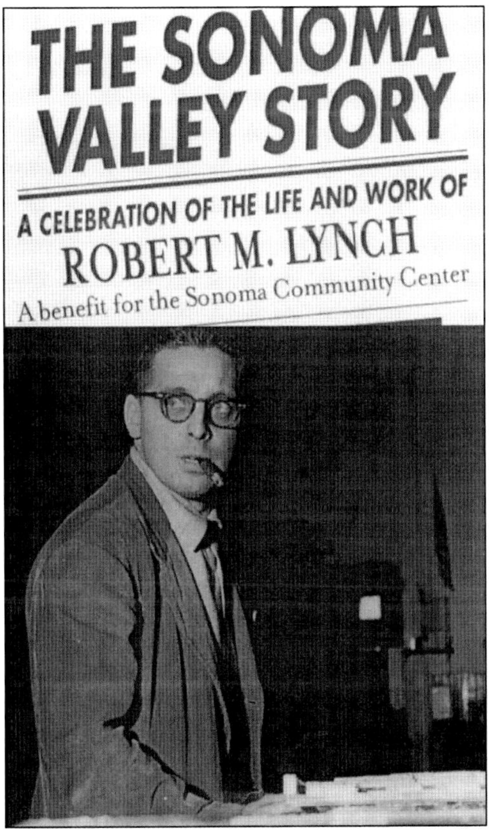

Each of the Muse events is designed to reflect the food and wine preferences of the person being honored. *Sonoma Index-Tribune* publisher Robert Lynch loved a good margarita, so SCC asked a local restaurant to create the very best margarita possible for the evening. The concoction was such a hit that "Bob's Margarita" is still served at Maya Restaurant in downtown Sonoma. (Courtesy of SCC.)

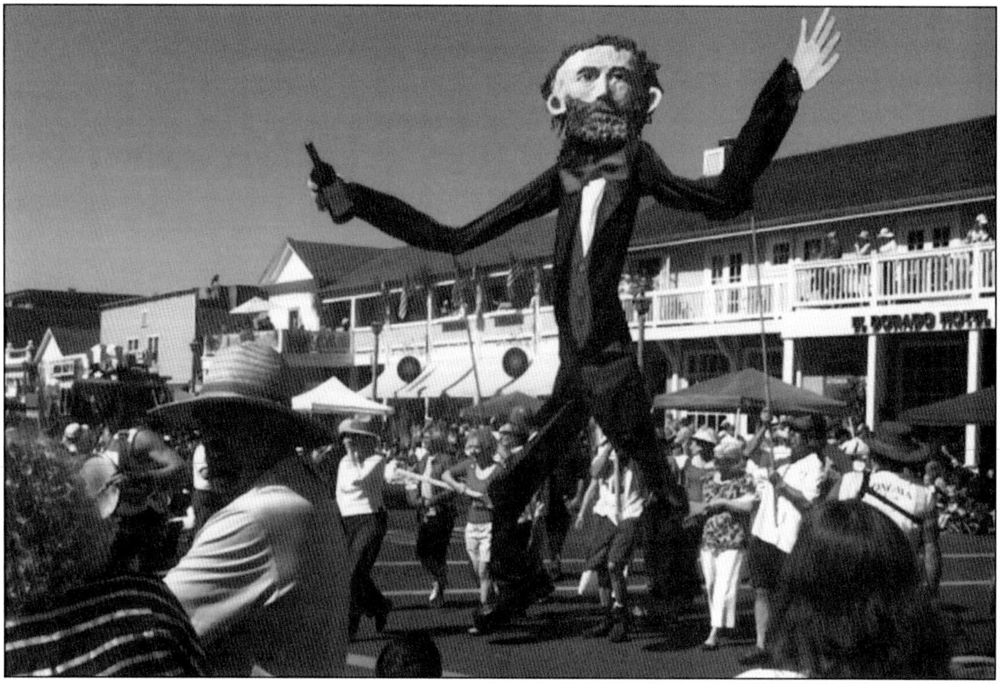

SCC strengthened and expanded some of its traditional events during this time by giving them a big boost of art direction. Under the direction of staffer Margaret Hatcher, SCC has used giant puppets to define each Fourth of July theme and lead the parade. Pictured is a puppet of Count Haraszthy, made when the parade celebrated his 200th birthday. (Courtesy of SCC.)

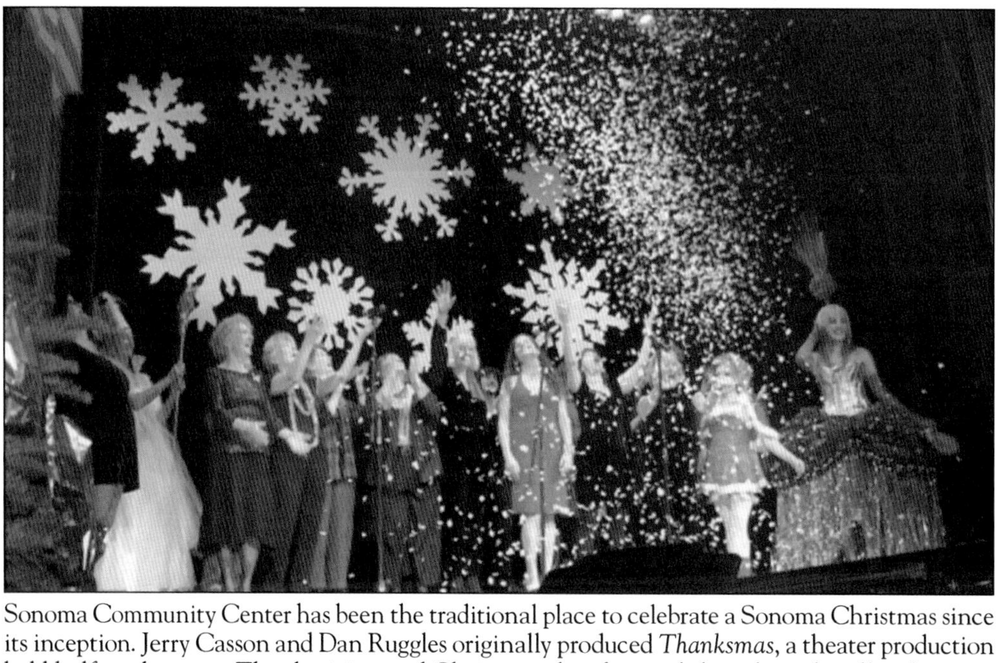

Sonoma Community Center has been the traditional place to celebrate a Sonoma Christmas since its inception. Jerry Casson and Dan Ruggles originally produced *Thanksmas*, a theater production held halfway between Thanksgiving and Christmas that featured the talented staff and renters of SCC. The updated, and slightly more sophisticated, version of that tradition is the *Fabulous Follies*, seen above. (Courtesy of Pat Reed.)

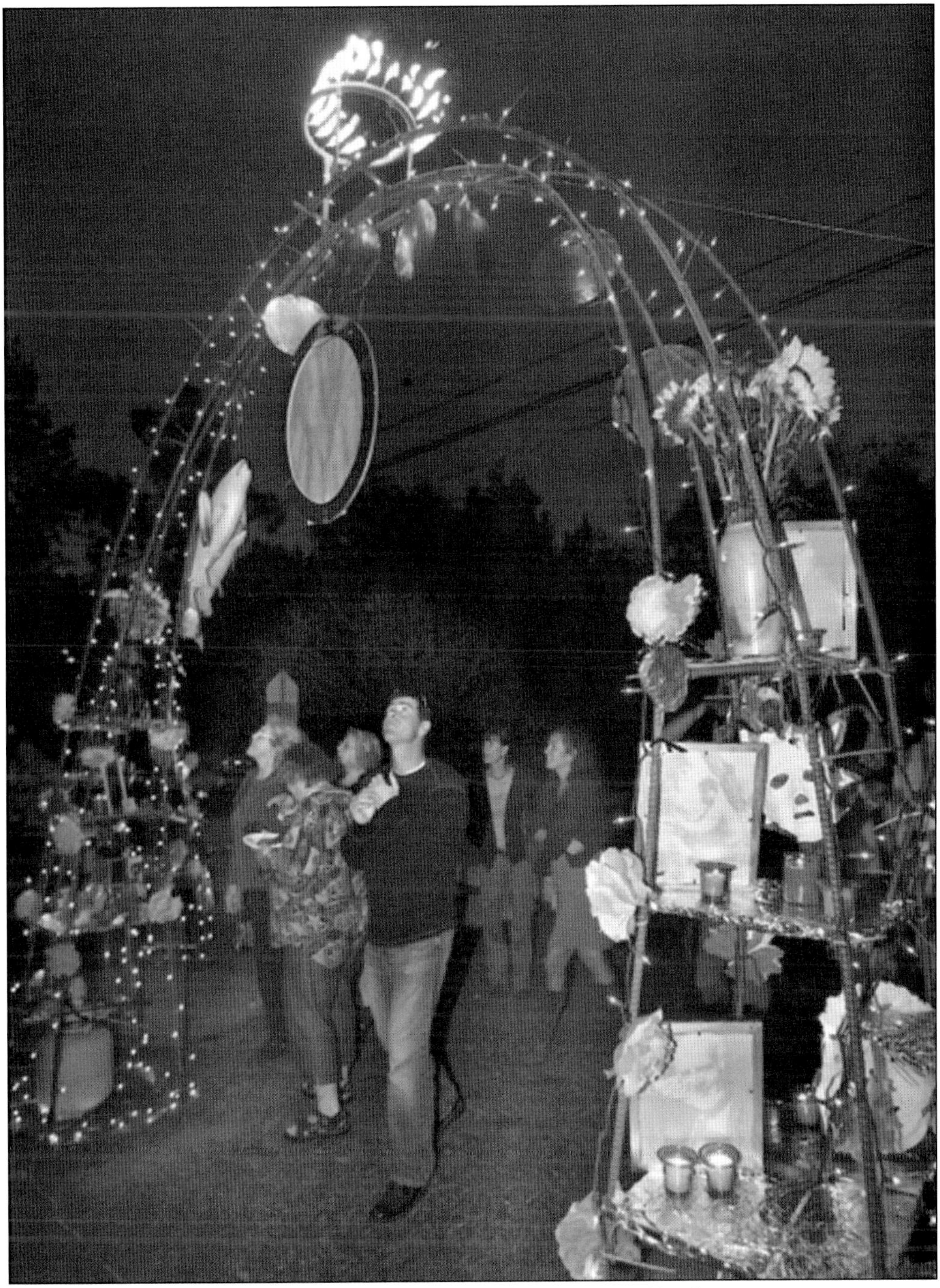

Each year, for Dia de los Muertos, SCC staff member Margaret Hatcher creates a community altar celebrating the family, friends, and Sonoma luminaries who have passed. The community is invited to post photographs of lost loved ones. (Courtesy of Christine Hansen.)

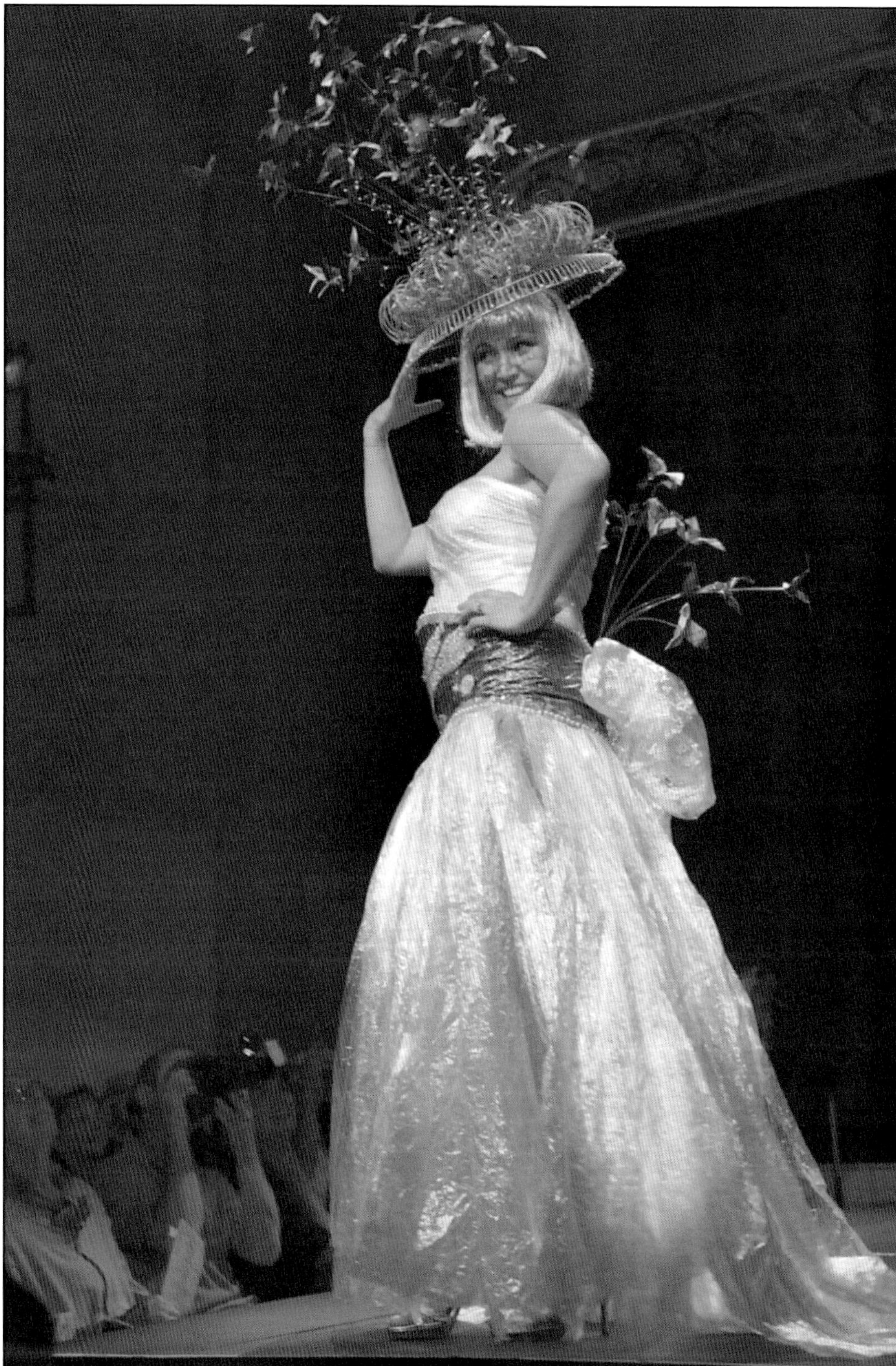

Several years ago, as a way of drawing attention to its sustainability program, SCC created its Trashion Fashion Show, headed by Margaret Hatcher. The shows feature designers who fashion gowns from used materials and consistently sells out. Here, Lauren Benward Krause is shown wearing Alexa Wood and Joanie Derricksen's creation. (Courtesy of Pat Reed.)

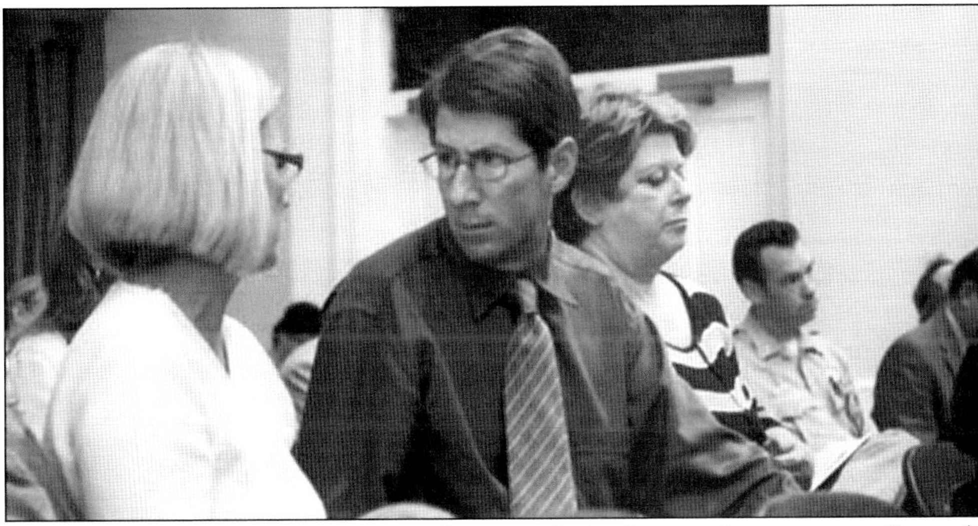

After three years of negotiation, the City of Sonoma's Redevelopment Agency vote to allocate $2 million to the restoration program of the Sonoma Community Center. Through compromise and hard work, SCC's team members Pam Gibson, Madolyn Agrimonti, David Goodison, Brock Arner, and executive director Kathy Swett (above left) won support from councilman Steve Barbose and the full council. David Goodison (above center), who served numerous terms as SCC president, was critical to the process. Above at right is board member Susan Goldstein. (Courtesy of SIT.)

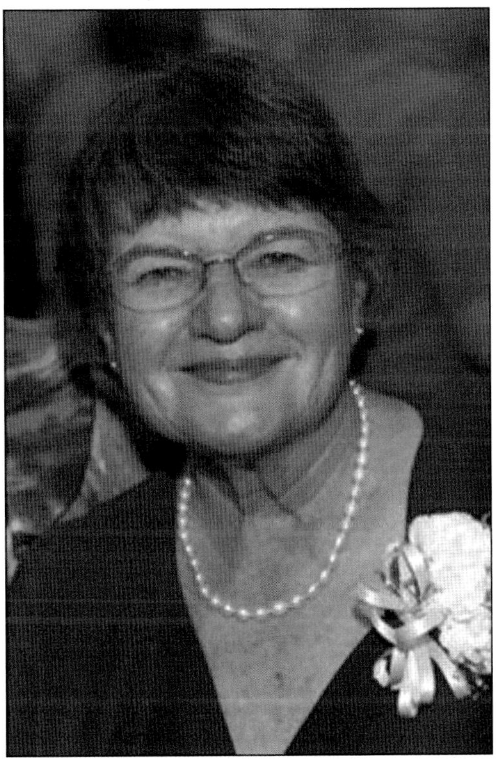

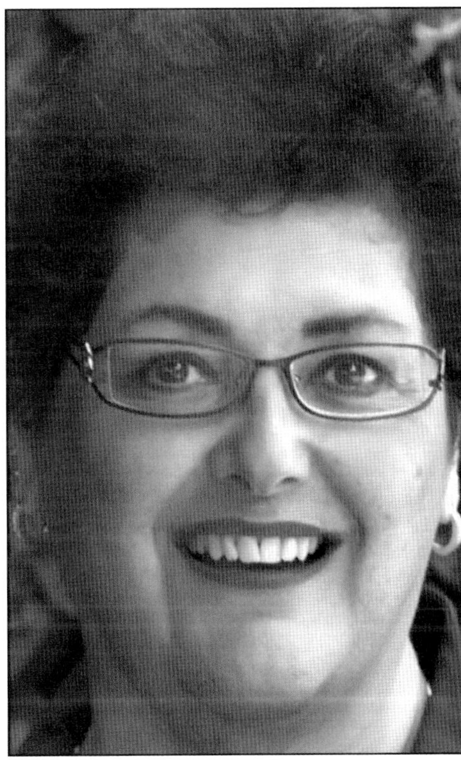

Pam Gibson (left) was a two-term SCC president during this period. She is a retired City of Sonoma city manager. Madolyn Agrimonti (right) also acted as an SCC board president. She also served as a member of the Sonoma Valley Hospital District's board of directors. (Both, courtesy of SCC.)

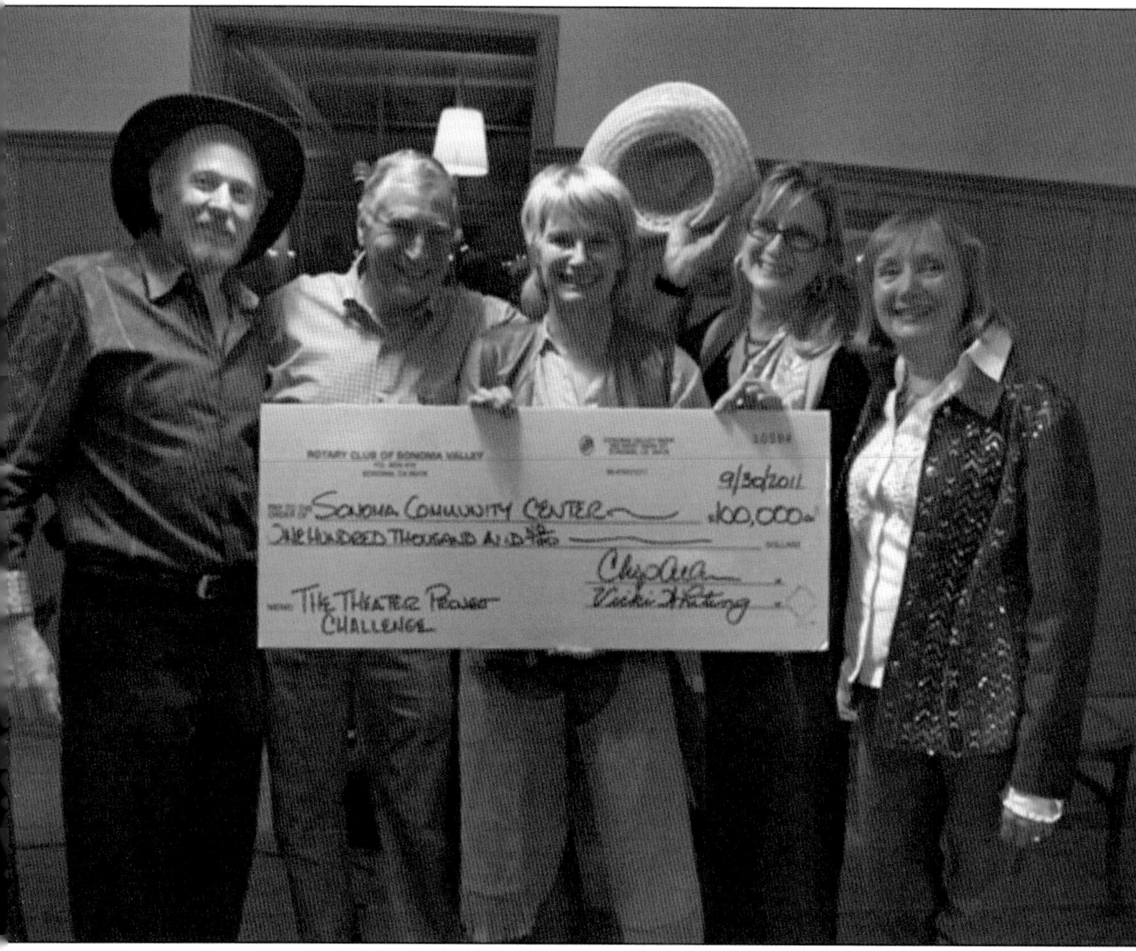

This substantial investment from the City of Sonoma leveraged additional fundraising. Rotary of Sonoma Valley pledged $100,000, the largest gift in its history. Les Peterson, an HVAC contractor on the job, donated $106,000 in in-kind service to the project. Additionally, individuals, families, and businesses from the community contributed over $150,000. In this photograph, from left to right, are Rotarian Gary Edwards, Rotarian Chip Allen, SCC executive director Kathy Swett, STA executive director Jaime Love, and Rotarian Vicki Whiting. This pledge check was presented during the Sonoma Valley Muse celebration in 2011. (Courtesy of SCC.)

Renovations included an HVAC system and new roof, upgraded electrical systems, a remodeled upstairs restroom, and new corridor lighting on both levels. (Courtesy of Owen Orser.)

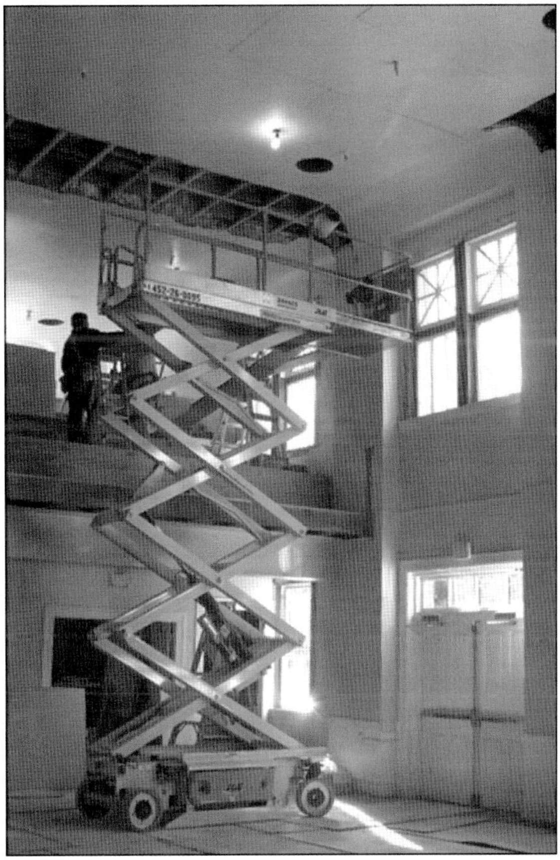

The work also included a seismic retrofit to code and a completely redone Andrews Hall, with new house and theater lighting, acoustical treatments, windows, flooring, stage rigging improvements, air conditioning, and an excellent sound system. (Courtesy of Owen Orser.)

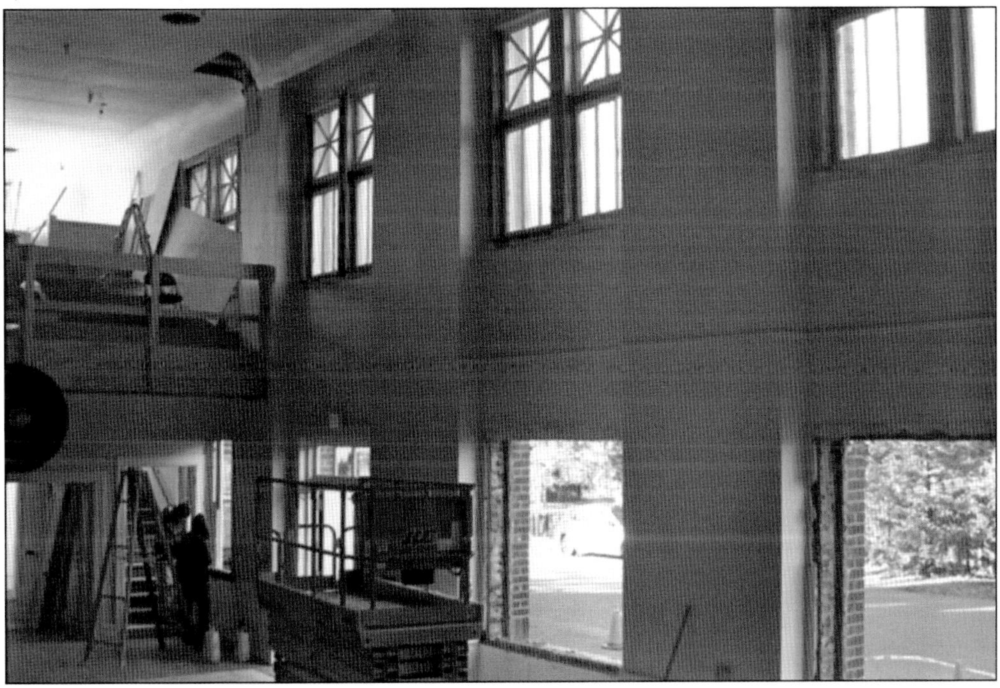

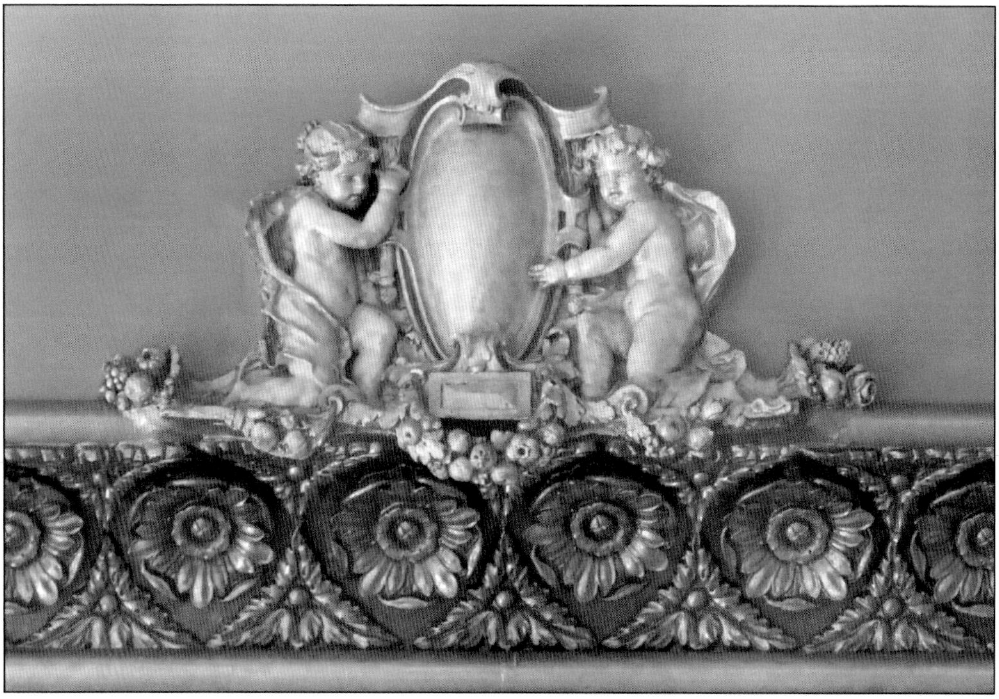

Local theater designer Owen Orser photographed the entire construction process. He also convinced the board that the rococo proscenium needed a new look and suggested Garen Patterson for the job. The completed work proved Owen right. (Courtesy of Owen Orser.)

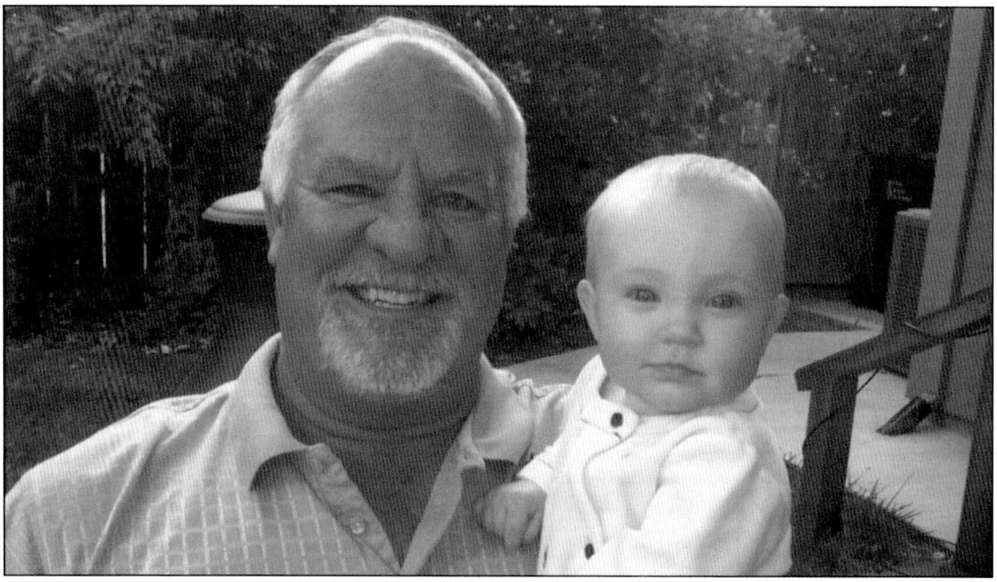

Over 30 years ago, young city manager Brock Arner argued for the demolition of the old grammar school so that residents could enjoy a new, efficient, usable community center. Ironically, Brock was president of the Sonoma Community Center when the city allocated funding to preserve SCC for the next 100 years. "I was newly arrived from southern California, where new was good, and old needed to be torn down," he remembered. "I was young . . . it took me a while to understand the importance of tradition and history." (Courtesy of SCC.)

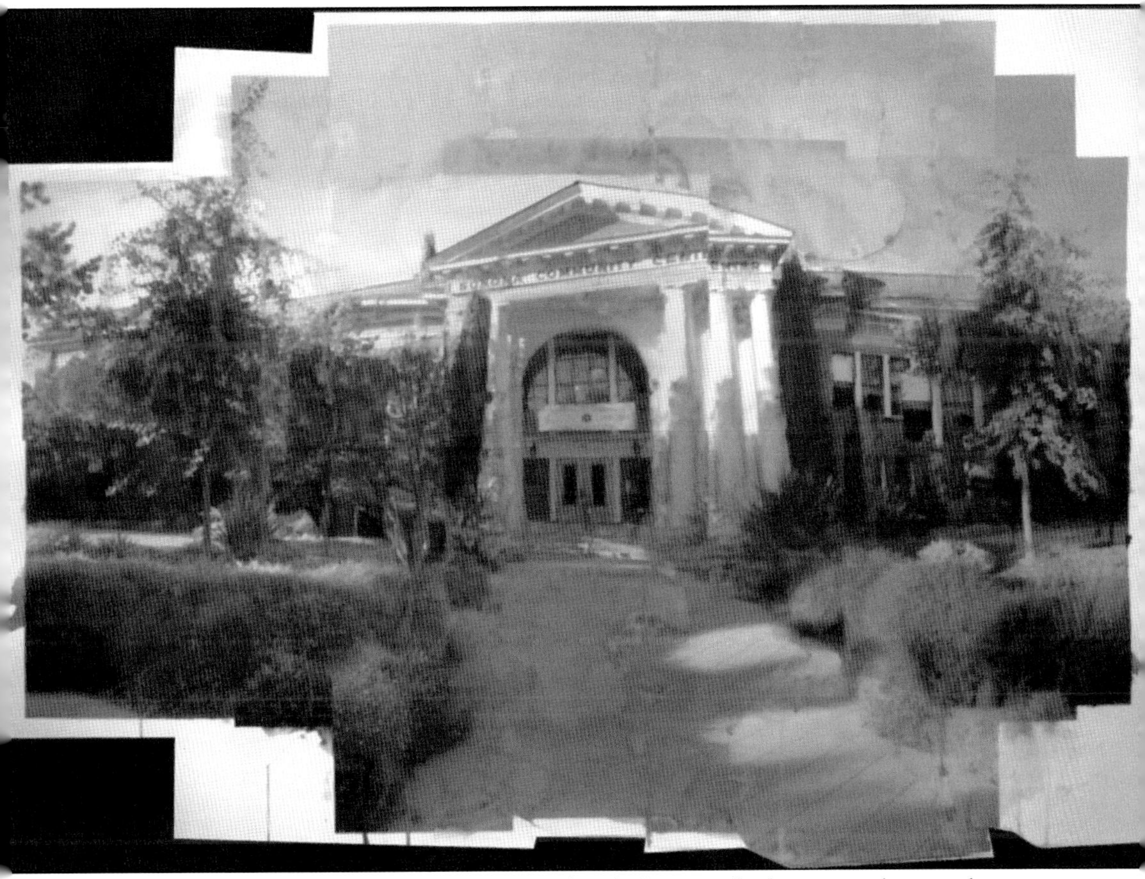

Sonoma Community Center has been painted and photographed extensively over the years. The latest rendition, shown here, is by artist and SCC staff member Michael Acker. (Courtesy of Michael Acker.)

Consistent with our mission to preserve history on a local level, this book was printed in South Carolina on American-made paper and manufactured entirely in the United States. Products carrying the accredited Forest Stewardship Council (FSC) label are printed on 100 percent FSC-certified paper.